THE LONG RUN

The

LONG RUN

Alfred Gover

PELHAM BOOKS

PELHAM BOOKS
Published by the Penguin Group
Penguin Books Ltd, 27 Wrights Lane, London W8 5TZ, England
Viking Penguin, a division of Penguin Books USA Inc.
375 Hudson Street, New York, New York 10014, USA
Penguin Books Australia Ltd, Ringwood, Victoria, Australia
Penguin Books Canada Ltd, 10 Alcorn Avenue, Toronto, Ontario, Canada M4V 3B2
Penguin Books (NZ) Ltd, 182–190 Wairau Road, Auckland 10, New Zealand

Penguin Books Ltd, Registered Offices: Harmondsworth, Middlesex, England

First Published 1991
1 3 5 7 9 10 8 6 4 2

Typset in Monophoto $11\frac{1}{2}$ on 13 pt Baskerville.
Printed in England by Clays Ltd, St Ives plc

A CIP catalogue record for this book is available from the British Library

ISBN 0 7207 1995 X

Photograph Acknowledgements

Alfred Gover Fig 27: *Associated Newspapers Ltd* Fig 16: *Central Press* Figs 4, 5, 6,
13, 14, 15, 19, 20, 22, 26, 30: *Dezo Hoffman Ltd* Fig 28: *Fox Photos Ltd*
Figs 9, 18: *P A Reuter Photos Ltd* Fig 17: *Sport and General* Figs 8, 11, 25: *The
Central News* Fig 3

Every effort has been made to trace copyright owners but if there have
been any omissions in this respect we apologise and will be pleased to
make appropriate acknowledgement in any further editions

Contents

Author's Note

I have called my autobiography THE LONG RUN for three reasons.

Firstly because I have been actively connected with the game in three capacities: as a player and a coach, as a journalist and broadcaster, and as a member of the Surrey County Cricket Club Committee since 1958.

Secondly because I was known for my long run up to the bowling crease

And, thirdly, for my *very* long run at Ajmer in India when a sudden attack of tummy trouble forced me to dash headlong to the pavilion.

I would like to dedicate this book to Marjorie, with love.

My thanks to my typist Janie for all her hard work and patience.

I

In the Beginning

MENTION EPSOM, the small town in the county of Surrey, and folk will immediately think of the racecourse up on the Downs. I always put the record right – I tell them that Epsom is famous for the Derby, Epsom Salts and the birthplace of Alfred Gover!

I was born, in February 1908, in a house overlooking Epsom Cricket Club ground and maybe my first glimpse of the outside world took place when my mother, dancing me up and down in her arms in an effort to get rid of my 'burps', faced me towards the Epsom Cricket ground. Well, my love of the game had to start somewhere!

I had two older brothers, Lewis who was nine years my senior, and Tom who was two years older than me; my sister Dorothy was born in between them. With three boys in the family Dorothy spent all her time 'out of our way' with Mum. Lewis was a very good and patient older brother. He was keen on cricket and tried to encourage us to play. When I was about six he fashioned a bat out of a piece of wood and started us on the game. He first showed us how to grip the bat (although I did try his patience when I kept getting the left hand below the right hand) and how to pick it up with a straight backlift.

The rule of the game was to hit the ball back past the bowler. Tom managed to do this by taking very little pick up and giving the ball a hard push. When my turn came to bat I swiped cross-batted; when I did manage to connect I was not too popular with Tom who had to chase the ball.

My father's profession as a chartered surveyor took him to all

parts of England and indeed the world. When he was posted to
Grimsby all the family moved with him to the attractive seaside
town of Cleethorpes, about three miles from Grimsby. I was then
about eight years old. Father's posting was for an indefinite
period, but in the event it only lasted two years, when he was
moved overseas to Aden and the family went back to Wimbledon.

My recollections of Cleethorpes are hazy but I have always
remembered an escapade by big brother Lewis. He had gone for
a walk around Grimsby Docks to look at the fishing vessels when
he suddenly received an invitation from the skipper of one of the
largest vessels to join up as a deck hand for ten days. The exciting
prospect of being at sea proved too much of a temptation and
Lewis duly signed on but unfortunately without informing his
parents. I remember my mother frantic with worry until father
had the bright idea of scouting around the offices of the shipping
companies until he found the company whose records showed
Lewis as a crew member on one of their boats. I feared the worst
when Lewis came home after the ten days but father simply said,
'Get those clothes off and wash them, you smell like a fish shop.'
Lewis told me later, 'Never again, I spent most of the time being
seasick.'

I do have one happy memory of our stay in Cleethorpes. One
Christmas morning Lewis took Tom and myself to call on one of
his friends and as soon as we arrived the friend's mother produced
some delicious homemade mince pies, inviting us to help ourselves,
which I did with great gusto. I have been addicted to mince pies
ever since and whenever I am dining out my hostess will invariably produce mince pies 'especially made for Alfred'.

As we three boys grew up and the age difference between us
narrowed we all played soccer together for the local YMCA. I
was in goal, from where I watched with some amazement my
gentle brother Lewis, a very solid right back, getting stuck in and
upending the opposition with his fierce tackling. Tom played on
the right wing.

After two seasons I stopped playing soccer fearing an injury
which could affect my cricket. Lewis also gave up soccer when he
became interested in the Boy Scout movement. He regarded it as
a builder of good character and leadership and he eventually
became a District Commissioner. In his early days with the Scouts
he brought his boys to the annual Jack Hobbs charity cricket

match at Wimbledon to give the organizers a helping hand. The Hobbs team used the upstairs dressing room and Andrew Sandham, leaning out of the window called to me and said, 'Alfred, your brother Lewis is down here in fancy dress.' There was Lewis in full Scout regalia, a broad brimmed hat held by chin straps on the back of his head, a khaki shirt and a pair of natty shorts to match.

Lewis and I were very much alike in build and features and this often caused him embarrassment. It started when I was playing for Surrey. He regularly visited the Oval to see the last two hours of play. When he came out of the pavilion at close of play he would be surrounded by youngsters asking for 'Alf's' autograph. He would always refuse telling them that he was not Alf Gover and then hurry away leaving the youngsters, books in hands, looking after him in disbelief. When this had happened several times I thought this could be getting me a bad name with the young fans so we solved the problem by Lewis leaving the pavilion from the west wing and then making his exit from the Vauxhall end of the ground. I then retrieved my good name by signing every book thrust at me, however tired I might be after the day's exertions.

Lewis qualified as an accountant and joined the Portman Office which is responsible for the administration of the Portman family estates in the West End of London, the Midlands, Scotland and Devon. He became their company secretary and on retirement lived quietly in Sussex.

Tom spent a lifetime with Shell Mex becoming an expert on bulk storage. Shortly after retiring, he was stricken with multiple sclerosis. This disease normally leaves the patient crippled for life. However, Tom leads a normal life and has a deep Christian conviction. He says that he owes his recovery to faith in God.

People find it hard to believe that I never received cricket coaching as a young schoolboy. Indeed the first coaching I ever received was when I turned professional with Essex in 1928.

My schoolmasters at St Marys, Merton gave little or no encouragement to sport of any kind. The school lacked a sports ground and any sort of equipment but a few of us were determined to play cricket. There was a small field near the school that was never used and no one appeared to own it. The field was covered in light grass and was quite bumpy. One of the boys managed to cadge the loan of a lawnmower from his parents; with this, and a pair of shears to do the preliminary work, we managed to cut the grass sufficiently to make an outfield. Working evenings and at weekends, we eventually created a twenty-two yard strip in the middle to make a pitch. Next we borrowed a roller from one of the boys' father who was in the building trade. He gave us strict instructions that the roller must be returned every night after use. As he lived two miles from our 'headquarters' the volunteers for the nightly push got less as time went on. But the threat of no push meant no game and it kept us all pushing!

Satisfied we had rolled our own pitch flat we 'prepared' it for our own trial match by giving the pitch plenty of water from watering cans overnight. In the morning we gave it a ten minute rolling and commenced operations. We made six stumps by cutting down tree branches, dispensed with bails and marked the creases with white paint obtained from the builder-parent. We bought two bats and a composite ball from a junk shop with savings from our pocket money. The ball had to last for the whole season. There was no question of lost ball for us. If it was hit into the long grass outside our boundary line then play stopped until it was found.

I had so many happy summers on that cricket ground. I always opened the bowling, being the fastest around, simply tearing up to the wicket holding the ball like an apple, and bowling straight at the stumps.

During our second year I became the proud possessor of my own bat, the only one of all the boys to do so. Though my father had been abroad for several years he took an interest in my cricket. To encourage me he took me along to the Oval on a non-match day to meet Jimmy Reid, the well-known dressing room attendant. In those days the rooms at the top of the pavilion contained the members' lockers and showers. The members were allowed to use the practice nets with a young player from the staff to bowl at them. The members in turn left old gear about and it was an old bat that Father bought off Jimmy and presented to me.

My bat had sticky tape round the middle and did look a bit worse for wear. But the edges were OK and I was in seventh heaven, the bat having pride of place under my bed. The bands of tape became bigger as time went on; it was not until four years later, when I had left school and was going out to work, that I was able to save up and buy myself a 'real new bat'.

In the second year on our ground we boys decided that leg

guards of some sort were a necessity. On our own not very reliable pitch the composite ball sent down by the bowlers was bringing bruises big enough on both sides to make mothers apprehensive about the dangerous game we were playing. Once again we were lucky. A parent who had given up playing found two pairs of pads in his loft. They were, of course, too big for us but with the help of some of the Mums they were cut down and the straps rearranged.

I have always looked back on those years with nostalgia. They were happy days. We never played matches against other schools; they were rather stuffy, turning their noses up at our 'composite ground'. Four evenings a week, and on Saturday mornings, all through the summer we played our cricket matches, usually England versus Australia. I always insisted on being England's opening bowler. Some of us went on playing in the holidays and, as I had seen Surrey playing Essex at the Oval, this game was brought into our repertoire. We kept score on bits of paper and the player who had a particularly good game either with bat or ball would be allowed to keep the 'score card'.

Leaving school I looked round for somewhere to continue my cricket. So I joined the local YMCA. They were then situated in a big house with a hall at the back which doubled as a chapel and a gymnasium. By now I possessed white boots, a pair of flannels, a shirt, a sweater and a bat, so I duly joined the cricket section and was given games in the YMCA first team (they ran two). They played on the local DunDonald recreation ground. Where our school pitch was not flat at least it was very slow, but the DunDonald pitch was bumpy, hard and fast. I relished in it. The ball often got up from a length to strike the unfortunate batsman in the body and, although I lacked experience, I knew the batsman would eventually back away. I soon had enough 'nouse' to bowl up on to his stumps.

After a season with the YMCA I decided to move on and picked on West Wimbledon, then a leading Surrey club. I obtained the address of the West Wimbledon secretary and knocked on his door one day to inform him that I was a fast bowler and also batted and was prepared to play for West Wimbledon. He looked somewhat amused at this gangling seventeen-year-old.

'And what makes you think you're good enough for us?' he asked.

'Don't worry about that,' I told him. The secretary invited me to a trial at the regular Tuesday evening net. I arrived a full hour before the net was due to commence, duly passed the 'examination' and turned out for the third eleven the following Saturday. Wickets and runs came my way so promotion to the second eleven followed three weeks later. Things continued to go my way and two games later I was in the first eleven. I soon found it a harder game but with encouragement from senior players held my place and achieved some success.

My first job was in the office of a building surveyor. In those days most people worked a five-and-a-half day week. I could hardly wait for twelve o'clock Saturday to come; then I finished work and was off, walking to my afternoon cricket. Very few people had cars and I covered several miles in a season, carrying my long, green carpet bag. My skipper was Murray Almond, the first eleven opening batsman, and I look back now on my good fortune in having had his tactical guidance and advice so early in my career.

Some years later, as a member of the Surrey eleven, I was playing for Jack Hobbs in an end of season charity match. Our opponents were fourteen players representing Wimbledon district. Given the new ball to open the bowling I found Murray Almond taking guard at the recipient's end. A wave of recognition, then I set off on my long run and sent down two half-volleys outside the off stump. These were followed by two long hops outside the leg stump and two outside the off stump. Murray gratefully hit all six deliveries to the boundary. At the end of the over I told him I owed him a few runs for old times' sake, but that now I would be bowling at my fastest. Although Murray was at a disadvantage, not being used to real pace in club cricket, he lasted another twenty minutes before being bowled not by me but by Amar Singh, the Indian Test match medium-pace bowler of swingers and leg cutters.

It was from West Wimbledon that I made my entry into county cricket. I was looking for some cricket in my two weeks annual holiday and a colleague in the office, who was a member of the Essex County Cricket Club, recommended me to them. They were short of players for several Club and Ground games during my two-week holiday period. A trial was arranged at Leyton (then the headquarters of Essex) and I reported to the secretary. He sent me out to bowl to a batsman just about to start his 'net'.

At the age of eighteen I always took a long run in the nets, hurling the ball down as fast as possible. It was a typical net wicket, the bounce of the ball varying due to the worn patches on the pitch. I got the ball past the bat occasionally and also hit the batsman several times in my fiery fifteen-minute spell. At the end of his knock, the batsman said to a heavily-built man watching the proceedings, 'I'll see this lad in my dressing room, Charles.' Charles turned out to be Charles McGay, the Essex coach. As the batsman walked off I asked, 'Who was that chap?' Back came the reply from Mr McGay, 'That chap is Mr Douglas, the Essex captain.'

So it was a very apprehensive lad who walked into the dressing room of the famous former England captain. But I need not have been frightened. He greeted me with a smile saying, 'Well bowled, you have the makings of a fast bowler young man. Would you like to play for Essex?'

'Oh yes, please sir,' I said.

Mr Douglas then asked me where I played my cricket. I told him West Wimbledon so he asked me where I was born. When I said, 'Epsom' he turned to McGay and said, 'We find one and he is not even eligible to play for us! Get him qualified.'

In those days to play for a county you had to be a permanent resident, or have been born in that particular county. If you wished to play in a different county side you had to undertake a two-year qualifying period.

Talking later to my office colleague I discovered he had recommended me as a fast bowler, forgetting to tell Essex I was simply looking for holiday cricket.

A room was booked for my use in Leyton with the purpose of gaining a residence qualification. When I told my parents of my good fortune my father was not too pleased as I would have to be away from home frequently in the summer. He knew very little about cricket and had a poor view of professional sportsmen, especially cricketers. However, mother persuaded him to let me do as I wished and two days later I was an Essex professional. (I might add that when I did make a success in the first-class game I had a very proud father who boasted to all his friends about his famous cricketing son.)

My move to Surrey was by way of being a complete fluke. Essex were due at the Oval for the Saturday start of a three-day game, and I asked the secretary of Essex if I could act as twelfth man. As Essex had no minor games that week permission was granted. I arrived at the Oval full of excitement. As a youngster I had spent all my spare time (when not playing) at the Oval, where I watched the Gods of cricket: Jack Hobbs, Andrew Sandham, Herbert Strudwick, Andy Ducat, Percy Fender and Bill Hitch.

Before the Essex game started one of these heroes of mine, Herbert Strudwick, the great ex-England wicketkeeper now retired and fulfilling the role of Surrey's scorer, introduced himself to me. He knew I was a fast bowler and wondered why I was not playing, as Essex had only one quick bowler in their side that day. I explained that I was still qualifying and had another half-season to go. He said, 'Where do you come from?'

'I was born in Epsom and live at Wimbledon.'

'You should be with Surrey, we are short of a fast bowler,' he said.

The thought of playing for my own county, playing for my heroes, those I had watched from the terraces, was too strong for me not to agree with him. Strudwick asked a friend of his who was a member of both Surrey and Essex about my ability and received a favourable reply. The Surrey coach, 'Razor' Smith, came to see me in action, approved, and the wheel was set in motion for me to move to Surrey. By mutual agreement my engagement with Essex was finished at the end of the season.

A happy partnership with Surrey County Cricket Club thus began. It was to last many years – first as a player for twenty years, then as a committee man for thirty-four years, later as chair of various committees and then culminating in the highest office, president of the club in 1980.

I was lucky to commence my career at the Oval during the era when the Surrey team included such players as Jack Hobbs, Andrew Sandham, Tom Shepherd and Andy Ducat. They were always happy to give me advice and encouragement, but none more so than my mentor, Herbert Strudwick. His advice was priceless to a young player, given from his years of standing behind the best batsmen of his time and watching the ball de-livered by the bowlers towards his gloved hands. He was a kindly man, but would not hesitate to 'chase' you during the intervals if he thought your bowling warranted hard words. Sometimes he would tell me I had forgotten a particular batsman's strength, pointing out that I had bowled a number of deliveries which gave the batsman a chance to play a favourite shot. He would show me his notes alongside his scorebook for my benefit. Herbert Strudwick was no respector of persons. If a rebuke was necessary, for the good of the side it was given.

I was to learn a lot from 'Struddy' – as everybody in the game affectionately knew him. In his role as scorer he travelled with the Surrey team and was a constant source of encouragement and wisdom to all the players.

2

Making a Start with Surrey

WHEN I LOOK at the Oval today and see every spectator provided with a bucket seat, two new stands providing the normal seating and the executive boxes and restaurants, I think of the extraordinary improvements made since my day. When I first joined Surrey from Essex in 1928, the public sat on wooden benches set in concrete terraces and, when we had a full house playing against such counties as Middlesex, Lancashire, Yorkshire, Notts, Kent and Essex, many fans would be content to stand up all day unless they were lucky enough to get a place on the grass around the playing area away from the members' pavilion.

The ground itself in those days was a dust bowl after the end of May when the hot weather arrived. There was little grass in the outfield, which was continually cut and rolled. The roller stood five feet high and was towed around by two horses, its weight continually making the ground harder and so helping the ball to travel faster to the boundary. The ground was so hard that running up to bowl was akin to running on a hard tarmac road and soon one's legs began to ache and jar, necessitating a massage from the trainer at the lunch and tea intervals.

Arriving from Essex did not mean I could claim a permanent place in the Surrey side immediately. I had to compete with two other fast bowlers, Ted Sheffield and Lew Lywood. Ted was a good all-rounder but not very effective on plumb wickets. Lew was short of stature and therefore had difficulty in obtaining bounce off the pitch. The skipper, Percy Fender, told 'Struddy' that he was a little perturbed about the 'big chap' (me) because every time he took me off I walked away muttering under my breath to myself. He felt I was being disrespectful. 'No,' said Struddy, 'he grumbles because you take him off and he wants to bowl all day.'

'Good,' said the skipper, 'he's the one for me.'

My approach to bowling has always been the same: if I stand in the field watching two other fellows bowling I am then deprived of the opportunity of taking wickets. As my career progressed, this attitude remained constant. Another of my Surrey skippers, Errol Holmes, would often ask, even on a very hot day in the afternoon session with the opposition batsman well set, 'Have you got any ideas, Alfred?'

'Yes,' I would reply 'I will have a go.'

'But you only came off four overs ago after an hour's spell.'

I usually had my way though, and many a time took a wicket straight away. Being a little stiff after resting would result in my first few deliveries being just below the normal pace and a batsman would often get out through mistiming his stroke. The skipper could hardly take me off after that success so I would stay on for another half-a-dozen overs. I would then be bowling to the lower order batsmen which would always give me an opportunity to improve my total of wickets. I had usually taken wickets with the new ball at the start of the day, so with my afternoon's efforts I often ended with a total of four or five wickets. A good reward for my bowling.

Of course, in those days I had plenty of stamina as in the off season winter months I used to do plenty of running. The Dulwich Hamlet Football Club let me use their perimeter track for my training schedule.

I was lucky in all my opening bowling partners at the Oval. First there was Maurice Allom who, off a short run, bowled fast-medium and was quite happy to bowl into the wind. When he retired Eddie Watts came along. Eddie became known as the up-wind fast bowler. The skipper at the start of an innings would give me the choice of ends. At the Oval in my day it was not a case of looking at which way the flags were blowing; as far as I was concerned it was a question of sniffing. If I could smell the wind from the gasometer and from the brewery down at the Vauxhall end of the ground I knew the breeze would be coming from deep long leg in a line towards mid-off. Ideal for my basic away-swing delivery. Sometimes I would decide after two overs that I had made a mistake and should go on at the other end. The skipper would call on Jack Parker to bowl an over of his medium-pace stuff to enable Eddie and me to change over. It would often happen that I had made a mistake in changing ends and would indicate to the skipper that I should go back to my original end. He would ask Jack to bowl another over saying, 'Alfred wants to change yet again, he just can't seem to make up his mind.' Eddie never grumbled, although he did say to me on one occasion when I had gone through my usual end-to-end trick, 'I'm beginning to get dizzy with all this changing around.'

Eddie was my great mate. He eventually became my brother-in-law, marrying my wife's sister.

I was lucky to have had an early lesson in discipline in my first year under Percy Fender. I had put in a lengthy spell with the new ball but without success. I had bowled quite accurately, beat the bat several times and had had a slip catch dropped. Umpire Joe Hardstaff, senior, an old Notts player and one of the game's senior umpires, was standing at my end holding my sweaters. After I had bowled the last ball in the final over of my opening spell I felt somewhat frustrated at the way things had gone and snatched my cap and sweaters from Joe. I realized my discourtesy only as I was walking away from him. I stopped, turned round and apologized, 'I'm very sorry Mr Hardstaff,' I said, 'I should not have acted like that.'

'Alright son, you said that just in time.'

I thought no more of the incident and as the game went on fortune swung in my favour and I finished with four wickets to my name. Percy Fender called me into his dressing room as we left the field and gave me the most severe reprimand for my fit of temper. I explained that I had apologized immediately to the umpire but Fender said that was not good enough: I was a Surrey cricketer, should be proud of it, should behave, should learn to control myself and should follow the example of my seniors in the pros dressing room. He added that, if there was another similar incident, I would never play for Surrey under him ever again. A very chastened young man went off to his dressing room where the senior players added their bit, telling me not to let the side down in future.

I had had my lesson and for the rest of my career always treated umpires with respect and never queried their decisions. Incidentally, I played many games later in my career with Joe's son, also Joe, who went on to play, like his father, for Notts and England.

The fans at the Oval soon began to get used to the 'big fella' charging up and down to the bowling crease and one particular fan was instrumental in changing my name from Alfred to Alf. He was a chap who sold morning newspapers outside the ground and would come in to watch the play. He used to encourage me with cries of, 'Wheel 'em out, Alf!' He kept this up until the cricket writers began to refer to me as Alf Gover and so 'Alf' became my professional name, although my fellow players and friends still addressed me as Alfred.

'Wheel 'em', as the players referred to him, did not appear again after the Second World War, but I often told my closest friend, Stuart Surridge, about this. However, he took the story with a pinch of salt until one night years later we were attending a first night at the Winter Garden Theatre. Wearing our dinner jackets and accompanied by our wives, we started to move through the crowd gathered to watch the celebrities go into the theatre, when all of a sudden there was a loud shout of, 'Wheel 'em out, Alf.'

'It's old Wheel 'em,' I said to Stuart. Excusing ourselves to the girls, we hurried over to find him on his paper stand with a big smile on his face. He greeted me warmly, saying that he had never forgotten the old days at the Oval but now his stand was in theatreland. He was obviously delighted to see me and his night was complete when I introduced him to Stuart, the man who had led Surrey to five successive Championship titles.

There was another newsvendor who always insisted on giving me an evening paper without charge. Several years after I had retired from first-class cricket I took my wife and daughter to a Putney cinema. Just as we arrived a voice said, 'It must be Alf Gover!' I recognized him as the donor of my evening paper of years ago. It was a cold night and he was obviously having a rough time but, against his protests, I pressed a little money on him in thanks for his kindness and memories of the Oval. My daughter, then a fifteen-year-old, remarked a little later, 'You do know some funny people, Daddy.' I impressed on her that throughout life, whatever a person's social standing, if he or she were of good character, always meet them on equal terms. I explained to her that the newsvendor was an old friend and I had been pleased to see him once again.

I was privileged in my career to play against and with many of the all time 'greats' and none more so than Jack Hobbs. For the first six years of my cricketing career I played alongside Jack, something I have always treasured. He was not only the master of his craft but had a great sense of humour. He accepted those decisions from the umpires that went against him as part of the game. I never heard him complain about what could be thought of as an error of judgement on the umpire's part. He was always saying, 'The umpire stands in the best position to see.' Jack accepted the success and adulation that came his way with a sense of humility and often remarked how lucky we were to be playing the game we all loved and to be paid for it.

He was not a distant type of person but nevertheless there was an aura about him that earned the respect of all who were associated with him. He was indeed the perfect professional and an example for all the younger players to copy. This certainly rubbed off in the Surrey dressing room during the years I was in the side with him. In my first two years I always addressed him as 'Sir', it seemed the natural thing to do. I still have a warm feeling about the day our relationship took on a different footing. We had fielded nearly all day and Jack had batted out the last half-hour. I was pretty tired after a long bowl and wallowed in the plunge bath. Jack took his time under the shower and we were the last two left in the dressing room. When I was leaving I called out, 'Good night, Sir.' He stopped me and said, 'We have been playing in the side together for two years, please address me as Jack in the future.' When he came into the dressing room the following morning he greeted me with, 'Good morning, Alfred,' but I could not get 'Jack' out in reply. He gave me an understanding smile and the Christian name came easier later in the day, and for the rest of the years that followed my respect for him remained and we became firm friends.

Such was my respect for him that I even let him alter the date of my marriage. In the August I announced in the team dressing room that I was getting married in September and I hoped they would all be there. They all accepted until Jack asked, 'What's the date?' On hearing it was going to be the 17th he said, 'You can't get married that Saturday – it's the day of my charity match at Wimbledon and all the boys always play for me.'

'But,' I protested, 'your game is always the previous Saturday.' Jack then explained that the annual game, Champion County versus the Rest, had been put back a week, so he had altered the date of his own game. As the Surrey team always took part in Jack's match, I had to tell my fiance, much to her bewilderment, that I could not marry her on that day. Her father, an avid club cricketer, was reading his paper and, after I had hurriedly explained the position, lowered it and said: 'Quite right.' Then, addressing my fiance, Marjorie, he said: 'Get married the next day and tell your mother to alter all the arrangements.'

One of my favourite stories about Jack Hobbs concerns Arthur Mailey, the greatest leg spinner of his time. Before England toured Australia for the 1924/25 series in Australia, Arthur decided he must do something about Jack, who was such a great player of spin and had always taken more than his fair share of runs off Arthur's bowling. So he worked out a different method of bowling his googly and practised it for several weeks until it was perfect. 'This,' thought Arthur, 'will catch Jack out and it will take him a long time before he spots the difference between my leg break and my googly.' Arthur kept his new weapon back when the tourists played his state team, New South Wales, waiting for the Test match a few days later.

The first Test found Jack in good form and going well before Arthur was given the ball. He bowled both his usual leg spin and the normal googly for the first few overs and then decided to use his secret weapon, the other googly. But as soon as the ball left his hand Jack called out, 'Googly, Arthur,' and, moving to the off side, cracked it to the leg-side boundary. Arthur told me this story years afterwards. I asked if it had annoyed him.

'No, you could never get annoyed with Jack', said Arthur, 'he was such a nice chap and was always full of humour, although this never upset his concentration as he was a great competitor.'

In the 1934 season, when Surrey played a match at Old Trafford, Jack was 52 years of age. He hit the Lancashire bowlers for 116 in the first innings and 51 not out in the second. It was to be Jack's last game on the Lancashire ground and, such was the measure of his popularity, that during the interval on the first day the Lancashire committee presented him with a silver trophy to mark his final appearance and as an appreciation of the pleasure he had given to Lancashire supporters with his many fine innings on the famous Test arena.

Two weeks later, against Sussex at Horsham, Jack scored 34 in the first innings, at a pretty slow rate for him; in the second innings he took four-and-a-half hours to score 79. The bowling had included that of the famous Maurice Tate whose good length and medium pace had made the ball come quickly onto the bat. Jack felt he could not move his tired legs into position early enough to make scoring shots against Maurice's accuracy. So he would now retire. However, Jack was talked out of such precipitate action but in his next game he scored only 57 in two-and-a-quarter hours and decided then to call it a day. We all felt very sad and the corner of the dressing room which was traditionally the senior professional's was left empty for the rest of the season with the heir apparent, Andrew Sandham, waiting until the next season before moving in.

I rarely found myself at the batting crease with Jack Hobbs but on one occasion, at Northampton when he was skippering the side in the absence of Percy Fender, he asked me to accompany him to the wicket as the nightwatchman for the last half-hour of the day's play. Surrey had been put into bat late in the day, so Jack wanted to risk me rather than any of his recognized opening batsmen, one of whom was Ernie Wilson who was deputizing for Andrew Sandham. Jack wished to give Ernie every possible chance to prove himself the next day (which Ernie did by scoring an immaculate hundred). There was, too, something against each of our top order batsmen opening, they were either slightly off form or did not relish the opening spot. I protested to Jack that I was tired, having sent down many overs from the football ground end, but Jack insisted and I duly found myself walking out alongside my illustrious partner to open the innings. The first ball was sent down by Nobby Clark, a tall left-hander and one of the quickest in the game. Jack appeared to have all the time in the world as he played the first ball away for a single. 'Hello,' I thought to myself, 'Nobby's lost a lot of his pace.' But I soon changed my mind as I sparred at the remaining five balls of the over and it was lucky Nobby bowled them all outside the off stump because I was much too late at every delivery.

Jack came down the wicket at the end of the over and asked me how I fancied Nobby. 'I don't,' I replied.

So Jack promised to arrange matters so that he would take Nobby all the time. This pattern continued next day with me staying at the other end and Jack scoring off Nobby. At one stage the frustrated Nobby turned to me at the non-striker's end and said, 'Why don't you go to my end?' To which I replied, 'Because you might get me out.' After one-and-a-quarter hours of play Nobby decided he had had enough; putting his sweater on, he announced that he was coming off as he was fed up having to continually bowl at the middle of Jack's bat. 'Well,' I said to myself, 'we have seen him and the new ball off,' and continued with my passive role in the partnership showing the bowlers the maker's name as I played straight up the line nudging the ball away for singles and twos.

Eventually, Jack walked up the wicket to me and said, 'Alfred, do me a favour.'

'Of course,' I replied. Jack continued, 'Do you mind getting out now? There's a lot of good players waiting to come in.' I duly obliged, getting out next ball.

In 1954 John Arlott and myself, with Frank Lee the old Somerset player, formed the 'Masters' club to honour the Master on his birthday, 16 December. The club meets on the day previous to the Lord's and Oval Tests. The 'Masters' club rapidly expanded and was soon to welcome 'Young Masters' such as Colin Cowdrey and Peter May, plus Stuart Surridge and Doug Insole, all happy to drink the only toast of the day to the 'Master'. During lunch I would relate the story of my opening partnership with Jack Hobbs at Northampton, embellishing it every time, much to Jack's amusement and to cries of, 'That's new!' from the assembled company.

Jack was a religious man, although he did not wear his faith on his sleeve. Whenever we played away at weekends he would slip away quietly on the Sunday morning to the nearest church accompanied only by his old pal, and my mentor, Herbert Strudwick. The rest of us would nip off to the nearest golf course, but we always respected Jack for his convictions.

3
Professionals, Amateurs, and Some Captains

THERE WAS A great deal of difference between the pro and amateur in my day. The amateurs had their own dressing room, and the professionals their private domain. Surrey in my time had fine amateur players: Percy Fender, Douglas Jardine, Freddy Brown and Maurice Allom. Middlesex turned out Gubby Allen, Walter Robins and Tom Killick. Worcester had the Nawab of Pataudi, Warwickshire had Bob Wyatt, Essex had Ken Farnes and Sussex had Duleepsinhji. All were successful at Test level. The only remuneration these amateurs received from the game was first-class travel and hotel expenses.

There was inevitably the shamateur, the chap who, usually for social reasons, did not care to join the pro ranks, but preferred to make money from the game by indirect means. The genuine amateur and pro had a mutual respect for each other. But, for the shamateur, the pro had no respect at all.

Although the financial rewards in my day were less than they are today, cricket as a career was an attractive prospect for many young men. The professional pay I received during my time at the Oval was quite good. I was paid a small weekly salary the whole year round and a match fee whenever I played in the eleven. The club also gave me a guarantee of earnings not less than £400, but playing all games I could top the £500 mark. We also took out personal insurances so that in the event of non-earnings through injury we would be assured of a sum commensurate with the lost match pay.

My salary being made up to £500, including the winter retainer, was good pay in those days when a bank manager would earn a similar sum for a whole year's work. I also had the advantage of a decent winter job in the building trade.

Amateurs, generally speaking, could afford to play without being paid. Most had private funds of some kind, or occupations which allowed them time off to take part in cricket. There were rumours that some amateurs, like the shamateur, did get 'behind-the-back' handouts. Whether this was so or not I don't know, but it does remind me of one occasion during the Second World War. I was a member of a sports panel quiz with Lord Tennyson, C. B. Fry and Sir Stanley Rous. A question came up as to what is the difference between the amateur and the professional games player. Sir Stanley spoke at some length on amateur and professional footballers (this was in the days when the amateur game was strong enough to attract 100,000 people to the Amateur Cup Final at Wembley). C. B. Fry also spoke at length going back to the days of Grace and Ranji. I simply said one can afford to play for nothing, the other plays for a living. Lord Tennyson then stood up and thrusting his right-hand palm uppermost out in front of him said the professional takes it this way, then putting his arm behind his back with the palm of the hand still uppermost he turned to Fry and, with a huge grin on his face, said, 'And we took it this way didn't we Charlie?' There was an eminent protest of denial from Charles Fry which brought laughter from the audience and from the rest of the panel at CB's failure to see through his Lordship's joke.

The cricketing authorities eventually changed what had become an hypocritical blight on the game. They created a two-tier type of player: the contracted, who would be signed on a county's staff as a regular player; and the non-contracted player who would be paid a match fee whenever he turned up.

I had my first taste of the good amateur player when Cambridge University played Surrey at the Oval in my second year. I was offered a rest for this 'friendly' match but refused, thinking I could pick up some easy wickets against the 'boys'. Boys indeed! On a plumb Oval pitch I found myself bowling at Maurice Turnbull, Walter Robins, Tom Killick and Duleepsinhji. To use a modern expression, they hit the inexperienced Alfred 'all over the park'. All these chaps, of course, went on to have distinguished Test careers. Never again in my whole career did I turn down the chance of a three-day rest when we played the Universities.

Going to Oxford or Cambridge today means studies first, sport second. In those days players, not only from home but also from overseas, would join 'Oxbridge' simply to get a Blue at cricket, rugby, etc. They only had to pass one subject in the year in order to stay up.

Today's first-class cricketers cannot, I am sure, possibly envisage anyone playing the game without remuneration of any kind, and the thought of having to pay an entrance fee and a year's subscription before being eligible and invited to turn out for the side as an amateur, would make them raise their hands in horror, or more likely in disbelief. But paying to play was what a great many amateur players did. Some of them went on to captain their county and others, such as Douglas Jardine, their country.

During my time at the Oval, I served under a number of such captains and it is pleasant to recall a few of them now, in an age when the distinction 'Gentleman' and 'Player' no longer exists.

PERCY FENDER
Percy George Fender, the Surrey and England cricketer, started his career with Sussex while still a schoolboy at St Paul's. His debut at Notts for Sussex was one run, one wicket and a catch, and it did not exactly hit the headlines, but he soon made them as the phenomenal Sussex schoolboy player, and he was judged good enough to be selected for the Gentlemen versus Players game at Lord's, a unique honour for so young a player.

He was now devoting all his time to cricket, which did not please his father, who told him to forget cricket and get down to making a living in the family wine business. He was, however, lucky in having a mother who was a cricket lover. She agreed he should come into the business eventually, but argued it would be an asset to the business in the meantime to have a first-class cricketer connected with it. So, putting heads together, the family found a solution. Percy should play for Middlesex or Surrey, so that he could still mix business and cricket and work from the firm's London office. Percy was born in Balham, South London, so having offered his services to Surrey and paid his subs, he commenced his long and distinguished service with them.

I was a lucky young man to join Surrey when they were captained by Percy Fender. He had a great depth of knowledge of the game and I could, I suppose, call him my 'guru'. He set out to teach me the finer points of the game from my first appearance in the Surrey eleven. He first inspired respect for his ability

20

as a player – his attacking batting could empty the bars when he went out to bat. He had a safe pair of hands in the slips and was a most versatile bowler. Apart from his stock leg-break bowling he could in an emergency open with the new ball, bowling both inswing and away-swing.

Fender was a great tactician and it was never easy to understand why he was not invited to captain England. Maybe it was because he was too outspoken which would not have pleased cricket's 'establishment' at that time. He did, however, have his off days. When the young Cyril Washbrook first played for Lancashire against Surrey he was of course an unknown quantity. On one occasion he was particularly severe on Fender's leg breaks, continually hitting into the turn, cracking the ball to the leg side. Our skipper persevered on the theory that Cyril must eventually hole out. At the tea interval he asked Struddy if he had got any ideas. 'Yes,' came the reply, 'take yourself off. Washbrook has taken far too many runs off your bowling already.'

Percy Fender rarely made such mistakes. He was an astute captain, making the most of a comparatively thin bowling line up. And what a cricketer to follow! In the six years that I played under his captaincy I saw him bowl inswing with the new ball, often making an early breakthrough, then, when the shine had gone off the new ball, revert to his normal leg-spin role.

I owe Percy Fender a great deal. He would invite me to his dressing room to discuss the tactics to use when bowling at the various batsmen we were due to face. He gave me a detailed description of what was required. He considered it a crime if the new ball was not directed at the stumps and on a full length. 'Make the batsman play at every delivery and don't give him room to hit you off the back foot towards the off-side field.'

Percy was a very superstitious cricketer. On one occasion in my first season I told the rest of the team that we looked like cruising to a comfortable win as the opposition needed 150 runs and only the last three in the batting order remained to be disposed of. A horrified look came over Percy's face and he said to me, 'Get on with your bowling and don't talk so much.' Rather mystified I trundled away and took a wicket, but the last player managed to hold on and the apparent victory became a tame draw. I was called to Percy's dressing room at the close of play. He said that I was partially to blame for our failing to ram home our advantage because I had tempted fate when I predicted a victory and I should never do that again.

In my first season I was a bit awkward in the field. I remember a game at Cheltenham when Wally Hammond was batting to the skipper's bowling. A hard hit ball was driven to me at mid-off and as I bent to stop it the ball suddenly kicked and went through my hands. So I was switched to mid-on, where this time I had anticipated the bounce of the ball only to see it shoot along the ground underneath my hands. At the end of that season the skipper told me I must do something about my fielding and suggested I should try to be a specialist short-leg fielder and to try and practise this in the winter. With the help of my two brothers, one bowling and one batting, the ball was hit at various angles towards me in the short-leg position and I had to dive at all angles to try and catch it. At the beginning of the next season I made several good catches. I received a quiet, 'Well done, Alfred,' from the skipper who added, 'You have made that your specialist position from now on.'

Percy Fender was a fine cricketer and, in addition to his ability as a bowler, was probably the hardest-hitting batsman of his day. I remember his knock at the Oval against Hampshire when he cracked three 6's and three 5's – yes, 5's. The playing area then was a vast expanse, yet Fender's score of 185 included twenty-four 4's.

I played alongside Percy some years later in a Sunday game at the Surrey village of Holmwood. The game was part of the Eddy Watts benefit year. The locals fielded a side of fourteen and batted first. Our side was skippered by Andrew Sandham who soon invited our old skipper to turn his arm over. Percy's old skills were still in evidence as he continually beat the bat, but he finished up with only one wicket. He had to go to Horsham during the lunch interval but said he would be back in good time. Lunch over, Andrew handed the bowling to Maurice Allom and myself. Maurice, my old opening partner, was still a fine fast-medium swing bowler, good enough to have toured New Zealand and South Africa with MCC. Owing to business commitments he now rarely found time for cricket. So, given the opportunity, he decided to stretch himself and soon the wickets were tumbling down. Not to be outdone I 'let it go' at the other end and within the space of seventy minutes the locals were all out. We had just started our innings when Percy Fender came back and asked 'Whatever has happened?' On hearing that the locals had been tumbled out he turned away saying, 'I wanted to have another bowl and had worked out the degree of turn of the pitch.' This, at the age of 60. Andrew Sandham, always a diplomat, suggested that Percy could go in number four and, 'Treat the crowd to some of your big hitting.' Percy hit up a quick 40 runs, including three 6's and five 4's and went off after the game a happy man.

During his career Fender had a good ally in Tom Shepherd who stood at first slip taking the catches induced by Fender's leg breaks. But on one occasion the ball had beaten the bat time and time again with the bowler getting more frustrated as time went on. Then he got an edge straight to Tom who dropped it. The skipper could hardly believe his eyes and raising his hands to his head said, 'Is there no God?'

Like all young fast bowlers I considered it necessary to take a long run in order to deliver the ball, but this was changed purely by accident. In a game at the Oval we had spent nearly four days out of six in the field. We lost the toss and the skipper threw me the ball at the pavilion end telling me he wanted a couple of early wickets. 'You'll be lucky,' I thought. 'It will be as much as I can do to get the ball up to the bowling crease.' I started measuring my steps back to my usual mark, but after seventeen paces I looked back at the wicket and thought, 'This will be far enough, I'll bowl from here.' It clicked. The run up was comfortable and the timing and the delivery correct, and so seventeen paces determined my run up for the rest of my first-class cricketing days. I learned sometime afterwards that the skipper had spoken to Strudwick about my inordinate length of approach to the crease, but Struddy had replied, 'Leave him alone. He will soon get tired of running so far and will sort it out himself.'

DOUGLAS JARDINE

Douglas Jardine was an amateur with a professional approach to the game. He first captained Surrey in 1932, causing Percy Fender to step down from the captaincy, much to the disappointment of the players. Jardine was already named as captain of the forthcoming England tour to Australia – the controversial 'bodyline' series – and it was said at the time that Jardine was given the Surrey captaincy so that he could gain experience. To his great credit, Fender continued to play in the Surrey team, and gave his advice on the numerous occasions that Jardine wanted guidance.

When Andrew Sandham, Surrey's opening batsman, with many a hundred to his credit, failed to score in three matches,

Jardine suggested he dropped out and had a game for the second eleven. We all felt this was a harsh decision, but Jardine was proved right. After four scores of over 50 in the reserves, Andrew came back into the side against Glamorgan at Cardiff and scored well over 200 runs. Jardine congratulated him, saying, 'Andrew, I am delighted, we have much missed your presence in the side.'

Jardine himself was a fine batsman. He had an unorthodox stance, standing side-on with the bat well away from himself. He was at his best in a crisis, and had plenty of courage. Following the 'bodyline' series against Australia, England met the West Indies the following summer. In the Old Trafford Test the two West Indian fast bowlers, Learie Constantine and Manny Martindale, consistently bowled short of a length at Jardine's leg stump, frequently hitting him on the upper thigh. He stood up to them, getting behind the line of the ball and refusing to give the West Indies fast bowlers the satisfaction of seeing him rub the bruised thigh. Yet the blows he received must have been painful; back in the dressing room when he stripped to shower it revealed his skin badly bruised and bleeding, but he never complained. We all agreed he could dish it out in Australia and now he proved he could also take it.

An example of Jardine's sense of humour was in 1933 when he skippered the England side in India. Nobby Clark, the Northants fast bowler, who I was to studiously avoid when partnering Jack Hobbs, rarely bowled at his fastest when operating on a plumb easy wicket. But he went flat out in the second Test, and on an easy-paced pitch he took six wickets. As the England side left the field at the end of the innings, Jardine called Nobby over. Naturally Nobby thought it was for a congratulatory pat on the back, but Jardine said, 'Nobby, I want to congratulate you on your much improved fielding.' The deflated Nobby found it very hard after that to extract pace from the plumb Indian pitches.

The Jardine sense of humour showed up again at the Oval. He had played himself in and looked good for a big innings on an easy-paced pitch when a wicket fell, and the incoming batsman, George Mobey, our reserve wicketkeeper who came into the side occasionally on his own ability as a batsman, went to the non-striker's end. Jardine immediately played a ball to fine leg. George, thinking the ball had gone past the leg-side fielder, called 'Yes' for a run. The batsmen set off, but George suddenly saw the ball being retrieved by leg slip and sent his skipper back with a loud cry of 'No!'. Jardine was well run out by two yards. In the second innings, with Surrey going well, George found himself joining the skipper again at the non-striker's end. Jardine played the ball in front of the wicket, called for a run and, when George was halfway up the wicket sent him back to be run out by yards. As George passed the skipper on his way back to the pavilion, Jardine said: 'That will teach you to say "Yes" or ruddy "No", young man.'

Jardine had his own ideas about close-in fielders cramping his style when he was batting, and this showed up against Worcester. Fred Root, who bowled a very late inswinger, had three fielders close up to the bat on the leg side. Before receiving a ball, Jardine turned to the three fielders saying: 'You will be in danger in a few minutes. When I hit hard, I hit hard.' Within three overs they were ducking and weaving as he deliberately moved his feet into position to hit Fred's inswingers straight at the short-leg fielders.

Not much was worn in those days in the way of protection, both for fielders and batsmen. Many old cricketers denigrate modern batsmen when they go out to bat looking like a 'knight in armour', with their helmets, forearm protectors, abdominal box, sidepads, leg guards and big batting gloves. It is said that all this protection is not necessary, that the batsmen of previous generations had to play against bowlers just as fast as today's 'quickies' and would have scorned the use of so many accoutrements. All they required was the abdominal box and the leg guards, plus of course batting gloves.

But I do not agree. The present generation of batsmen have been brought up on poor pitches and in an era when the fast ball aimed in an intimidatory way to hit the batsman has become the norm. Poor pitches have been endemic in all Test match countries, except India and Pakistan. There was an improvement in the pitches provided for the 1990 Test season in England and I noted that at times batsmen took off helmets and forearm guards when the fast bowlers were resting. But the suspicion of pitches remains in the minds of the majority of batsmen. If pitches do improve I would like to see the forearm guard and the extra leg protection, sometimes worn inside the trousers on the left leg, disappear. But I would keep the helmet, except on a slow wicket.

Today, the fast, short-pitched, bouncer is continually hurled towards the batsman's head, which is the most vulnerable part of his body and should always be protected. A batsman could be killed if hit on the head by a ball travelling at 80 to 90 miles per hour. I know because I nearly killed a batsman. It happened in 1932. Douglas Jardine was skippering Surrey in the annual Whit Bank Holiday fixture at Trent Bridge. Frank Chester, the leading umpire of his day, stood at my end. Frank handed me the new ball. It was very greasy and as I walked back to my seventeen-pace mark I kept rubbing the ball on my trousers to get the grease off and stopped at my mark still rubbing the ball in an attempt to get it clean. Jardine called out from the slips, 'Bowl up, Alfred', and Frank said 'Come on, get on with the game. We are already two minutes late.'

George Gunn, the Notts opening bat who was still a renowned player of fast bowling though near the end of his career, stood ready to receive the opening ball. Then came the tragedy. I arrived at the crease, jumped into my delivery stride and swung my right arm round ready to deliver the ball. But just prior to that moment of release the ball slipped out of my fingers and went down the wicket at full speed 'a beamer', straight at George's head. George made an attempt to hook it, missed and got a frightful blow on the side of his head and collapsed to the ground completely unconscious. The club doctor, accompanied by the trainer, rushed out and George had to be stretchered off the field. I called to see him in hospital that evening. he looked pretty rough with his head covered in bandages. He put his hand out to me and said, 'Not your fault, Alfred, I lost sight of it and thought it was a bouncer and picked it up too late.'

The doctor told me that had the ball hit George an inch higher it would have probably killed him. George, thank goodness, made a full recovery, but this accident undoubtedly helped towards his retirement at the end of the season.

In these days of short-pitched intimidatory bowling it is worth recalling how George dealt with it in his time, thereby helping establish his reputation for playing fast bowling. A few years before my 'beamer' hit him, George was selected to tour the West Indies with the MCC team 1929/30. He was such a good player of fast bowling that in the final Test Constantine and Martindale bowled at him with seven men on the leg side and only two on the off. This was a similar tactic to that which Jardine later developed in the controversial 'bodyline' Australian tour – and from which Jardine himself, facing these same two bowlers, was to suffer during the bruising summer at Old Trafford. Remember

26

that these two bowlers were just as fast as any of the present-
day West Indies quick bowlers, Marshall, Ambrose, Bishop and
Tony Gray. George proceeded to play them by walking up the
wicket three or four yards and meeting the bouncing ball by
hitting it hard onto the left side or playing it down in front of
himself. In the latter case, when the bowler grabbed the ball in
his follow through George would turn his back and stroll back to
his crease making sure he was blocking the line if the ball should
be thrown at the stumps in an attempt to run him out.

I got on quite well with Douglas Jardine, principally because I
was always willing to have a bowl, but it was without having the
same close player-captain relationship that I had with Percy
Fender. Jardine was a more detached character than Fender and,
although at a stretch he might forgive a player a temporary lapse,
he came down hard on any player who lacked ambition and
team spirit.

MONTY GARLAND WELLS

Of the captains I played under when the line between amateur
and professional was closely drawn, Monty Garland Wells was
the captain closest to his players. Monty was a rarity. He was
'one of the boys' but he still kept the respect of his players. He
was full of refreshing and sometimes unorthodox approaches to
winning a game, but he usually discussed his proposed tactics
with his senior professionals. However, if he wanted to go his own
way, we always backed him 100 per cent, whether we agreed or
not with the policy in hand. In the normal way the professionals
did not encourage the amateur into their dressing room: it was
their domain and they liked their privacy. However, Monty was
different. He had a friendly manner, treating all his players as
friends, always having a quiet and encouraging word with the
younger players. On the field and in the pavilion he was always
addressed as skipper, but away from the ground and off parade,
to his senior players he was simply 'Monty'.

He was a good all-round sportsman, a double Blue at Oxford
at cricket and soccer, and a single-handicap golfer. His other
sport was greyhound racing. He was a director of Clapton Greyhound Stadium and often invited us to watch the races from the
comfort of the directors' dining room. It was Monty's connection
with the greyhounds that led to a unique experience when Surrey
were playing Gloucestershire at Gloucester. During the second

day's play Monty told us he had on our behalf accepted an invitation from the directors of Bristol greyhound stadium where we would be their guests at a champagne supper. So after the match we set off in a convoy of four cars. We were looking forward to the evening as, apart from the promise of the champagne supper, Monty said we would be given tips on the winners from the experts at the track. We were welcomed with the champagne supper and soon had our racing cards marked. What a let down! Not one recommended dog came home in the first five races. The boys were now disconsolate, most of them were down to only the loose change in their pockets and this in the days when they paid their own hotel bills.

The situation was more than serious. I still had a few notes left and walked down the lane of bookies' stalls to make a bet. I looked at the list of dogs running and chose one called 'Woolley Three' who was quoted at long odds. 'Five pounds to win, Woolley Three,' I said. The bookmaker looked kindly down at me and said: 'I know you are one of the cricketing boys. Now Woolley Three hasn't a chance. Go down the line and back any dog with the odds of about 4-1. They always have a chance.'

'No,' I said. 'I want £5 on Woolley Three.'

'Why,' asked the bookmaker, 'are you so insistent on backing such a hopeless dog?'

'Because,' I replied, 'Frank Woolley bats at number three for Kent.' The bookie looked up to heaven, shook his head and accepted my bet.

When the dogs paraded, I saw my choice was a big black fellow. When the race started my dog was the last out of the traps, well behind the other runners, no sense of racing but just galloping along. I thought 'there goes my fiver'. Suddenly, the leading dog on the inside swerved into the dog challenging him for the lead, and a fight started with all the other dogs joining in, thinking no doubt 'why should we miss the fun'. But not my big black dog. He ignored them, refusing to join in, and galloped on to the winning post. My bookie paid me out, saying, 'Son, I reckon you could walk on water after that.' I dashed off with great excitement to my hard-up team-mates clutching my bundle of 'life saving' notes in my hands.

With the evening's racing over we were invited into the directors' hospitality room where discussions started on the merits of the dogs who had been racing and of course a great deal of leg-pull on my method of choosing my winning dog. The conversation then veered round to how young athletes would fare running around a greyhound track. Someone suggested the team should have a go. All the boys agreed, and bets were struck on the likely winners. Sandy Tait, our trainer, who supervised my training sessions on the Dulwich Hamlet football ground in the off season winter months (where I always commenced with 15 laps around the perimeter of the pitch to help build up my stamina for my job of fast bowling) had that inside knowledge so made a small wager on me, the 'big feller'. I was long odds against so I had a small bet on myself. Backed at short odds were the batsmen who spent their time sprinting about the field and retrieving the ball when it was short of the boundary. When our race started they looked to be the right choice. The sprinters were quick off the mark and at the halfway stage were all ahead of me but by now running out of wind and steam. They were used to a sprint of no more than about 30 to 40 yards, but for me it was the same as one of my winter training sessions. I just kept going, leaving them all well behind and for the second time that night I had another handful of notes thrust into my willing hands.

Apart from being a useful middle order batsman, Monty bowled a leg cutter quite accurately at a little under medium pace and was always keen to turn his arm over. When we played Essex at Clacton in 1938, Essex won the toss and decided to bat on a 'green top' pitch. Eddie Watts and myself opened as usual and both had early success. After an hour, Monty decided it was time for a change of bowling and announced, 'I will have a go myself.' I said, 'You are not surely suggesting that I come off without taking full advantage of the pitch conditions, are you? And Jack Parker is our third seamer and he must relieve Eddie.'

Monty insisted. 'I am captain and I am going to have a bowl at Eddie's end.' He then proceeded to upstage me by taking five wickets for 27 runs and never stopped talking about that performance all season.

Monty was due to skipper Surrey in 1946, but on the death of his father had to take over the reins in the family law business. He became a well-known figure at Wentworth Golf Club for many years until he gave up golf and retired to live in Brighton, where he took up bowls and played the 'Drakes' game for his adopted county. I still see him at the Oval in the summer, and, bless him, he is still the same old Monty.

ERROL HOLMES

All captains have their own ideas of how to approach their job and Errol Holmes, skipper of Surrey in the late 1930s and in 1947, was no exception. He played it like an Old Corinthian in the highest sporting spirit. At times we pros, intent on our job of producing results, thought him too sporting, especially in a game at the Oval against Essex. Errol was absent injured but watched the game from the pavilion. The side was skippered in his absence by Bob Gregory, the senior professional, and on the third day of the game we had Essex in a hopeless position. I was bowling from the Vauxhall end to amateur Jack Stephenson, batting at number 8 with number 10 at the other end. With one of these out and only an hour to go we knew that number 11 was usually lucky to survive two or three overs so we were licking our lips in anticipation of a win. To stop Jack pinching a single at the end of the over I bowled the ball just short of a length in line with the stumps. To my surprise Jack played forward at full stretch with both knees bent and tried to play the ball cross-batted towards the leg side, resulting in a top edge deflection hard into his mouth splitting his lips and loosening his teeth. I rushed down the wicket and helped him to his feet.

'Sorry, Jack,' I said.

Through his shattered mouth he muttered, 'Not your fault, Alfred, I should have been on the back foot.' As he was being helped off the field, acting skipper Bob said, 'Come on, Alfred, Errol is waving us in from the pavilion.'

'He can't do that,' I remonstrated. 'You are the captain and we have only one wicket to go for the win.' But Bob, to my chagrin, took us off the field.

For my part I went straight to Errol's room and in the politest way voiced my protest. 'Jack will tell you it was his own fault and I have been bowling on and off all day to get us into this winning position.' But in spite of my vigorous protest Errol said, 'Alfred, we cannot possibly win a match under these circumstances – it just isn't on.'

In the 1947 season the Surrey attack, mainly Alec Bedser and myself, had struggled on some very plumb flat Oval pitches. Now we were due for an away match at Chelmsford against Essex and I told Alec we would have a 'ball' on the Essex ground because I had been told that it was a 'green' seam bowler's paradise. We won the toss and persuaded Errol to put Essex in on a pitch looking like a green bowling rink. I could not get my sweater off quickly enough to get hold of the ball, with my field strung up for pace bowling: three slips and two gullies and wicketkeeper Arthur McIntyre behind the stumps twenty yards back. They were all hopefully awaiting a catch off a high bouncing swinging delivery; so, full of joy on this gift of a green pitch, I put everything I had into the first delivery. I was horrified: instead of the expected bounce off the pitch the ball took off very slowly taking three bounces before reaching Arthur McIntyre at ankle height. Within two overs I came off.

Jim Laker came on with his off spinners, operating at my end where he obtained prodigious spin and turn, albeit slowly. Standing at leg slip I stopped more of the deliveries than the 'keeper until Jim went round the wicket and aimed well outside the off stump. Alec Bedser cut down his pace and, taking advantage of the turn off the pitch, concentrated on off-cutters taking five wickets for 30 runs and Essex scrambled only 182 runs total.

They improved in their second innings, knocking up 301 after dismissing Surrey for 104 runs. On the third day with five wickets gone Surrey required another 201 runs to avoid defeat. The pitch had quickened up and was still taking turn, and Essex had two fine spinners in Ray Smith and Peter Smith who could exploit the pitch conditions. Surrey were in a hopeless position.

But not for Errol. At the start of the third day's play he said, 'We are going to win this game by hitting them over the top. And furthermore, I will bat in one of my old caps that used to bring me luck when I was at Oxford.' He dug deep into his cricket bag and produced a cap of many colours. It was that of I Zingari, the exclusive club for top amateur players. What an extraordinary way to get the runs, and only for the loss of another three wickets: Arthur McIntyre, Eric and Alec Bedser, plus Errol himself hitting 65 not out in twenty minutes. The Essex bowlers were visibly shaken when their turning and popping deliveries were continually hit over the infielders' heads. However much they swapped field placings, they could not put a stopper on our battling heroes and, with five minutes remaining before lunch, Surrey had won and Errol's boast of winning from our hopeless position was justified. What a performance, 201 runs in five minutes under two hours!

On the way to Chelmsford, the night before the game started, Jack Parker who was travelling in my car, suggested we call in at a club run by a friend of his for a quick evening meal. During the evening we boasted of Surrey having an easy win on the 'green' Chelmsford pitch and laid several small wagers on a Surrey win. On Thursday evening with Surrey looking defeat in the face we called at the club and settled our lost wagers. On Friday after the game we called at the club and the money changed hands once again.

We were back at the Oval for the next game against Notts and we persuaded Errol this would be a good time to wear the 'crisis' cap of many colours to bring us a win in front of our own supporters. Poor Errol, as soon as he appeared on the field one of his cockney fans called out in a stentorian voice heard all over the ground, 'Who do you think you are Errol? Bloody Joseph.' Poor Errol was so embarrassed the cap came off at once in favour of his brown and white Surrey cap. What a pity, that was the last we saw of the lucky piece of headgear.

I was genuinely fond of Errol. He was a kind and friendly chap but at times made decisions difficult to understand. Every bowler dreams of taking all ten wickets some time in his career. My chance came at Kidderminster when we were playing Worcester. In the first Worcester innings I had taken seven wickets for 35 runs in 14 overs on a pitch made helpful to the bowlers. In their second innings on the second day of the game Worcester were in a hopeless position. They needed 99 to win. I had taken the first seven wickets and, apart from Reg Perks, the last three Worcester players were 'non-batters' and with five minutes to go Reg, batting at number 8, suggested I ask Errol to claim the extra half-an-hour. 'We don't want to come here tomorrow just to go through the formalities and we will also make sure you get all your ten wickets,' said Reg. On my asking Errol to claim the extra thirty minutes he replied, 'Sorry Alfred, that is impossible. I am dining with Charles Lyttelton tonight at 7.30 p.m. at Hagley Hall.' (The Honourable Charles Lyttelton, later Viscount Cobham, was then the Worcestershire skipper.) So a rather disconsolate bowler followed his skipper off the field. A normal healthy young chap, I was always a sound sleeper but this particular night I was awakened about four o'clock by the sound of heavy rain beating on the bedroom window. It rained for the next eight hours, bang went my chance of all ten and, as I pointed out to Errol, in the politest way of course, his dinner party had also lost the side 15 championship points. Errol, always a supreme optimist, replied,

'Alfred, you will have plenty of chances to take all ten in the future.' Now I really did have to swallow hard to take that one.

Errol provided some exciting entertainment with a fine exhibition of stroke play once he had played himself in. He disliked slow scoring batsmen, 'The bat is there to hit the ball', was his favourite expression. If quick runs were called for he would ask his fellow amateur batsmen in the side to 'have a go', knowing they did not have the same apprehension of failure as the professional batsmen. The skipper together with Freddie Brown and Monty Garland Wells were known to the pros as the 'Biff Bang Boys'. In 1935 against Somerset the three of them hit an incredible 195 runs in ninety minutes.

As I have said, Errol was always the supreme optimist. In 1947 the annual Whitsun game at Trent Bridge versus Notts had a full house, which saw Surrey bowl Notts out for 401 just before the close of play. The pitch was a batsman's dream, made especially by Walter Marshall, their famous groundsman, for runs and entertainment for the Bank Holiday crowd. It was not a fair contest between bat and ball. Coming off the field I said to Errol, 'We have done well to get Notts out for 401 on this wicket. I reckon we will get 1,000.'

This remark was not well received: Errol regarded the Notts total as a failure on the part of his bowlers. Well, I am quite sure we would have made 1,000 if Errol had not declared at 706 for 4. In addition, when Stan Squires, our number 3 batsman, was on 154, Errol sent out a message to Stan to say, 'Swing your bat.' Stan obeyed instructions and got himself out. The skipper then came in and enjoyed the luxury of the pitch, hitting 122 runs. When Notts went in to bat after lunch on the third day, Errol addressed Alec Bedser and myself, 'Now, you two, come on – bowl this lot out for me.' He had no chance and neither did we. We managed to get four Notts wickets down but in the process they scored nearly 300 runs.

During Errol's pre-war years of captaincy he decided that when the county eleven had rest days they should go round the county showing the flag by playing one day games against the clubs. We were due to play at Farnham against the local club and Errol told me they had a very promising young fast bowler named Cannings. Errol asked me to give my opinion on the lad. The Farnham Royal ground has quite a big playing area, and when Errol strode to the wicket the bowling change was made straight away. The unfortunate Cannings was hit by Errol for three 6's and three 4's in his initial over and was at once taken off. After the game Errol said, 'Well, Alfred, which bowler was Cannings and what did you think about him?'

'Cannings,' I pointed out to Errol, 'was the chap you hit for 30 in one over.' The young Vic Cannings, knocked out by Surrey, later played for Warwickshire before moving on to Hampshire where he had a long and successful career as part of their opening attack. On retirement he spent many years as coach at Eton college. Whilst he was there we often played golf together and often had a laugh about his one over for 30 'trial' for Surrey.

Errol had a great deal of charm about him and this attribute helped to get him the job leading an MCC (England) team to tour Australia and New Zealand in 1933/34. This visit was the first by an England team since the acrimonious 'bodyline' tour which had disrupted relations between the cricket authorities of Australia and England and indeed alienated the Australian public.

The Holmes tour consisted of matches against all the Australian state sides, plus a full tour of New Zealand playing three Tests. Errol made several broadcasts and public appearances in Australia. His charm and public school approach made the Australians think, 'Here was a good honest pom who respects our cricket and tradition.' I was told by players on the tour that Errol did a tremendous job in healing the wounds of the previous winter.

As a batsman Errol was essentially a front foot player. He had a peculiar habit just as the bowler arrived at the crease prior to delivering the ball: he would take his right hand off the bat and tap his gloved hand against his right leg. Apparently, he had batted in his schooldays with an old glove bereft of elastic and this tapping habit stayed with him through his cricket career. Errol had a straight pick up towards the stumps and played everything off the front foot, even against the fastest bowler. For the bouncer he would simply sway out of the way and swing the bat at the ball. He rarely lofted his hook usually hitting it downwards towards fine leg. He rather helped the ball on its way letting the ball do the work rather than giving it a hard slam. His cutting off the front foot to all types of bowlers was most unorthodox and called for a fine degree of timing. As a medium-fast bowler he could come on and be an integral part of the attack.

One of Errol's best shots was hitting the under-pitched half-volley over mid-off's head and he would often say to his players, 'You must always be prepared to hit the ball over mid-off's head if it is an under-pitched half-volley.' He reiterated this so often that we decided to make the shot 'legal'. Unbeknown to Errol, the boys formed the 'OMO' club and each player in the side, including the tail enders, had to put at least one delivery over mid-off's head in order to qualify for membership and wear the brown tie with the white OMO motif. When all had qualified we asked Errol to come to our dressing room at the close of play to join us in a glass of champagne. Errol was delighted at the invitation and on arrival was handed his glass of champagne and on his inquiry as to what we were celebrating, we gave him his tie and said we had elected him president of our new club. 'What club?' he asked. On being told it was the OMO – 'Over Mid-Off' – club he called us a lot of idiots but we know he enjoyed the joke. He would often wear the tie and enjoyed telling the story.

In the Middlesex and Surrey game at Lord's in 1936 Errol tried to force a Middlesex declaration. The non-bowlers in the side were to send up inviting donkey drops, but the Middlesex batsmen would not 'play ball' so Errol, to the dismay of wicketkeeper Ted Brooks, put himself on and bowled two overs of wides down the leg side. However, Errol was a member of the 'establishment' and after the game told us to back him up if there were any repercussions from MCC, then the supreme rulers of the game. He panicked somewhat when we said 'No' but relaxed when we told him we were joking. Of course he could be assured of our support and we would deal with any awkward questions from the press. But in the event it was a storm in a teacup, the press ignored the incident and there were no disciplinary measures by MCC.

NIGEL BENNETT

In 1946 Surrey had a captain appointed by a quirk of fate. The 1939 skipper, Monty Garland Wells, had had to withdraw due to the death of his father.

Leo Bennett was the player the Surrey committee had in mind as his successor. Leo had played several games for the county second eleven pre-war, then had gone into the Army where he saw service in the Middle East and Italy and was now awaiting demobilization in the rank of major.

Whilst the club were busy inquiring as to Major Bennett's

whereabouts, a visitor entered the outer office of the Surrey club at the Oval dressed in a major's uniform. He said he wished to renew his membership of the club, was on demobilization leave during the coming summer and would like to get some cricket – perhaps in the county second eleven. He had played two or three games for that side pre-1939. The clerk filled in the details on the visitor's membership application form then hurried into the secretary, who happened to have the chairman with him. The clerk reported to them that the 'Major Bennett' they were looking for was outside, would be free all summer and wanted some cricket. Nigel was invited into the office and, after confirming that he had appeared for the seconds pre-1939 and had served in the Middle East and Italy, was told of the late withdrawal of Garland Wells. He was then asked to take over the captaincy of the county eleven. The very surprised major accepted. Having been a number 4 or 5 batsman only in club cricket Nigel was a brave chap to have accepted the job.

Our first game of the season was the traditional match at Lord's against MCC and we players soon realized the inexperience of the new leader. I opened the bowling with my usual array of slips, gulley, third man, short leg and silly-mid-on. Nigel took up position at cover point, the only man in front of the wicket on the off side. My second delivery was played towards his left hand and the batsman took a comfortable single. I was up the wicket in my follow through. The stumps at my end were unguarded with the batsman cruising through comfortably. To my amazement and horror Nigel returned the shiny new ball to me underarm and all along the ground. The ball rolled past for overthrows. After the same thing occurred again in the next over I muttered, 'For heaven's sake! Somebody tell him we struggle to keep the shine on the new ball and not to get it off by rolling the ball along the ground.' The nearest player drew the skipper's attention to the facts of life over the new ball and the unnecessary waste of its effectiveness. To Nigel's credit the point was taken with good grace, whereafter the ball was always returned through the air in the normal way.

In the next game, at a crowded Oval against the Indian touring team, both Nigel and myself had more to contend with. I sustained the first ever injury of my career. The bright sunny day cracked the ground and after a few overs I had asked for some sawdust. Although the pitch was hard my front foot was slipping as I delivered the ball. Before my next over started I waited for the sawdust to arrive. It was so long coming that the groundsman must have been sawing logs in an effort to create some. The umpire said he could wait no longer and ordered me to get on with the bowling.

But calamity. As I was delivering the ball my front foot slipped on the heel of my boot. I limped off the field with a strained Achilles' tendon. I sat on the balcony watching the boys getting on well without my bowling until numbers 10 and 11, Sarawate and Bannejee, got together. At the tea interval they were both going remarkably well. I had played against these two players in India so I mentioned to Nigel and our bowlers it might be best not to attack them as tail enders as both were capable batsmen. My advice went unheeded and a bit of cricket history was added to the record books when both batsmen scored a hundred runs each.

I was out of the side for a month getting treatment from Bill Tucker, the leading orthopaedic surgeon of the day. During this time Surrey were having a lean time on the field and the attack badly needed reinforcements. Andrew Sandham, then the club coach, and Nigel Bennett approached me and asked me if I would have any objection to giving my ankle a fitness test in the county second eleven.

I was quite happy to do this but put to Nigel and Andrew: 'Why not in the first eleven?' Bill Tucker agreed but gave me a stern warning that at all times my ankle must be strapped up, that I should take only a short run up to the wicket and then only in spells of three or four overs at a time. Furthermore, I was not to attempt to run after the ball when fielding and only very slowly between the wickets when batting.

The game chosen for my return was the traditional Whit Bank Holiday match at Trent Bridge against Notts. We lost the toss and Nigel, with a touch of humour, gave me the ball and said, 'Come on, the walking wounded, see what you can do in three or four overs.' The pitch was one of the greenest I had ever seen at Trent Bridge and the ball swung around so much that even off a five-pace run up I could get late movement and trouble the batsman. I had instant success and heard one of the slips tell Nigel, 'You won't get the ball from him after only four overs.' I finally bowled 27 overs in four spells, picking up six wickets.

Our next game was at Leicestershire on the Grace Road

ground, the new headquarters of the Midlanders. Conditions were then a little on the primitive side (today it is a first-class enclosure). The sightscreen at the pavilion end was a piece of canvas tied between two trees. Surrey batted first on a pitch of unreliable bounce. We lost wickets at regular intervals except for left-hander Laurie Fishlock. When I joined Laurie at number 11 he said, 'I feel like Horatio standing on the bridge when all but he had fled.'

Facing the pavilion end I discovered that I occasionally lost sight of the ball from the bowler's hand, then picked it up just before it hit the pitch. This happened when the bowler delivered the ball from wide of the crease. At this point his arm was outside the width of the sightscreen and the ball left his hand in the darkness of the trees behind it. This did not worry Laurie who, being left-handed, received the ball from a different angle.

When Leicestershire's turn came to bat I opted to bowl at the pavilion end, although Nigel pointed out to me it was into the wind. I delivered the ball from wide of the crease concentrating on bowling short of a length straight at the stumps. Occasionally a batsman would peer into the gloom, then depart stroking his head in disbelief. I was quite happy to see them go, finishing with match figures of 14 overs and seven wickets for 37 runs, and 21 overs with four wickets for 56 runs.

Then onto Lancashire for the last of our three-match tour. What a comedy of errors it was. The game, traditionally played during the holiday 'Wakes Week', attracted large crowds. Lancashire won the toss and decided to bat. But five minutes before play was due to start a dark cloud appeared, down came a quick, heavy shower of rain passing over so fast it barely obscured the sun. The damage was done. Umpires and groundsmen reported no play before lunch. With a full house and the sun streaming down from a clear blue sky there was panic amongst the Lancashire authorities. The prepared pitch was soaked and there was no guarantee of play until at least three o'clock. So the groundsmen were instructed to cut and roll another pitch on the dry area at the edge of the square in order that we could start straight away.

Out came Cyril Washbrook and Phil King to open the innings. Cyril took guard against me with great confidence, anticipating a delivery from me off my five-pace run up. He lasted one ball. It is said that a ball cannot go faster off the pitch than in the air. Well, this delivery did just that. Pitching on a good length, it took off at additional miles per hour and flew upwards, striking

Cyril a fearful whack on the head, felling him to the ground – fortunately without serious damage, but hard enough for him to be assisted back to the pavilion.

Our wicketkeeper, George Mobey, had been standing up, at my request, to my short run, medium-pace stuff in the two previous games of our tour. He now announced that he was a married man with two kids and saw no justification in standing up. He stalked a dozen paces back in spite of my appeals.

An over or so later Phil King was a recipient from my end. The ball took off in similar fashion to the delivery that had hit Cyril. Phil shoved his bat up in desperate defence, deflecting the ball over the slips' heads. 'To hell with this,' he said, 'I'm getting out, I can get a better living working at the dog track.' (He occasionally acted as a tic-tac man.) He proceeded to stand a yard outside his leg stump and invited me to bowl a straight one.

The Lancashire captain, Jack Fellows, like our Nigel Bennett, was inexperienced. Under instructions from the Lancashire committee, Jack came dashing out of the pavilion to confer with Nigel. He wanted an agreement that the fast bowlers would pitch the ball well up to the batsman. I pointed out that I could hardly be designated fast off my five-pace run, to which the two captains agreed. However, Alec Bedser, at fast-medium, was in his first season and inclined to obey orders, so he pitched the ball well up. But I soon pointed out to Alec that batsmen would always take advantage of bowlers on a plumb batting pitch and that he should now take the opportunity to 'make hay whilst the sun shone'. (He did and finished with five wickets for 65 runs.)

As the game went on, the pitch progressively improved into a firm, safe batting strip with runs coming from Surrey and from Lancashire in their second innings. Eventually Surrey required eleven runs to win. Arthur McIntyre was still at the crease. I reminded him we had plenty of time to get the runs and also to remember I could only do a very slow trot so the ball must always be well away in the deep before we attempted a single.

Mac was known in the game as one of the quickest runners between wickets. The first ball he received he hit to mid-wicket and called for me to run. I set off but had no chance. The ball had gone to John Ikin, one of the best fielders and accurate throwers in the game. Mac passed me when I was only three yards from my ground. I was run out by three-quarters of a length of the pitch.

Mac often batted with Jack Parker, a number 5 or 6 batsman. Jack was tall and a little slow off the mark between the wickets and was often the victim of a McIntyre run out. Mac was selected for the Australian tour in 1950/51 as the reserve wicketkeeper-batsman. He played in his batting role in the first test at Brisbane. Jack was at home in England. In the winter close season he was in business, so he followed the cricket on the radio. When Mac came into bat, Jack was having his breakfast, together with his daughter aged five. His wife was upstairs making the beds. The commentator suddenly said, 'McIntyre has played the ball a little wide of deep third man. He is going for two. He will have to hurry. Good Lord, he's trying for three – he will surely be run out. He is by five yards.' Jack, a passionate supporter of English cricket, could not contain himself, abusing Mac with many adjectives. Returning home that night from his office he had a frigid reception from his wife.

'What's the trouble?' he asked.

'You should be ashamed of yourself. Your daughter came upstairs and asked me what was the meaning of various words Daddy had said.'

Nigel Bennett almost lost us the last match of the season at Hastings, when we had to circumvent his instructions. We wanted 48 runs to win in twenty-nine minutes. Nigel decided that Laurie Fishlock, who normally opened, should stay back. Nigel believed that Laurie, being a left-hander for whom the field would have to keep changing, would waste time. We disagreed. Laurie was our hardest-hitting batsman and we reckoned he was the one who could knock the runs off. We told Laurie to pad up and go to the side of the pavilion out of sight. If a wicket fell he was to rush straight on. With 27 runs required a wicket fell and out dashed Laurie to Nigel's astonishment and annoyance. But he scored only 3 runs in the first two overs he received. Whereupon Jack Parker picked up a loaf from the dining room table, walked to the front of the pavilion, put two fingers to his mouth and emitted a whistle which could be heard all over the ground. This caught Laurie's attention. Jack held the loaf aloft and pointed to it, the message being 'Use your crust.' The message was understood and Laurie started swinging his bat to the ball and the balance of runs was knocked off in the space of four overs.

A few weeks later we were at Derby playing Derbyshire. They were well on top throughout the game until the late afternoon of the second day. When I went out at number 11 bat to join Laurie he was still at the wicket. He said, 'Let's try and make a fight of it,' and our last wicket partnership put on 79 runs.

We made Derby fight for their runs and, in the later stages of their innings, Alec Bedser and myself had bowled, apart from the tea interval, for three hours unchanged. We had eight Derby men out. If we could only get another wicket we would be home and dry, the last Derby players being known as 'non-batters'. But we never got at them. Our slip fielders dropped five catches in the space of three overs, leaving only two very tired and frustrated bowlers to console each other.

We had to travel on immediately to Leeds for our next match, against Yorkshire, on the Headingley ground. We arrived too late for dinner at our hotel. Food rationing, a year after the war had finished, was still in operation so the team went to bed that night hungry as well as tired.

I was so hungry I woke up early next morning and arrived at the dining room before the staff had started to serve breakfast – only to be beaten to it by Alec and his twin brother Eric. When we did have breakfast, it was so sparse we were still hungry. We toured the nearby area and found a café. The proprietor proved to be a cricket fan and, after listening to our tale of woe, produced three plates of eggs and bacon and toast and marmalade.

Our skipper won the toss and although the wicket looked to have a touch of grass decided to bat. A grateful Bedser and Gover stretched themselves out in the dressing room for a 'spot of shut eye' after the previous day's efforts. But at 3.30 p.m. we were on the field and bowling again. Frank Smailes, the Yorkshire pace bowler had bowled Surrey out. The only batsman to hold him off had been Stan Squires and he fell not to a swinging delivery but to a 'beamer' straight at his head.

Nigel Bennett retired at the end of the season. He had become very popular with the Surrey side and made many valuable contributions, scoring over 850 runs.

4

Learning the Technique
of Fast Bowling

AS A YOUNG schoolboy I used to save up my pocket money in order to go to the Oval in the summer, but not only to watch Jack Hobbs and the other famous batsmen; my special hero was fast bowler Bill Hitch. He had an unusual run up to the wicket of about twenty-one paces, with a little hop every seven paces, and then a final charge to the bowling crease. He stood about five feet ten inches and built himself a reputation as one of the greatest short-leg fielders of all time, and also as a hard-hitting number 8 batsman. I used to be fascinated by the speed he could generate, and in our pick up games at school I was always 'Bill Hitch'.

I suppose I was a natural fast bowler. Whatever age group I was in I was the quick bowler. The finer points were not for me. I just charged up to the bowling crease and hurled the ball down as fast as possible, often inaccurately, but in junior school cricket the straight ball usually brought a result. I tried hard to think about my action. I always fell away towards the off side before I released the ball, unlike my hero Bill. It was in my second season of watching him that a chance came to sit in the stand at the Vauxhall end of the ground when Bill was operating from the pavilion end, and on this occasion I used a pair of borrowed field glasses. This enabled me to see a close-up of Bill's action, and after a while I tumbled to the fact that, on delivering the ball, his whole body seemed to go over his front leg and both arms swung towards the batsman. 'That's it,' I said to myself, and off I went to emulate Bill. It took some time and many hours of practice before I began to get the feel of going over the front leg towards the batsman.

As I developed physically and progressed from school to first-class club cricket, I was always told I had a good action. However, when I first played at the Oval my knowledge of bowling was limited. I simply held the ball alongside the seam and let it go as fast as I could. All the coaching as regards the action came from Herbert Strudwick. Struddy said, 'Keep your left arm up and look at the spot where you wish to pitch the ball.' Percy Fender advised me on the tactics to employ in getting batsmen out. Then, after three years, came Frank Foster of Warwickshire and England, who, in tandem with the great Sidney Barnes, had bowled Australia to defeat in Australia in the 1910/11 Ashes series. The series was won by four matches to one: Foster taking thirty-two wickets at an average of 21, and Barnes thirty-four wickets at an average of 22.

My meeting with Frank came about at the Oval during a match when I had time on my hands. Surrey, having won the toss, were batting and, as usual, were occupying the crease all day. Just after lunch Percy Fender asked me to go to his dressing room. 'Alfred,' he said, 'I want you to meet Mr Frank Foster, who will talk to you about swing bowling.' I had read all the cricket books I could lay my hands on, so I knew I was about to meet one of the legends of the game. Frank was only 42 but had been retired for several years. He said that, although I had a good action, he might be able to improve it and also my ability to get lateral movement on the ball in the air and off the pitch. Would I mind a few suggestions? 'Mr Foster,' I said, 'I would be grateful for any help you could give me.'

We talked for well over an hour. He stood me in front of the big mirror in the dressing room going through the motions of the action, the correct way to hold the ball and the importance of the hand behind the ball at the moment of release, the position of the left shoulder on arriving at the bowling crease and the importance of the co-ordination of both arms for the delivery of the ball, as well as the mental approach before each delivery. 'Remember,' he said, 'to be able to bowl fast is a gift and an art.' I confessed to him I might have thought the former but had never regarded it as an art. He said that, to be able to control length and direction, and to also control the swing on the ball by using the crease, and the timing of releasing the ball, is an art. And, he added, 'Never forget it.' He went on, 'You will have to put in a lot of hard work and practice.'

So I started to practise early next day and when Percy Fender walked into his dressing room at 11.00 a.m. ready for an 11.30 a.m. start the dressing room attendant said, 'Your young fast bowler will kill himself. He has been bowling by himself in the nets since 9.30 a.m. this morning.'

I had arrived at the Oval and gathered a dozen balls from our dressing room, polished them on one side with an oily rag and then tried to put into practice Frank Foster's advice. I started with a short run and after the first twenty frustrating deliveries I suddenly clicked and the balls started moving away. I was very chuffed but going on to my long run I could not attain the same degree of control over the ball. I kept going and there was a slight improvement, but when I finished the practice at eleven o'clock I realized I had much hard work ahead.

Taking the field thirty minutes later the skipper made no reference to my net practice simply putting me on to open the bowling. He did ask if I wanted any different field placements to my normal setting so I asked for a third slip in place of the long-leg fielder. This was granted and I found the odd ball swinging away when I pitched it outside the off stump so I aimed the ball outside the leg-stump area. The ball now went straight outside the leg stump so out went my third slip back to deep long leg. The odd delivery still moved away but without any sort of consistency. But at least it was an improvement, whereas before my talk with Frank Foster I had simply held the ball seam up and delivered it in the direction of the off stump, quite accurately until I tried for extra pace. Then I could not analyse my action; now I knew the 'break-down'. I knew what I was trying to do. I finished up with four wickets out of the first seven for 60 runs; that, I reckoned, was a good performance on a plumb Oval wicket. When the innings finished Fender asked me to go to his dressing room and, after a pat on the back and a 'Well bowled', he said, 'It's fine to make the odd delivery move away, but difficult for me to place the field for you if you are going to fire some deliveries down the leg side. I think when you saw the ball moving slightly away when it was in line with the off stump that you tried to make it move by pitching on the leg stump and just outside.' He added, 'You were asking the ball to do too much – to swing from the leg-stump area towards the slips the degree of swing must be much bigger.'

He said he would be in the nets at ten o'clock the next morning and would bat against me for thirty minutes. From the batting crease he would be in the best possible position to watch the whole action and delivery of the ball and my follow through. This was followed by a long session in his dressing room going over and over the advice Frank Foster had given me. 'We will put it down on paper.' We did this at some length analysing as we went along. 'Now,' he said, 'keep that on you at all times. Read it in the dressing room, at home, on the train when we are travelling away, and there will come a time when you can run up to bowl and go through the delivery of the ball quite naturally without having to think about it just before you start your run up. You have lots of hard work ahead', he went on, 'you are lucky to have had help from such a great bowler. I know you will make the most of it.'

I carried on with my net practice at every opportunity for the rest of the season and gradually my arms, legs and body began to co-ordinate in the 'Foster' way. In the following winter I spent all my spare time with Herbert Strudwick in the indoor nets and at the end of the close season my practise had paid off; I had greater control over the delivery and had added at least two yards of pace.

I could now open the bowling with a full complement of slips and move the new ball towards the off side from the leg-stump area. I realized also that Frank Foster had not interfered with my basic action but simply improved it by a small adjustment to my natural fast bowler's delivery.

In 1936, when I was on the way to my first 200 wickets in the season, C. B. Fry wrote: 'Alf Gover may not have a graceful run up to the wicket but once he gets to the crease and delivers the ball he looks like a "thoroughbred".' Looking back to my 'Foster' learning days I realize it gave me a good insight into not only how the bowling action should be delivered but also the mechanics of how the action is achieved. This is something that I am quite sure helped me later, both in my coaching career on my retirement and in my indoor cricket school. I had many first-class and Test match bowlers under my wing, fast, fast-medium, medium and spinners and any success I had with them was helped by the picture of the art of bowling given to me by Frank Foster.

But what it is that makes a fast bowler 'tick'? They all want the magic secret for hurling the ball down at the batsman at 80 miles per hour and more. I give them all the same frank answer. I am no magician. Fast bowlers are born, not made. Gather together a crowd of good young cricketers at the nets and invariably the majority will try to bowl as fast as they possibly can. Inevitably, one boy will stand out above all others. He will have a natural whip and pace that is lacking in the others. He might (at that tender age) lack style, but he will have balance and co-ordination, and that little bit of natural ability that goes to make a 'quickie'.

The outstanding fast bowlers have all had the one common ability to whip the bowling arm over, at the pace necessary to get the ball moving down the wicket at speed towards the batsman. Fast bowling is no game for weaklings, especially in county and Test cricket, when stamina and strength are an essential to get the fast bowler through the match. The main physical requirements are a good sound pair of legs and a strong back. I have yet to meet the first-class pace man who did not possess good back muscles.

The fast bowler should be able to co-ordinate his leg, arm and trunk movements before and during delivery of the ball, in such a way that he can bring his bowling arm up from behind and over at a speed which will accelerate the arm until it is going at its quickest at the moment of releasing the ball.

Using an orthodox action, the fast bowler will go through the following drill (assuming he is a right-hander): as he commences the final delivery stride he turns sideways on, and lands with the weight on the back leg, with the right foot parallel with the bowling crease. Simultaneously with the turn of the trunk, the right (bowling) arm is taken to a slightly bent position, with the hand holding the ball about level with the bowler's forehead. The left arm follows the right arm up, fractionally later. He will now be looking at the batsman over the left shoulder and past the left arm, and his back will be arched. At this stage the balance of the body is thrown away from the objective (the batsman), the left shoulder directed towards it. The bowler is now wound up and ready to deliver the ball. The right arm begins its downward swing a split second before the left arm starts to swing forward and down. The left leg which has been brought up in a bent position when arriving at the crease is now thrust forward and braced as it hits the ground. The left arm co-ordinates with the right arm, and assists the body in its forward movement over the left leg, as the weight goes forward towards the batsman. The bowling arm is helped by the forward swing of the left arm, as both arms must work together. The hand must be behind the ball.

But to bowl fast the bowler must have body swing. This is the real secret of the genuine 'quick' bowler. This is the ability to turn the trunk back from the sideways position to face the batsman at the moment of delivering the ball – in the shortest possible time. The hips begin to rotate just before the left leg hits the ground. The right side of the body has been released as the bowling arm comes up from behind the trunk, at its greatest possible speed.

The arms in fact work against the body. The left arm goes through a half-circle, but the bowling arm performs a full circle. It is this full circle of the bowling arm performed at speed and working with the trunk turn that gives the fast bowler his pace. The quick release of the right side means that the right hip will come round as the bowling arm swings up, the back now changing from its arched position to a more rounded one. Now the body swing gets to work. The right hip movement releases the whole of the right side, and the shoulders turn back with a jerk to bring the chest facing the batsman. This jerk of the trunk (hips and shoulders) assists the right arm to accelerate in its upward swing. The weight goes forward on to the braced left leg. The right leg follows, the bowling arm fractionally later, working with the hips. The left arm goes forward and down, past the left side. The bowling arm then follows the left arm round the left side of the body, as the weight goes forward and the right leg comes past the front leg. The rotating hip movement and trunk turn allows the back leg to step in front of the left, and the bowler to follow on towards the batsman, but away from the centre of the pitch.

The fast bowler usually takes a lengthy run. Why? Because he wants to be going fast when he arrives at the bowling crease. This speed of run will allow him to obtain the body swing of a quick sideways turn of the trunk, and consequent quick turn back to deliver the ball. When the 'quickie' really wants to let one go, he will get extra acceleration from his last few strides to the bowling crease, and strive to obtain an even quicker turn of the trunk as he delivers the ball.

When the pace man begins to lose his fire at the end of the day, it is not his arms that are tired but his legs. He can't get up to the bowling crease with his former rhythm. When he does get there, he has lost his body swing, and so takes longer to go through the movements of delivering the ball. His early pace has now gone.

Pace is, of course, one of the fast bowler's most potent weapons. However, it did not always work for me. For example, I am often asked how many hat-tricks I performed in my first-class career. The questioner who expects me to recite several occasions is always surprised when I reply, 'Only once, against Worcester on their New Road ground at Worcester.' Though pace had no part in it, it was nevertheless a rather splendid hat-trick, four wickets in four balls, a feat performed rarely, and for Surrey only by Pat Pocock with his off spin, Alan Peach with his medium-pace swingers, and the fast bowler who took 1,000 wickets in four seasons – the legendary Tom Richardson, in the early 1900s.

Strangely enough, it was not off my seventeen-pace run but off a shortened version of seven. This was because early in the season I had strained a muscle in my left side and, as the team were short of bowlers, I strapped my side up and reduced my pace. I bowled medium-quick off the pitch outswingers, with the occasional break back, and, lacking pace, I had to concentrate on a good line and length. Any delivery now lacking a good length would be hit, whereas off the long run up with pace I normally employed I could often get away with a little inaccuracy.

Off medium pace I learned how to make better use of the crease compared to my long run and to deliver from a point where my back foot almost touched the near stump at the bowling crease. This was a great advantage when the shine had gone off the ball and I could let the ball go from a different angle. I was always a willing learner, and took the opportunity to have a long discussion on the art of medium pace with Maurice Tate, the Sussex bowler who had performed many feats for England. It was Maurice who had given Jack Hobbs such a torrid time just before Jack's retirement. He was renowned for his pace off the pitch.

'Alfred,' he said, 'always bowl at the stumps and keep the batsman playing at the ball, have your 'keeper standing up and try to make your away-swing move off the pitch towards the 'keeper's hands. This will help you to keep the ball up on a good length. If tho 'keeper stands back you will tend to bowl too short in an effort to bounce the ball off the pitch into his hands.' I talked years later to Alec Bedser about always having the 'keeper standing up to the stumps. Alec agreed about bowling into the 'keeper's hands. He would know, of course, as he had two great 'keepers: Arthur McIntyre with Surrey and Godfrey Evans for England. Other 'keepers found it difficult standing up to Alex and most stood back.

Maurice also advised me to persevere when bowling on a plumb wicket when the shine had gone off the ball. 'Keep it tight', he said. 'Wait for the batsman to make a mistake or for the ball to do the unexpected off the pitch, in this event surprising both yourself and the batsman.' This is, of course, an entirely different approach for a bowler who is used to attacking a batsman at all times.

At the commencement of the 1936 season I was fully recovered and although I had taken 130 wickets the previous season with the medium-pace stuff I never enjoyed it as well as when I was charging up to the wicket with my long run.

I had always been a fast bowler since my schoolboy days, and then right through to the best stages in club cricket before I became a professional. Like all fast bowlers, I enjoyed the prestige of being the opening bowler. I had to battle with my skipper Errol Holmes who thought I looked a better bowler off my short run and in the first match of the season against MCC at Lord's I was not pleased when he told me I should keep to the short run up. The opposition made over 400 runs, with Patsy Hendren knocking up 202 and my return was two for 132. After the first innings was over I told Patsy of my difference of opinion with Errol Holmes on the length of my run up.

'Get back to your long run and the fast stuff.' said Patsy. 'Off your short run the batsman knows you have to keep on or around a good length, but when you are charging up to the bowling crease off your long run there is more freedom in the length and line and the batsman is not so comfortable, especially as he is wondering if the next ball is to be a short-pitched bouncer.'

To strengthen my case I went to Errol with the current copy of *Wisden*. It had reported on the 1935 season: 'Mention has been made of the heavy toll undertaken by Gover, again he was the only bowler in the Surrey side to take 100 wickets, but his number of victims might have improved had it been used in short spells and allowed his full run up to the wicket. As it was he seldom looked natural.'

So, much against his wishes, Errol gave way. When MCC in their second innings came out to play the remaining three hours left on the third day of the match, I went back to my full run and, in an effort to prove my point, put everything into every delivery. Two wickets were soon down. In came Patsy Hendren, smiling because I had taken his advice. My first ball to him was nudged to the leg-side boundary. The next delivery got up from short of a length and hit him a resounding whack on the left elbow joint (the funny bone). Patsy threw his bat away, rubbing his arm and letting out 'Oohs' and 'Aahs' and making faces, no doubt wishing he had not advised me to change to my old-style run up. Being the leg puller he was, at first we thought Patsy was fooling about, until he told Errol that he would have to retire. I was of course upset, and went straight to him in the dressing room after the game, but he was very generous, saying, 'Well, Alfred, it shows that I was right in my advice to you.'

I was happy to be on my long run again and with the experience of the 1935 season I was not only quicker but much improved in both line and length and control over my outswinger. Given the right condition I could now straighten the ball when delivering from wide of the crease and finished the season with 200 wickets – the first English fast bowler to do so since the legendary Tom Richardson had performed the feat 39 years before. I was also able to take just over 200 wickets the following season.

Years later, long after my pace bowling days were over, I did manage to perform another hat-trick. Three years after I had given up playing any form of cricket, I was talked into playing for a team called 'The Old Parisians'. They were so called because they played a weekend's cricket in Paris every year.

It was a bitterly cold day on the second Sunday in October, though fortunately it was only to be a half-day game and I wore two long sleeve sweaters and a slipover, plus a scarf. I declined an invitation to field in the slips, instead taking my freezing hands to the comparative safety of the deep field. When numbers 8 and 9 came together the skipper persuaded me to leave my lonely patrol in the deep field and join in the game by turning my arm over at the tail enders. Still wearing 'full kit', to my surprise I took successive wickets with the fourth and fifth deliveries. Before number 11 arrived to take guard I turned to the umpire and said, 'I have only had one hat-trick in the whole of my playing career and I would like to do another, especially as this is probably my last game.' Number 11 missed the final delivery which struck him on the inside of his right leg close to his abdoguard. I let out a yell, 'How's that?' and up went the umpire's finger, followed by, 'Well bowled, Mr Gover.'

I must confess that I never had the cheek to use this performance to 'double' my record of hat-tricks!

5
Thoughts on Umpiring

UMPIRES WERE, of course, very much part of my life in cricket. My youthful discourtesy to Joe Hardstaff, senior, – and subsequent telling off by Percy Fender – had taught me that umpiring is a difficult job and that the umpire's decision should not be queried.

In a game against Yorkshire I saw an exceptional piece of umpiring by Frank Chester. Frank had lost a hand in the First World War and, on the resumption of cricket, had taken up umpiring at a comparatively young age. He had quickly become the leading umpire of the day – an automatic choice to stand in Test matches. On this occasion I was bowling to George Macaulay, who played forward, bat and pad together, at a ball short of a half-volley pitched in the off-stump area. There was a loud click as the ball went past the inside edge of the bat. Up I went, accompanied by loud appeals from wicketkeeper and slips. To our astonishment, Frank turned the appeal down. However, at the end of the day's play, the wicketkeeper told me the ball had in fact been diverted by the outside edge of the off stump without disturbing the bails.

Frank also made a quick decision in another Surrey versus Yorkshire game at the Oval. Yorkshire's attack was weakened by the absence of Bill Bowes, their opening bowler, and on a plumb Oval track we batted on well into the morning of the second day. Hedley Verity, the England left-arm spinner was bowling to Freddie Brown, a renowned clumper of the ball. We had over 500 runs on the board when Hedley, to show his disagreement with the whole proceedings, without warning ran up to the crease in his usual way and let go an underarm job. The ball had hardly left his hand when Frank's shout of 'No ball' resounded round the ground. Freddie Brown, the receiving batsman, showed his appreciation by hitting the ball clean out of the ground, over the wall on the gas holder side of the ground.

I always looked forward to playing against Yorkshire. They were an uncompromising lot on the field, great competitors, although friendly enough off the field. They were either winning the championship or challenging for the title in those days although Surrey, with their powerful batting line up, always gave them a close game. However, on one occasion in 1938 we were very much the underdog. Travelling up to Leeds by train Struddy told us that in his early days under similar circumstances bowler Tom Richardson had enquired about the best train back to London on the last day of the game and was told that it was 3.20 p.m. Tom said that he and Bill (Lockwood), his fast bowling partner, would see that the side were on that early train – and they were.

On hearing this story I said that what Tom and Bill could do so could we, Alfred Gover and Eddie Watts (my fast bowling partner). But how wrong we were – we caught the 3.20 p.m. train alright, but we lost by an innings and 185 runs. Herbert Sutcliffe scored 129, Len Hutton 103 and Maurice Leyland 103 in a Yorkshire total of 519. Alfred and Eddie proved 'humpty dumptys': Gover got two for 111 and Watts one for 113!

Sutcliffe did well that day – and did so again when I bowled to him at the Oval during another Surrey versus Yorkshire fixture. This time, though, I could claim luck was not on my side. Herbert, who often opened for England with Jack Hobbs, had a remarkable temperament and was always confident in his ability, no matter how many deliveries he might have played at and missed. In this game conditions were ideal for swing bowling and I surprised myself by beating him five times in the first two overs, just outside his off stump. Herbert, playing at the ball without getting an edge to the behind-the-wicket fielders, said at the finish of the second over, 'Well bowled Alfred, it's obviously my day and I must score a hundred having got away with these two overs.' He was right and now full of confidence duly hit up his one hundred.

The Yorkshire approach to the game was typified when Surrey played at Bradford in the year that George Macaulay had his benefit. George had toured South Africa the previous winter, one of his team-mates on the tour being Andrew Sandham, so when George had a benefit game arranged on the Sunday he asked Andrew to play. Andrew accepted and on his return on Monday morning told us that he had scored a 50 and had a most enjoyable time staying with George who proved to be a first-class host. Andrew had been a few runs not out on the Saturday night and was due to take the first ball of the day to be bowled by George on the Monday. This, to Andrew's surprise, was a 'fast beamer' straight at his head. He dodged it and looked up the wicket to see George, hands on hips, glowering down the wicket, as if to say: 'Yesterday is forgotten – now it's business as usual.'

Brian Sellars, the Yorkshire captain during most of my career, was a down to earth person. Skippering a side containing so many great players he had to be a stern disciplinarian, but he kept his sense of humour. On one occasion when playing at the Oval he said to me, 'I haven't scored a run lately, what about giving me one to start?'

'Sure,' I replied and proceeded to bowl a bouncer at him. 'You asked me to give you one so that's it,' I said down the pitch.

'Fair enough, now let's have a do,' he replied.

In 1947 at the Yorkshire game at the end of the season I was having a beer with him after the game and he said, 'I hear you are retiring Alf. Well, if you had been born in Yorkshire I would have been pleased to have you in my side.' I was flattered, it was a great compliment coming from a Yorkshire man.

A few players do go on to be umpires after retiring from the first-class game. My own experience of umpiring was, however, not a great success. In 1945 after my discharge from the Army I joined my wife and children, who had been evacuated from London to near Ascot. Shortly after my arrival I heard that the West of England XI, a team made up of professionals, was due to play a charity match at Reading. I decided to hop on a train and meet up with a few old cricketing friends. The local organizers thought it would be a good idea for me to be seen on the ground and pressured me into umpiring. That was my first mistake. I had never even umpired at school, always playing and leaving the umpiring to other boys. Opening the bowling at my end was Lofty Herman, the Hampshire fast-medium bowler, whose main line of attack was the inswinger mixed with the occasional leg cutter. The conditions were ideal for swing bowling, a green wicket and low clouds. His first ball, delivered from wide of the crease started in a line towards the batsman's middle and off stumps and swung so much it finished wide of the 'keeper's hands standing back.

'Now Lofty,' I said to myself, 'bowl nearer the stumps, aim outside the off stump. With this degree of swing you should have a chance to hit the stumps if the batsman misses.' I mentally bowled the next few balls for him as he moved progressively closer to the stumps. 'Now Lofty,' I thought again, 'this is the time to bowl your leg cutter from wide of the crease, pitch it on the middle and leg stumps and the ball will straighten.' But before my wishful thinking could come off Lofty turned to me saying, 'When are you going to call "Over", Alf? I have bowled eight already!'

Just before lunch Lofty came back for a second spell. With the shine off the ball the degree of swing was much less and I was interested to see the mixture of cutters and seamers that Lofty bowled. In his last over before the interval he gave a loud appeal for a catch at the wicket. I had heard nothing and stood undecided on my decision so called out to the batsman, 'Did you get an edge?' On receiving the reply in the affirmative I raised my forefinger. As we trooped off the field I took off my white coat and handed it to the match organizer. 'I don't think I am cut out for this passive role,' I said, 'give the job to someone with better hearing than mine!'

Frank Chester was caught out in the nicest possible way in a Surrey versus Middlesex game at the Oval. I was bowling to Denis Compton, who four times in three overs stepped back just before I reached the bowling crease refusing the delivery because something white was being waved about in the pavilion behind the 'bowler's arm'. Frank was getting irritable when, despite his having shouted and gesticulated towards that area, the waving in the pavilion continued. Eventually, Frank, accompanied by myself and Denis, walked to the pavilion only to find that the culprit was my dear wife using the scorecard as a fan to keep cool in the heat of the day. Both Frank and Denis were old friends of ours and Denis had a broad grin on his face when Frank said, 'Now, Marjorie, I know Alfred wants all the help he can get bowling at Denis on this wicket, but I can't allow you to assist him this way!'

And help I did need. The scorecard at the end of the day read: 'Compton, caught and bowled Gover, 99.' Nearing his hundred, and with only number 11 at the other end, Denis had kept taking a single off the last ball of the over. I decided this must stop so I placed my field with the majority in front of the wicket. Bowling straight half-volleys, and making Denis play in front of the wicket, I had hardly commenced delivery of the ball when he was out of his crease and smacked the ball straight back at me. It was in sheer defence that I managed to catch the ball in my midriff before I had completed my follow through. As we went off I congratulated Denis on his knock, adding that it was a pity that he did not get that single before getting out. He thanked me and said, 'I enjoyed that last little bit.' Denis was not a bit worried about missing the magical three figures; he played the game for enjoyment as well as for his side.

A contemporary of Frank's on the umpires' list was Bill Reeves, an old Essex player and a quick witted cockney. In 1934 I had been in the twelve for the Lord's Test but was left out at the last minute. Later on in the season Surrey were playing Notts in the Bank Holiday fixture and Bill was standing at my end. I knew that 'Plum' Warner, chairman of selectors, was there so I put the maximum effort into every delivery, but without success. The ball was edged through the slips several times and when I beat the bat with a ball pitched on the stumps I saw it sail past without connecting. At the end of my opening spell with nothing to show for it I noticed the flag on the pavilion was at half-mast. I turned to Bill and asked who the flag was at half-mast for. Quick as a flash Bill replied, ''Cos you aint got a wicket yet.' However, I did pick up wickets later in the day and was in the twelve selected for the Oval Test, only to be left out once again at the last minute.

Of all the laws of cricket there is no explanation in the rules for 'kicked out'. I was involved on two occasions when the decision could have been 'kicked out' in place of run out. One was at Coventry, when we played Warwickshire. Jim Laker was bowling to Peter Cranmer and I was one of two covering the cover-point area, the other being John McMahon, an Australian left-arm spinner. John had played Australian Rules Football and had been one of the specialist kickers in his side. I was playing with my left side strapped up and found difficulty in making a quick swoop at the ball. Peter Cranmer played the ball towards my right side so I kicked it towards John saying, 'Yours Mac'. Mac took a flying kick at the ball with his left foot; the ball hit the stumps at the non-striker's end and out went the unfortunate Peter. He was a rugby international so knew something about footwork, but his remarks as he departed were somewhat unprint-able towards Mac and myself.

Another left foot, this time a more famous one, was involved in similar circumstances at the Oval in 1946 during the final Test against India. I was bowling at the opening batsman V. J. Merchant, Denis Compton was fielding down the wicket two or three yards deeper than for the normal silly-mid-on position. V.J. played the ball gently to the right-hand side of Denis and set off for a run. Denis pivoted on his right foot and swung his left foot, which he had used to good purpose on the soccer field for both Arsenal and England, to boot the ball onto the stumps. Poor V.J. was run out by yards.

During a Middlesex versus Essex game at Lord's, Bill Reeves was on duty and Middlesex were in the field. The morning had commenced with a cool breeze blowing across the ground and as the day progressed the breeze stopped, sending the temperature up. Bill stood with the bowler's discarded sweater and slipover round his waist and the batsman's sweater round his neck. The Middlesex emblem on sweaters was three swords and when Walter Robins, the Middlesex skipper, threw his sweater across to Bill as well Bill said, 'And what am I supposed to do with this?'

To which Walter Robins replied, 'You can stick it where the monkey sticks his nuts if you like.'

'What!' said Bill, 'swords and all?'

6

India

EARLY MORNING, the sun streaming through the cabin portholes, the smiling steward waiting with my morning cup of tea, and the luxury liner *The Viceroy of India* sailing smoothly on the Indian Ocean towards Bombay. It was hot even in the air conditioned cabin – not that I cared a hoot. I pinched myself once again to remind myself that I was on my first ever overseas trip. I was living a life of luxury and this was to go on for the next five months whilst I toured the sub-continent with Lord Tennyson's team playing unofficial 'Test matches'.

It was a pretty good cricket side that he had assembled to take on the might of All India Cricket. The batting line up was Lord Tennyson (Hants and ex-England captain), Tom Jamieson (Hants), Joe Hardstaff, junior, (Notts and England), Norman Yardley and Paul Gibb (both Cambridge undergraduates but also regulars in the Yorkshire side during the summer vacation), Jim Parks (Sussex and England), and Bill Edrich (Middlesex and England). The all-rounders consisted of Stan Worthington (Derby and England: right-hand bat, medium-fast outswing and off cutters), George Pope (Derby: right-hand bat, medium-fast in-swing and off cutters), and Jim Langridge (Sussex: left-hand bat, left-arm leg spin). The specialist bowlers were Alf Gover (Surrey and England: fast right-arm), Arthur Wellard (Somerset and England: fast right-arm), Peter Smith (Essex and England: leg spin), and Ian Peebles (Middlesex and England: right-arm leg spin). The wicketkeepers were Neil McCorkell (Hants) and Paul Gibb. Paul was reserve, but in later years played as wicketkeeper-batsman for England.

For the first few days we relaxed, resting from the season not long finished and keeping fit by playing the various deck games. This tranquillity was soon to be rudely shaken. Lord Tennyson, a cheery extrovert, discovered a cricket net on board and a search of our cricket gear in the hold brought up one cricket ball. We were now on the hottest part of our journey and we were told to prepare for net practice. It would, Tennyson said, be good for us and it would be entertainment for our fellow passengers. The skipper took first knock showing his full range of shots, helped by his bowler who pitched the ball under instructions in the appropriate places for the particular strokes. He then retired to take a shower and a cool drink letting us get on with it for the next two hours. This, we thought, cannot go on. We must lose our solitary ball. A little financial help for the crew member responsible for erecting the netting left a gap in the top. Then a ball from myself pitched on the appropriate spot to allow batsman Joe Hardstaff, junior, to hit it through the hole and plop it into the sea.

The skipper said it was a put up job to end the practice but thereafter we went back to the quietness of the deck games, protesting our innocence.

Our trip was, of course, before the Partition of India. We stayed mainly in maharajah's palaces, or in top-class hotels such as the famous Taj Mahal in Bombay. Each player had a personal bearer who wore the team's colours in his turban and around his waist. My chap was called Nathaniel, and I was informed he had become a Christian just for our trip. The skipper soon became known as 'My Lord the Captain' to the general populace. On our long journeys by train whenever we stopped, and at any time of the day, the locals would meet the train to give a passing greeting to the team. Tennyson in reply to a local chief's message of welcome was always magnificent, but his speech became repetitive, though word perfect. However, his loyal team always enthusiastically led the clapping at the end of his speech as though it was the first time they had heard it.

The maharajahs were great hosts and at Porbander the ruling prince laid on a panther shoot for the skipper who had a reputation as a first-class shot. We left the main palace to travel to a small building in the jungle where dinner was laid on. After the meal we set off in cars. When we reached the thicker part of the jungle we set off up a path about five feet wide. It was quite eerie,

Alf Gower
With every good wish
Jack Hobbs

1. Bob the Butler, here seen with Douglas Jardine, was a well-known character and the recipient of good humoured banter from the Oval fans, especially during Tests and representative games when he would don his tails and white tie. He always had a special drink for me – orange juice laced with lots of sugar. 'It makes for energy', he would say always adding: 'Come on bowl them out'.

2. I opened the batting once – at Northampton, as the Night Watchman, with the Master, Sir Jack Hobbs.

3. My marriage to Marjorie in 1932. We're now nearly 60 not out.

4. Early golfing days with Jack Hobbs and Eddie Watts. This was taken at our Golf Club – Malden in Surrey and this one went down the middle. Jack played off a handicap of seven, Eddie off sixteen and myself off twelve.

5. Off to India in 1937 and saying goodbye to Marjorie and the boys, David and John, on the steps of Wandsworth Manor House. David is obviously aware the farewell cuddle was being set up for the benefit of the cameraman so he directs a peep out of the corner of one eye towards the camera.

6. Lionel Tennyson's team leaving for India. From left: Jim Parks, Bill Edrich, George Pope, Stan Worthington, Neil McCorkell, Peter Smith, Paul Gibb, Lord Tennyson, Joe Hardstaff, Arthur Wellard, Lady Tennyson, Norman Yardley, Ian Peebles, myself, John Langridge.

7. Gentlemen v Players at Lords 1936. The players team coming out of the professionals dressing room (now part of the Warner stand), from left: Wally Hammond (Captain), Maurice Leyland, Harold Gimblett, Joe Hardstaff, myself. At back Bill Copson. Over Hardstaff's right shoulder, Charlie Barnett and Keeper, Neil McCorkell.

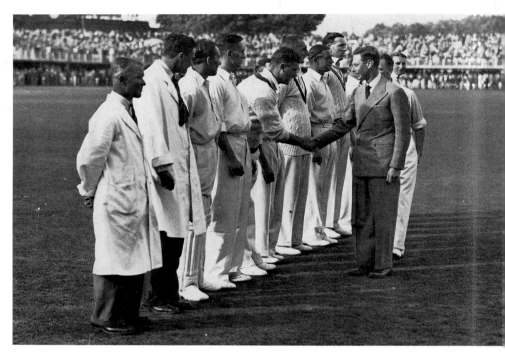

8. At Lord's in 1937 and meeting King George VI. From left: Fanny Waldon and Frank Chester, umpires. Les Ames, Len Hutton, Bill Voce, Hedley Verity, Wally Hammond, myself, Walter Robins, Charlie Barnett.

9. In the Metropolitan Police War Reserve, stationed at West Malden. I joined the War Reserve in 1938 when the Surrey President urged the players to show public spirit by joining one of the services. In the event only myself and Eddie Watts and Laurie Fishlock made the gesture and on the outbreak of War in 1939 we were called up. Eddie and myself left to join the Army within three weeks. The picture was taken outside the Cricket School.

10. The raw recruits, Eddie and myself on the first day in the Army.

11. The British Army Cricket Team at Lords 1942. From left: Back row: Sgt C Harris, Lt J Mercer, Capt B O Allen, Lt A R Gover, Csl Wilkinson, L/C L Compton, Sgt D Compton, Sgt M Leyland, Lt H Palmer, Lt Maxwell. Front row: Brig M A Green, S Christopherson, Major A B Sellars, Major Sloan.

12. The children in 1944 (from left) David aged 11, Elizabeth aged 3 and John aged 9.

13. England v India, The Oval, 1946. From left: Sandy Tait, Len Hutton, Joe Hardstaff, Cyril Washbrook, myself, Denis Compton. Len was odd man out for this stage of the game, played when rain stopped play. We only played for very small stakes. Joe usually won being a very good card player.

14. Surrey v Old England, The Oval, 1947, meeting Field Marshal Lord Montgomery. From right, Jack Hobbs, Arthur Gilligan, myself, Andrew Sandham, Donald Knight, George Duckworth.

15. The Surrey team in 1947, my last season. Back row from left: Andy Sandham, Arthur McIntyre, Tony Lock, Eddie Watts, Eric Bedser, Jack Parker, Alec Bedser, Geoff Whittaker, Laurie Fishlock, Sandy Tait, Herbert Strudwick (Scorer). Sitting from left: myself, Bob Gregory, Errol Holmes, Tom Barling, Stan Squires.

16. H.R.H. The Duke of Edinburgh's Eleven v The Duke of Norfolk's Eleven. An informal match at Arundel with, from left: R W V Robins, Bill Voce, Jim Sims, myself, Errol Holmes, H.R.H. The Duke of Edinburgh, Mike Parker. The game was played in aid of the National Playing Fields Association. H.R.H. was President of the Association for several years.

17. At the Cricket School in 1953 coaching Hanif Mohammad who holds the world individual batting record of 499. Hanif's batting technique was sound and I did not coach this part of his play but simply advised him on the placing of his strokes and the way to build an innings.

104.1.
£ P3a

18. Coaching members of the Pakistan team in 1953. From left: Andrew Sandham, Rosi Dinshaw, Imtiaz Ahmad, myself, Khan Mohammed, Agar Sadaj. Only Imtiaz and Khan Mohammed showed outstanding ability. Rosi and Agar were good club cricketers but not with the ability to rise to first-class standards. Imtiaz and Khan went on to be outstanding cricketers for Pakistan.

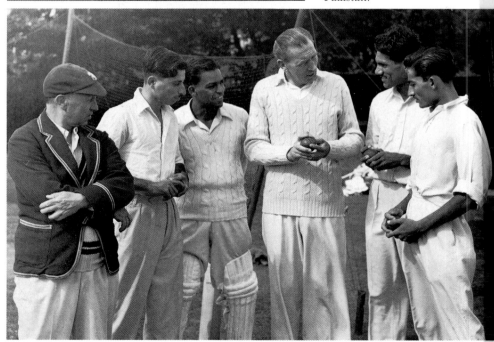

104.1.   P3B

dusk had just fallen and we had all read about the jungle stillness. It was quite uncanny, with not a sound to be heard, no birds singing or any movement in the surrounding undergrowth. We proceeded in single file, escorted by the maharajah and with a shikari (gamekeeper) at front and rear with their rifles at the high port in the ready-to-shoot position. I asked the maharajah why their rifles were being carried in that fashion. 'Well,' he said, 'the damn fellow might hop out on to the path in front of us.' Seeing the look on my face, he added that it was only a precaution. The panther would be curious, he said, and, if we kept walking, it would hop back into the jungle and go away!

On arriving at the 'killing ground' we went into the muchan, the building accommodating the shooters. We were led up to the first floor; here were holes (slits) in the wall which were big enough to hold the 'shooter' and for him to push his gun through and see to take aim. Some thirty feet away on a stone plinth, about ten feet high by six feet wide, was a small goat tethered to a pole which had a light fixed to the top. We were told that the panther would soon be here, attracted by the bleating of the goat, so the maharajah handed Tennyson a rifle.

Now the skipper had dined and wined very well and as he worked himself into a comfortable position pushing his gun through the hole in front of him we reckoned the panther had a sporting chance of escape. The panther duly arrived and with a great leap and a swipe of the paw knocked down the goat and stood still making a perfect side-on target. 'Now,' said the maharajah to the skipper who immediately pulled the trigger. The panther was away like a flash of lightning. The goat in it's death throes jumped and then lay back still. 'My God, skipper,' I said, 'You've shot the ruddy goat!' We had been accompanied by an agency press man who stayed behind after dinner and when we told him about the shooting of the goat he reported it and the story reached around the globe. Tennyson was not too pleased to receive cables from other shooting pals congratulating him on 'getting his goat'. But, bless him, he forgave us later, especially after we looked after him when he contracted a bad dose of dysentry.

We were to travel from Porbander to Bombay by a small passenger boat which, in the absence of a dock, lay some half-a-mile offshore and we had to travel by barge to board it. The skipper was in a bad way with his dysentry and was not capable of getting up the gangway by himself so we had to assist him. He was a big man, broad shouldered and well built, and we had a job getting him up to the ship's deck. However, with grunts from us and groans from our 'patient' we heaved him up the gangway steps. When we eventually made it to the deck we demanded that he be made comfortable in the best cabin and be given medical treatment at once.

Three days later in Bombay we were due to open the newly-built Brabourne Stadium with a game against the Universities eleven. The skipper turned up for the opening ceremony in Ascot-style dress suit and top hat. We were all proud of him but a little nonplussed when he announced that he would play and lead us on this historic day in Indian cricket. We thought it unwise on his part as he still looked rough from his illness but he not only played – he hit a sparkling hundred. What a man!

We had all looked forward to visiting Jamnagur because this was the home of Ranji, a former ruler of the state. Ranji had been a great batsman both for Sussex and England in days gone by and the present incumbent, the Jam Sahib of Nowangur (that being the ruler's title in Jamnagur) was uncle to Duleepsinhji who had likewise played for Sussex and England. The Jam Sahib arranged a day's shooting for the whole team and I asked the skipper if I could be excused as I had no idea how to shoot, in fact I hardly knew one end of a gun from the other. However, he said that as a refusal might offend our host he would put me with one of the experienced shots in our party. This was Arthur Wellard, my fast bowling partner, who had made up the number in many shooting parties in Somerset during the winter off season. I had thought we would be on foot, but found we had to be mounted on elephants where we sat side-by-side in a howdah on the animals' backs with the 'driver' sitting in front steering by prodding the elephant with a pointed stick.

We had been told to only shoot at game running from right to left as the beaters were driving from the right-hand side. Arthur instructed me on how to use the gun, his last words being, 'Whatever you do, don't point it towards me.' I sat with the gun across my knees, finger round the trigger, ready for action. I had not long to wait. A hare burst out and up came my gun, but, while I was trying to remember which eye to use to look down the barrel, the hare did an about turn. My eye being adjusted, I followed it and, satisfied that it was in my sights, pulled the trigger. However, my delight in my achievement was somewhat shattered when Arthur said, 'You idiot!' and, before I could ask why, an officer from the state army galloped up with the request that I hand him my gun as I had just shot back into the line of beaters – fortunately, it transpired, without causing bodily harm.

My bearer, Nathaniel 'the Christian' or 'Natty' as I called him, was a chap who would tackle any situation that arose. In Patiala on the morning of the first day of the match I missed the cars laid on to take us to the ground as I was in my room writing letters. When I realized that I had been left behind I called Natty, and asked him to find me a vehicle, but he reported back that no cars were available. 'Well, get me something,' I said, 'I must get to the ground as soon as possible.' He was away a few minutes and came back to say that 'all was ready to go to the cricket ground, Sahib', and led me out to the front of the hotel where he proudly pointed to an elephant waiting ready with the steps against it's side for me to climb up onto the howdah. Not to let the side down, I gravely thanked Natty and climbed up, followed by Natty who went forward to sit by the 'driver'. The spectators laughed and applauded as I came through the gates of the ground but Tennyson did not appreciate either my late arrival or my wave to the spectators as I descended backwards down the steps from the howdah.

Natty surprised me on another occasion, too. We were travelling by night train to Lahore, and when we were about an hour from our destination, I decided I could not arrive unshaven. Unfortunately, the train lacked hot water, so I handed a jug to Natty and said that I must have some hot water. He had been gone some ten minutes when the train started to move out of the station. 'Where the heck is Natty?' I asked my mate, Stan Worthington. 'There he is,' he said, pointing towards the back of the train. Natty, short of the train by about a hundred yards, was running as fast as possible, holding my jug aloft. He never made it. When I reported the incident a few minutes later to the Indian managing the side, he said: 'Don't worry, he will find a way to catch us up.' And, no sooner had we arrived in Karachi, than Natty reported to me with the jug still in his hand. I asked the manager how Natty could have caught us up so quickly, and received a shrug of the shoulders. I never did find out, as all Natty would say was: 'Train went without me so I come quick.'

At Peshawar, near the Afghan frontier, we played a British

services Northern Command side, made up from the Army and RAF troops stationed in the area. We were given a party in the Officers' Mess prior to the start of the two-day fixture and Arthur Wellard and myself enjoyed ourselves so much that it was 3.00 a.m. before we left. Our hosts turned up later in the morning and on hearing that we were fielding decided that, in view of our late bedtime, Arthur and myself would have little success. In the event, between us we dismissed them for a very low total and explained to our hosts afterwards that a few weak Indian beers was like medicine to us.

We were given a flying farewell two days later when we boarded our train to leave. Four RAF officers in biplanes hedgehopped and buzzed our train for some three miles until, with a waggle of their wings, they flew off. There is an interesting postscript to this flying episode. Paying my first visit to La Moye Golf Club in the Channel Islands years later I was greeted by the course ranger who also acted as starter on the first tee. 'You must be Alf Gover,' he said, 'Do you remember after a game during your tour of India being buzzed farewell by four planes? Well, I was one of the pilots and I have often told the story of the two fast bowlers who saw all their hosts off in the mess until the early hours of the morning and then saw off the opposition the next day.' Small world.

The Indian team in those days was not professional and relied in the main on 'sponsors giving them jobs'. Many players had commissioned rank in their state's army, such as Colonel Naydu and Captain Mustaq Ali. Fast bowler Mohammad Nissar, I was told, was given a stationmaster's job on the state railway but told that he should not go near it; rumour had it that the limit was 200 miles.

When we played a state game at Ajmer we found that, owing to the lack of hotel accommodation, we were boarded out on the English residents. I stayed with the chief of police and found my accommodation was a large tent in his compound fitted with all mod. cons. – bathroom, shower, etc., writing desk, full electric lighting and the entire area carpeted. After dinner he escorted me to my accommodation waving a big torch in front of him. The reason for waving the torch, he explained, was that if there were any snakes around they would go away, and he doubted if there were any about at that time of the year. I was just getting over a dose of dysentery at the time and his words did nothing to improve my condition. I kept the bedroom light on all night and had my bat across the bed at the ready.

Two days later after doses of pills from the local doctor I reported fit to play. We lost the toss and as usual I was given the ball to open the attack. I commenced my long run up, but in my final stride to the bowling crease, just prior to delivering the ball, my faith in the local doctor quickly evaporated and, still clutching the ball, I tore up the wicket and past the batsman, who was backing away in some trepidation. The skipper called out to me as I passed and I tried to explain in one single word what had happened, only to receive the answer, 'That's ridiculous, you are fit to play.' Still at full speed I called out again, using the simple word that referred to dysentry, and carried on. I had almost reached the boundary in a time worthy of an Olympic sprinter when my long-leg fielder, Joe Hardstaff, called out, 'What's the matter, Alf?'

I threw him the ball. 'I won't need this where I am going.' Tearing up the steps I met the twelfth man coming down. 'Out of my way!' I cried, shoving him to one side. But all to no avail, I lost by two yards.

It was, despite the dysentry, a marvellous tour so I jumped at the opportunity to visit India again. In 1964 I was invited to take a team to Calcutta for a short trip playing a four-day game against the Universities and a five-day unofficial Test match against India's full Test team.

I made my side up of past and present international players: Peter Richardson (Kent), who skippered the side; Colin Cowdrey (Kent); Brian Close (Yorkshire); Barry Knight (Essex); Keith Andrew (Northants); Bill Coldwell (Worcestershire); John Mortimore (Gloucestershire). From the West Indies were Basil Butcher, Gary Sobers, David Smith and Lance Gibbs. And from Pakistan, Mushtaq Mohammed.

It was a pretty good side I had assembled with an in-depth batting line up: Richardson, Cowdrey, Close, Basil Butcher, Gary Sobers and Mushtaq Mohammed, plus all-rounder Barry Knight – a fast bowler who could bat for runs at number 8. Bill Coldwell was there to open the attack with Knight, plus the medium pace of Brian Close and David Smith, the off spin of Lance Gibbs and John Mortimore, and the dual talents, pace or spin, of Gary Sobers.

It was Gary that I had to meet off a plane from Australia – he had had to miss our first game because of prior commitments there. He was due to arrive in Calcutta on the afternoon prior to the Test match. In the event he arrived at 3.30 a.m. in the morning. Our game commenced at 10.00 a.m. and when Gary appeared at 9.30 a.m. ready to be driven to the Eden Gardens ground five minutes away he looked very tired and I discovered that he had not slept at all. It made no difference to his play, he hit a magnificent hundred in a little under two hours with Cowdrey and Brian Close partnering him in succession, playing attacking knocks but without keeping pace with Gary. The capacity crowd roared with delight at this feast of run-getting although their full Indian Test attack was on the receiving end. At close of play I said to Gary, 'Do me a favour Gary, do not go to bed tonight you are obviously at your best without sleep.'

I dropped a 'clanger' on the first day of the match. As manager of my team I was expected to sit in the VIP enclosure and help to entertain the distinguished guests. I was sitting next to a chap I presumed was a British Army officer. He wore the regulation off-duty dress, felt hat with a small feather at the side, silk shirt, a gunner's tie, grey trousers and suede shoes. When the players left the field for lunch they were replaced by three Army bands marching around the ground and playing martial tunes. I was most impressed and turning to the British Army officer said, 'I wonder who arranged this entertainment?'

'I did,' he replied.

I said, 'I did not know that British Army officers were still being seconded for duty to the Indian Army.' He replied, 'I am an Indian Army officer.' I asked him what job he did in the Army. 'I am General Officer commanding Northern District Indian Army.'

I apologized, saying that his whole manner and appearance had misled me. He put me at ease saying that confusion was quite understandable as he had gone through Sandhurst and, in fact, started his career with four years in the British Army before commencing his service in the Indian Army.

There was a lot of difference in the look of Calcutta compared with my last visit twenty years before. The statues of the last viceroys and generals looked undressed. The vandals had stolen all the lead. Right arms were held high but without swords, and hands and arms were extended to grip non-existent reins, plus boots without spurs. In various parts of the city I saw these dignitaries looking most undignified; they were a bizarre sight.

I took the opportunity to visit the Royal Calcutta Golf Club where I had played several rounds when in India with Tennyson's side in 1938. Colin Cowdrey and myself arranged a game for 7.00 a.m. on the day we were scheduled to leave India. The environment near the golf club had not changed for the better. The area adjacent to the clubhouse was even worse than on my last visit. The overcrowding and abject poverty were in stark contrast to the 'green oasis' of the golf club which was enclosed by a high brick wall all around the perimeter of the course. Colin and I were two very silent golfers for the first few holes of our round.

7

Army Days

MY TWO VISITS to India, of course, spanned the years of the Second World War. Eddie Watts and I had joined the army on 2 October 1939, having already served four weeks in the Metropolitan Police War Reserve. We became policemen as the result of an appeal by the president of the Surrey County Cricket Club, H. D. G. Leveson-Gower in August 1938. During the Munich crisis he had asked the players to show an example of public spiritedness by volunteering to join one of the civilian services. In the event, the only player to respond to his appeal were Eddie, Laurie Fishlock and myself.

We signed up as policemen and when the crisis was over simply forgot all about it. We received a reminder from the police in September 1939 when war broke out. I was living in Wandsworth and had to report to Wimbledon Police Station, likewise Laurie, who was domiciled in nearby Merton. Eddie, living in Surbiton, reported to Malden (Surrey) Police Station.

I reported for duty on a Sunday, 15 September wearing a light grey (new) summer suit but was issued with only a steel helmet, armband, truncheon and a gas mask and whistle. Laurie and I received a warm welcome from the station inspector, an avid cricket fan, who instructed us to take it easy for a while and go off to the basement café for coffee. We seated ourselves in the far corner of the crowded room full of regular and war reserve policemen.

Suddenly, all hell broke loose. The air raid siren went off like a wailing banshee and the station inspector and his sergeant appeared at the door to issue instructions. They sent officers out in separate bunches, some to help women and children onto trains at nearby Wimbledon Station for evacuation to the country and other officers to clear the streets. I said to Laurie, 'They must have missed us, we will order another coffee.' Suddenly there was a bellow from the door. Our friend the station inspector, all thoughts of cricket forgotten, shouted, 'You two, get going and fill the sandbags to cover the roof.' We tossed up to see who would take the bags on to the roof or to fill them. I won the toss and opted to fill the bags; soon Laurie was climbing the rickety ladder with a heavy sandbag across his shoulders. After an hour's work Laurie was near collapse and I was bemoaning the ruination of my new suit. Two days later we were issued with uniforms and I was told, 'Suede shoes should not be worn, only black leather.'

Eddie, in the meantime, had telephoned from Malden to suggest that, as my family had extended their holiday on the South Coast, I should arrange to stay in my brother's house in Malden. 'Ask the Wimbledon station inspector to transfer you,' he said. I did and it was agreed, so I reported for duty at Malden the following Monday.

I was put on night duty, with orders to patrol a beat which included the BBC Sports Ground. An old friend, Arthur Sellick, was manager there, and on the first night I called on him. He suggested that I only walk the beat three times during the night, and, handing me a key, said, 'Why not spend the times between beats in my office with your feet up?' – an offer I gratefully accepted.

The following week I was on day duty, and at midday I was sent to relieve the regular officer on traffic duty at Shannon Corner, a junction where four roads met. I must have been the worst traffic controller ever – cars coming from all directions were soon in a mess so I walked off the traffic point throwing my arms in the air and left the motorists to sort themselves out! I had let my wife and family know of my transfer to Malden and on the day of my traffic fiasco they had decided to travel up from the South Coast on the A3 to collect some belongings from Wandsworth. On approaching Shannon Corner and seeing the chaos ahead my wife said, 'I bet Alfred's the traffic officer.' How they roared with laughter, when they eventually reached the corner and there was 'Alfred' standing at the side of the road.

Eddie and I decided after three weeks that the life of a policeman was not for us and we made arrangements to join the

Army. On telling the station inspector of our plans he said, 'You can't,' but we showed him the papers from the Army and were released immediately. Three days later we were on a crash course of four weeks at the headquarters of the Army Physical Training Corps (APTC) in Aldershot.

The colonel commanding the unit was Michael Green. I had last seen him playing for Gloucestershire against Surrey. After the war Michael became secretary of Worcestershire and managed the MCC team to Australia in 1946/47. The course members included many sporting stars, mainly from the world of soccer: Frank Swift, Stan Cullis, Joe Mercer, Tommy Lawton, Warney Cresswell, Arthur Rowe, Matt Busby, etc. From cricket came Len Hutton and Stan Nichols. We spent the first three days square bashing. It was all new to us and we tried hard but occasionally it went all wrong. It was my turn to act as drill instructor and my squad of 24 were marching in three files. I was to give them the command 'about turn', so I walked alongside my squad watching their feet waiting for the left foot to go forward at the correct time in order to start the 'about turn' drill. But I waited so long my section sailed 'concertina fashion' into a wall. They broke up in laughter.

Later Eddie Watts managed a half-right instead of half-left to march his men straight into another section marching in the opposite direction. Both sections roared with laughter at Eddie's expense. The colonel was watching the scene accompanied by Regimental Sergeant Major Hopkinson. The RSM complained to the colonel about our behaviour. 'Mr Hopkinson,' said the colonel, 'these chaps are used to discipline in their own walks of life and although household names in sport have accepted the discipline of the Army. Give them two days to settle down and they will master the drill.'

At the end of the first week we were kitted out ready for the gymnasium; plimsoles, running vests, athletic shorts and tracksuit. I enjoyed the gymnasium since, as a lad, I had become familiar with all the equipment and exercises. We also became experts in unarmed combat and were shown how to score the points if judging a boxing competition. This was called the Black and White Exhibition as the two boxers wore singlets marked in black and white squares to show the points marking. The boxers went through the motions of boxing but were not allowed to land a blow to the head.

Eddie went into the ring with Matt Busby. Both Matt and Eddie had boxed at school and for some time all went well, with our instructor stopping the contest occasionally to show us how many points had been scored with blows to the white squares. The punches of course had no beef behind them and both boxers kept their guard down, having no need to cover the face. Suddenly Eddie unleashed a perfect straight left on Matt's left eye (he said afterwards that it was an instinctive punch) leaving Matt with a lovely black eye.

In the evening a game of football was arranged and the staff, strengthened with four footballers, played a team from the Corps. They gave Eddie a game for the Corps team, then discovered that he was a rugby player so put him out of the way on the right wing. He didn't get a kick for the first twenty minutes of the first half, then a corner was given from the opposite side of the field. Eddie decided to join his team-mates crowding the goal area. A high ball came over and Eddie jumped, arms out, elbows bent. In an effort to get up to the ball he flung his bent arms out and Matt, who was next to Eddie, jumped at the same time but never reached his full height, being impeded by a tremendous whack from Eddie's left elbow on his right eye. Two black eyes in one day! We met Matt at Chelsea just after the war and Eddie was introduced as, 'This is the chap who gave me two black eyes in one day!'

Both Eddie and I were made NCOs and posted to detachments of the Officer Cadet Training Unit (OCTU) in Aldershot as physical training instructors (PTI). It was the 'phoney' war period and life was comparatively pleasant. My wife and family had left London to live in the small village of Winkfield, two miles from Ascot, just a month after I was attached to a Royal Engineer OCTU. A month later I obtained a living out pass. I must have been a fit chap in those days, cycling seventeen miles both ways between home and camp and having plenty of exercise during the day. My best effort was two six-mile endurance tests in one day following my cycling.

The Aldershot command soon had a cricket team playing sides such as the Navy, RASC, Sandhurst, RAMC and Civil Defence. Our side called on Company Sergeant Major A. R. Gover, Sergeant E. A. Watts, Sergeant Denis Compton, Captain R. Tindall (New Zealand Test wicketkeeper), Sergeant A. Brown, and Sergeant T. G. (Godfrey) Evans. Our captain was Major Brian

Sellars, the Yorkshire skipper. We also found Officer Cadet R. J. (Bob) Crisp, the South African Test fast bowler, in a Royal Tank OCTU. He turned up without gear of any sort for his first match, fielding and bowling in Army-issue brown canvas shoes, khaki denims and khaki shirt but by the following week we had made a team collection: I found him a pair of flannels, Eddie a shirt, Brian Sellars a sweater and, scrounged from the NAAFI stores, a pair of white shoes. Bob took many wickets for us and he subsequently had a fine war service in tanks with the Eighth Army, gaining a decoration.

The war seemed a long way off until we had an interruption during a two-day game against the Civil Defence. We finished the first day's play and Eddie and I went off to Winkfield in Eddie's car. We had all sold our cars on joining up but Eddie had recently bought an old open Austin for £5. It was so old we swore it went faster uphill than downhill. We went back to the cricket ground early on Sunday for the resumption of the Civil Defence game but by the official start time we were the only persons on the ground. We waited until 2.00 p.m. thinking that the game may have been altered to a half-day for Sunday. We motored back to Ascot, being stopped several times at road blocks to prove identification and we presumed this was part of a big exercise.

Going back to my unit in the morning I found a deserted barracks and my first parade missing. I went off to the Orderly Room. 'Where the heck is my first parade?' I demanded of the lonely occupant, a young sapper.

'Don't you know, Sergeant Major, it's "Cromwell"?'

'What are you talking about? Who is "Cromwell"?' It turned out that 'Cromwell' was the signal for an invasion, that's why everybody had been turned out last night, but it proved to be a false alarm.

Following the false alarm all APTC personnel were summoned to the headquarter's gymnasium and told that, in the event of a real 'Cromwell', we must take our part in defence against enemy paratroopers. The question was immediately asked, 'As the APTC is a non-combat unit, how can we possibly deal with paratroopers?' The reply was, 'You are all experts in unarmed combat and ju-jitsu.' To which we in turn replied, 'That would be useless against bullets.' However, soon afterwards, we became a combat corps and were all given a weapons training course at our various units.

My family lived in a house situated opposite the village cricket ground in Winkfield. The village cobbler, Mr Weller, was the old-fashioned type, sitting at his workbench with his mouth full of nails, surrounded by pieces of leather of all sizes. He had been mending the footwear of the locals and the gentry in the big houses for thirty years. He did complain to me one day about the gentry: they wanted the best attention and service but they always kept him waiting at least six months for his money. He knew the business of all the villagers and of many of the gentry, and whenever I was with him I let him do the talking.

Sergeant Instructor Denis Compton came to see me for help one day. He had recently got married, had been posted to a unit stationed in the stands at Ascot racecourse and he asked if I could help him find accommodation. I took him over to Mr Weller. He was delighted to meet Denis and, after some thought, said, 'I have a friend who is barmy about cricket and he will fix you up.'

Our fame as cricketers did not always open doors for us as it had for Denis. The Winkfield Cricket Ground is on the small side and Eddie and I were invited to play in a Sunday afternoon game one day. Eddie kept belting the ball over the leg-side boundary and into the houses beyond. That was the last invitation we received.

My wife's mother was staying with us, accompanied by Ethel, her life-long maid. Ethel loved my two sons, David and John, and in the summer of 1943 she walked them up to play cricket on Ascot golf course which was laid out within the perimeter of the racecourse. When she returned home she complained about the behaviour of people on the course. Ethel told my wife that she had found a nice green patch with a red flag in the middle which she had thrown away. David and John had then banged their stumps into the grounds three at each end and happily started their game, with Ethel fielding for both sides. The game had been in progress for about half-an-hour when two men appeared carrying some sticks. They ordered Ethel to pack up at once and to take the boys with her. Ethel had indignantly refused saying, 'You should be ashamed of yourselves – their father is away in the Army and you seem to have nothing better to do than to walk around here!' My wife tried to explain to Ethel that the flat grass patch was used by the golfers to putt their ball into the little hole on the green.

After two years at Aldershot I was posted to the South Coast.

My unit's headquarters was at Worthing and we were to train troops in an area between Bognor Regis and Brighton. The commanding officer was Colonel Jordan, a sports journalist by profession, and on my joining the unit he immediately arranged a cricket match on the local recreation ground between his team and a nearby regiment. The game started at 5.00 p.m. I was the only player in whites in my team with the rest in brown canvas shoes and denims. Four other matches were being played at the same time so each game was a little cramped for space. We won the toss and my turn to bat at number 5 soon came. The opposition bowling was moderate and I was soon 49 not out, and looking for the single for my 50, when a fielder from another game came chasing a ball across the middle of the pitch just as the bowler was going to deliver the ball. I stepped back but the bowler let the ball go and hit my stumps. I stood my ground but the umpire said, 'You should know better than that,' and gave me out. The next day I was playing for the Army at Lord's and, looking round the crowded ground, contrasted it with my experience on the recreation ground the previous evening. What a great leveller is our game of cricket!

I now decided to apply for a commission. My application having been accepted, I was summoned to the first of the War Office Selection Boards (WOSB), set up in the Surrey countryside for the last three days of the week. On Thursday and on Friday morning I negotiated all the tests satisfactorily. On Friday afternoon the test was a two-mile run followed immediately by an obstacle course. Both tests were easy for a PTI such as myself. As I came off the obstacle course I was taken at the double into an interview room in front of the five-man WOSB. Because I was so fit and showed no sign of exertion, the colonel in charge found it hard to believe that I had just taken the physical test. I was questioned at length on a variety of subjects, gave what I thought were the right answers and, at the end of the interview, the colonel told me the programme for the next day. I said I would be away, playing for the Army at Lord's, and explained that it was an official duty as the instructions had come from a department of the War Office, the Army Sports Board. On producing the summons to Lord's, the Board gave me permission to be absent.

Later I was given the rank of Cadet Officer and sent to Dunbar in Scotland for officer training. The course consisted of weapons training, lectures in tactics and map reading. I was on my map reading test well out in the hills and looking puzzled at my map, when the commanding officer, Lieutenant-Colonel Coldwell, who had been secretary of Northampton County Cricket Club, pulled up in his staff car and said, 'You should be two miles ahead by now.' I explained that, according to my map, there were two wooded hills on each side of the road but I could see no sign of trees. He glared at me and replied 'Use your initiative, look at the terrain, the trees have obviously been cut down since the map was drawn.'

A few days later Coldwell arranged a cricket match between the staff and the 'course'. He opened the batting for the staff and I opened the bowling for the course. I ran up to bowl thinking, 'Now use your head, get the CO "off the mark" with an easy ball.' My good intentions went sky high and so did the CO. I caught my foot in the matting and hit him smack on the joint of the left elbow (funny bone), and for the second time he looked me in the face and glared. I thought, 'Bang goes my commission.' But the game was, of course, 'off parade' so all was well.

Coldwell returned after the war to be secretary at Northants again. When we met at post-war matches we often recalled 'war games' in Scotland and the painful cricket match.

After the cricket match against the staff, it was back to work for the course. The following day the whole unit went out on exercise in the Lammermuir Hills. I enjoyed the 'war games', but not sleeping on my groundsheet on a cold Scottish October night. The next evening we arrived at Abbey St Bathans, a 'dry' town with not a sign of a pub, much to the disappointment of my section. We settled down for the night in an old barn warm and comfortable after the previous night's freeze, but as soon as we put the lights out, there came the scurry of rats on the rafters and the odd one across the floor. Now, being a 'townie' I am scared of rats, so after sitting up listening to the creatures scampering around I gathered up my clothes and bedded down outside – reckoning that the cold night was the lesser of the two evils.

Duly commissioned as a Lieutenant at the end of the course, I rang Eddie Watts to let him know my exalted rank of two pips, only to hear that he too was now a commissioned officer. I was sent back south again and made several journeys. On one of these I 'bought' an injury to my right knee. Later, doing exercises on a troop ship going to Capetown, we were just three days out of

Freetown when I aggravated the knee and had two operations in Westlake Hospital in Capetown.

The operations were not a success and I was shipped back to England. Here my cricket connections came to the rescue once again. On board the ship taking me home I found my sleeping quarters were in the mess deck, three decks down, in a cramped space having to accommodate 200 officers. The 'beds' were hard mess tables with three blankets each to make a mattress. However, I had been allotted one of the hammocks which were slung up between the 'beds', and with my injury I knew I could never climb up into one. Neither did I cherish the thought of the heat once we had sailed under 'darkened' ship orders when the portholes (painted black) had to be shut tight. All ships, of course, sailed without showing any sort of light.

I knew it would be of little use appealing to the officer commanding the troops on board. He would probably have sent me to the ship's hospital. The ship was the same line as the *Viceroy of India* which had taken me with Tennyson's team to and from India in 1937/38, and I wondered if by chance any of the officers who had served on the *Viceroy* were serving on this ship. I asked a member of the ship's crew the name of the captain, and he told me it was James Carver who had served on the *Viceroy* so I made my way towards the bridge. He was just coming down when I hailed him. He looked at me without recognition at first, until I took off my cap and said, 'Remember the *Viceroy of India*?' He gave me a hard look and then, with a big smile and, putting out his hand, he said, 'Alfred, it's good to see you.' I quickly explained my position, and he said he would send for his chief steward, Fred Tester, a cricket 'nut' who had 'taken' Jack Hobbs and Herbert Sutcliffe to India when they played a series of games for the Maharajah of Vizianagram.

Fred did me proud. He had two cabin suites, one used as a spare office and the other as his own quarters. He moved his office into his own cabin and said that I could have the spare suite. I lived like a lord for the rest of the voyage: a different menu for dinner every night, with a wine list to choose the best vintages. All Fred wanted in return was for me to talk cricket with him and I was only too willing to oblige.

I had two more operations in England performed by Brigadier Rowley Bristow, Consultant Orthopaedic Surgeon to the British Army. After three months physiotherapy treatment at Ascot I finished up with a right leg which would not straighten 100 per cent and the Army dispensed with my services with the verdict that I would never play cricket again.

Of course, I did play again but not before a stint with the Entertainment National Service Association (ENSA). I had a vague idea of what this was, some sort of entertainment for the troops, but never thought I would one day be part of it. I joined ENSA by sheer chance. In November 1944, I was walking down Fleet Street when I met an old friend, the Reverend Sir Herbert Dumnico, who was at that time helping Sir Basil Dean to run ENSA. I was at a loose end, so Herbert asked me if I would consider joining. I replied, 'No, I am not a song and dance man, especially in my present state with one leg and "a swinger" and walking around with the aid of a shooting stick.'

Herbert explained that what he had in mind was for me to visit hospitals and to talk about cricket to Services patients. He added, 'I have heard you make many after-dinner speeches and I am sure you could speak for an hour, about cricket, and then answer questions.' He told me that I would be provided with a car and free accommodation, plus the normal ENSA fee of £15 a week for a one-man show. Within five days I had started on my travels.

My ENSA car was a little Ford 8. The sidelights were very small, being reduced to slits for normal night driving during the war, and I had instructions that the headlights were only to be used in emergencies. The car lacked any sort of heating so in the cold weather I resorted to wearing cycle clips.

My first assignment was in the West Country, visiting hospitals. I enjoyed this new experience but found it diplomatic to first explain that, although I was in civilian clothes, I had served in the Army from October 1939 and had only recently been discharged. I made a habit of prefacing my talks with this information for the next five months.

To get the maximum audience possible most hospitals would arrange for me to give my talk in a ward where the patients were bedridden, so other lads could be brought in from the other wards. I would then extend my allotted time by going round the ward talking to those confined to their beds and who had asked interesting questions about cricket.

After four weeks ENSA decided to transfer me to the main circuit, visiting Army bases in South-Eastern Command. This involved addressing an audience of between 300 and 400 troops.

I was lucky before my first 'performance' in meeting a professional comic whose company were staying in my hostel. He told me, 'Always open up with a joke, against yourself if possible, as that way you get a laugh and sympathy.' Now, I had often made after-dinner speeches to 100 diners, but they were, of course, wined and dined and already in a convivial and receptive mood. Standing up on a stage with up to 300 or so faces looking straight at me and waiting to be entertained was a little daunting, to say the least.

I confess that on that first night I was very nervous. The audience were seated according to rank, the commanding officer and his senior officers in the front row and the junior officers behind them, followed by the warrant officers and sergeants, then the corporals and way back in the back rows were the 'erks'.

I followed the comic's advice and opened up with a joke against myself. It got a big laugh, my nervousness disappeared and I was 'off the mark'. I gave them plenty of entertainment in the next hour, including stories about some of the great cricket players. One story, which always went down well, concerned Don Bradman in the final Test at the Oval in 1934.

I had been picked in the original twelve for England, only to be relegated to the twelfth man's job at the last moment. Part of my duties as twelfth man was to go to the visitors' dressing room at close of play and collect all the bats sent up from the England dressing room for autographing. Whilst I was busy sorting out bats, Don Bradman was dismissed in the last over of the day and came into the dressing room obviously upset, though he did not throw his bat about or show any signs of temperament as he was not that kind of person. I asked Clarrie Crimmett what was the matter with The Don as he had made 254 runs. 'Oh,' said Clarrie, 'he had a look at the pitch before start of play and he reckoned that it looked so easy he could make 400 runs if Australia won the toss.'

I saw my comic again the following morning. Thanking him for his professional advice I told him how well I had been received. He then gave me a further tip. 'What happens in your game when you have performed very well? Do you put that behind you next match?'

'Yes,' I replied.

'Entertaining is exactly the same, you can't live on last night's laughs.'

I showed him the script I worked to and he advised me to learn to memorise as soon as possible as I would get across much better without having to refer to it. 'You can always write reminders on the palms of your hands,' he said. I followed his advice again and within a week was word perfect, but six weeks later I had a 'black' in the middle of my talk. I suddenly dried up and my mind went blank. I wondered what the heck I was doing standing on a stage in front of so many people. It only lasted about 30 seconds but it seemed an eternity before my memory took over again and I carried on. I learned later that stage folk in a long running play, their lines being repeated every night, sometimes have a 'black' and their fellow actors have to 'prompt' them to bring them back to reality. But I was all on my own so I linked in my 'prompters' on the palm of my hands once again. I did have another 'black' in front of the television cameras years later, but that's another story.

My tour of South-Eastern Command came to an end and I was posted to Scotland. On the way, I was ordered to a base near Darlington. My stay was very pleasant, with sunny mild weather. Most of the units were not too far away, but one visit was to a unit stationed well off the main road. My roughly-drawn map brought me to the top of a hill and then instructed me to turn right at the bank at the bottom of the hill. I thought, 'What an extraordinary thing to build a bank in the middle of nowhere with only miles of ploughed fields to be seen.' I stopped a chap driving a farm cart and told him I was on my way to an army unit and that, according to my map, I had to turn right at a bank but could not see any building. He fixed me with a baleful glare and said, 'Bank? Aye, there's bank – that steep bit going up there.' He pointed to the hill opposite. As he walked his horse away, I distinctly heard him mutter. 'Bloody fool!'

My first call in Scotland was at Dunbar, the small coastal town in the Scottish Borders, a place I knew well from a four-week stay there during my Army days. I travelled long distances in my seven-day stay, up to North Berwick, famous for its golf course, and across country to Dalkeith. After Dunbar came Berwick-on-Tweed in Northumberland. The snow had now arrived, and, though the main roads were comparatively clear, the smaller side roads which I often had to use had twelve feet of snow banked up on either side. My little car would go 'bumpty-bump' over the frozen lumps of snow. This, plus the restricted lighting, often made it hard going. But I always said to myself that I was in comfort compared with many other fellows still in uniform.

My next stage was at Alnwick, and although the snow was still thick on the ground that was not my biggest worry. When I looked at my engagement list I found I was booked to talk to a unit of the WAAF (Womens Auxiliary Air Force). I envisaged standing in front of 200 women who would be completely in the dark if I gave my usual cricket talk. When the night came, I still hadn't found a solution. On arriving I asked for the commanding officer, expecting to see a mannish and matronly figure, but I had a lovely surprise as she was about my own age, with good looks and a trim figure.

I said that I hoped her girls would not be bored with listening to me to which she replied, with a twinkle in her eye, 'I thought you might be concerned so I have arranged that only the girls who played cricket for the Women's Cricket Association Clubs can attend your talk. I will also be interested to hear you as I play for the Brondesbury Ladies Club.' The WAAF proved to be a delightful audience, enjoying my stories, and plying me with questions about the great players I had played with and against. They wanted to know more about the technique of batting and bowling and I told them that I had coached several England Lady Test players. They then produced a bat and a ball and the CO suggested that I took my 'pupils' to the gym. It was another hour before I could get away. The girls all had some cricketing ability and were apt pupils. It was one of my most enjoyable evenings.

I then travelled inland to Newcastle and there made my first effort to prove the Army medics wrong when they had told me, 'You will never play cricket again.' Directly I arrived in Newcastle I went to see Stan Seymour, a famous international soccer player. He ran a sports shop in the town and knew me by name. I told him the reason for my visit was to use the Newcastle ground to exercise my wasted muscles. Stan was, at that time, Newcastle's manager and was able to arrange for me to meet his trainer, Andy Mc-Crombie. Andy was an old Newcastle player of about 60 and he was a nice loveable chap. I kitted up with tracksuit and plimsolls and Andy took me out onto the running track and told me to run a lap. I had to explain that my right leg was only a 'swinger', so we went straight back to his treatment room. After a thorough examination, the verdict was physiotherapy and deep massage for three days and I was to stop driving to the ground from Jesmond in the north of the town and walk the two miles every day.

My tour of duty in Newcastle lasted four weeks and at the end Andy's hard work found me not only doing four laps round the pitch but also running up and down the terraces. Stan Seymour told me that I must not offer Andy any money as he would be offended. I will always be grateful to Andy and I sent him tickets for the Oval Test for several years. It was always a pleasure to meet this rough Scot who was one of nature's gentlemen.

Then on to Leeds where the Leeds United Football Club gave me the freedom of their Elland Road ground and dressing rooms on weekdays. I followed the schedule of training set by Andy — plenty of lapping plus terrace work and soon my leg muscles began to show signs of 'life'.

At my next stop in Nottingham, Nottingham Forest Football Club were also kind and hospitable, allowing me to use all their training facilities in the gym as well as the pitch area. Two weeks later I was in Derby and was given permission by Derby County Football Club to use their 'Baseball' ground. I decided that my condition had improved so much I could step up the amount of work, so I went up to 20 laps and a double dose of terrace work plus trunk and arm exercises. I left Derby after three weeks; I felt on top of the world and fit enough to bowl at Don Bradman.

I was coming to the end of my tour. Lincoln was my next and last town. Lacking the facilities of the football club I did some 'roadwork' until I met Bill Tucker, the famous orthopaedic surgeon, who had just returned to England from a prisoner-of-war camp in Germany. Bill had stayed behind with his field hospital after the fall of France in 1940. He was barely recognizable as the big burly ex-Irish rugby international he had been, having lost so much weight. Bill was playing some golf as part of his self-imposed rehabilitation and invited me to join him. He told me that running on hard roads could harm my right knee so I took his advice and swapped to an early morning run round the golf course for the next two weeks.

A few days later I handed in my little car to the ENSA workshop in London. I had enjoyed my tour, meeting many nice people and, I hope, giving pleasure to those I visited. I shall always be grateful to those football clubs for their kindness and generosity. In providing facilities they helped me prove wrong the medical experts who had said that I would never again play cricket.

8

The Post-War Years and
The Gover Cricket School

I HAD MY first taste of League cricket in 1945. I decided if I strapped my knee up I could get away with a Saturday afternoon game. I signed for Royton, a Central Lancashire League Club. I must confess I did not enjoy the greatest success in the League, where the clubs expect their pro to do his stuff every week – which is fair enough as they are paying him a good salary.

Unfortunately, on the slow League pitches, I bowled a fraction too short. I found it difficult to divorce myself from the short of a half-volley length I had bowled in first-class cricket. It was not until later in the season when George Duckworth, the Lancashire and England wicketkeeper, told me to bowl a full length and aim at the stumps that I had any success.

There was an amusing incident early in the season. I walked out to bat at the non-striker's end. The next ball went down to the batsman who hit it in front of the wicket and called me for a run. When I was halfway down, he sent me back. I was out 'by a mile'. As I climbed the steep pavilion steps to a deadly silence, a loud voice called out, 'Call yourself a ruddy batsman?' Now I did think that was a little hard.

Royton released me on the following Saturday to play for England at Lord's against the Australian Services side, made up from Australian Army and Royal Australian Air Force cricketers stationed in England. It was a good side, captained by Warrant Officer Lindsay Hassett and included: Flying Officer Keith Miller, Flying Officer Bob Cristofani, Flying Officer Ross Stanford, Squadron Leader Stan Sismey, Captain Dick Whitington, Sergeant Charles Price, Flight Sergeant Jim Workman, Warrant Officer

Reg Williams, Captain Arthur Cheetham, Flying Officer Reg Ellis and Flight Lieutenant Carmody. The tour's experience did much for Keith Miller. In the five Tests he hit 443 runs with an average of 63 and a top score of 118. Lindsay Hassett was the most experienced of the touring side, having toured England as part of Bradman's 1938 team. Sergeant Cecil Pepper, Flying Officer Jack Pettiford, Stan Sismey and Bob Cristofani made up the rest of the batting in the touring party. Miller had bowling support from fast bowler Reg Williams and fast-medium Jack Cheetham. The spinners wre Bob Cristofani, Reg Ellis and Charles Price.

They played the first of the five Victory Tests at Lord's. Sir Pelham Warner, who was running cricket at that time, 'phoned and asked me to play. At first I refused, on the ground that my knee would not stand up to a three-day game, but eventually I accepted.

I had bowled for just over an hour before close of play on the Saturday, bowling Jim Workman, but overnight my knee 'blew up' and I spent the whole of Sunday giving it the hot and cold water treatment. I took the field on Monday with the knee heavily bandaged and felt no discomfort in my first three spells. But in mid-afternoon, with Doug Wright bowling his leg spinners to an off-side field, I found myself the only fielder on the leg side at mid-wicket. Lindsay Hassett, hitting against the spin, hit the ball towards the long-on boundary. Wally Hammond called out from first slip, 'Leave it to Alf', but, having just come off a lengthy spell of bowling, my knee had stiffened up. So I set off with one leg and a dragger to vociferous shouts from the obviously Middlesex supporters on the ground. The ball stopped inches short of the boundary ropes, and when I eventually arrived back from the deep field, I noticed Lindsay at the non-striker's end. 'So you ran three?' I said. 'No,' said Lindsay, 'we ran five.' Oh well, maybe those Middlesex supporters did have something to shout about.

England hit up 267 and 294, the Services 455 and 107 for four wickets. Pepper hit the winning runs off the fourth ball of the last possible over just after seven o'clock on Tuesday, and who did he hit to the boundary? Why, Hopalong Cassidy, Alfred Gover. After six years of war cricket was 'off the mark', 67,500 people having watched the game.

By embarking on a programme of nearly fifty fixtures, including five Victory Tests against England, the Australian Services team made a valuable contribution towards the recovery of cricket. They played in all parts of the country, providing enjoyment above all else to all kinds of people seeking relaxation from the long war years. After the tour finished, the team returned to Australia, but several were to come back. Miller and Hassett, after playing at home against England in 1946/47, returned with Bradman's triumphant Ashes team in 1948. By this time Miller was showing the class that was to make him one of the game's leading all-rounders of all time, an exciting cricketer to watch, with his fast bowling let go from his full height of six feet, and his hard-hitting batting.

The diminutive Hassett (affectionately known as The Little Mouse) came again as captain of the 1953 side, only to lose the Ashes in the final Test at the Oval. Bob Cristofani returned as a trade official in the Australian High Commissioner's Office in Australia House, and he became a familiar figure in London club cricket, with his leg spin and batting for the Australia House Cricket Club team. Jack Pettiford returned to become a regular member of the Kent championship side, batting at number 6 or 7, and with his leg spinners, he gave several years' service to the 'hop' county. Cecil Pepper returned to play Lancashire League cricket. His leg spin was the ideal type for success in the League, and, combined with an attacking style of batting, made him much in demand. After a long and successful career in the League, he retired to become a familiar figure on the first-class grounds as an umpire. Dick Whitington, a working journalist, returned to report the Test series in 1948, 1953 and 1956. Jim Workman, who had taken an English bride to Australia, came back to settle in England in 1949. I was able to introduce him to an Australian friend of mine in business in Covent Garden who took Jim on his staff where he remained for the next 26 years. Jim also coached in my cricket school at weekends for the next 24 years until his untimely death from a heart attack.

After taking 114 wickets in the 1947 season I decided it was time to retire whilst I was still on top. I had several lucrative offers from Lancashire League clubs but the contracts would have entailed me staying in the north of England to coach the club's members in the weekday evenings. The Birmingham League on the other hand only required their professional to play on Saturdays in the afternoon games, and when West Bromwich Dartmouth offered me terms I accepted. I used to drive up on Saturday morning and drive back immediately after the game was over. I had three happy years with the 'Dartmouth'. They were one of the leading clubs in the League but had been out of contention for championship honours for several years when I first joined them.

The Dartmouth had a good side but lacked an opening bat and a wicketkeeper. I suggested that I approach Jim Workman to fill the roll and a deal was struck for liberal expenses, only one pro being allowed in each League side. It helped me of course bowling to a first-class 'keeper and, coupled with the firm wickets on all League grounds, I had three very successful seasons. The club won the championship in each of the first two seasons and finished close runners-up in the third.

I have one abiding memory of a game played in my second season in the middle of a hot dry spell of weather. We arrived on our opponents' ground to find a pitch which had obviously been heavily watered. We batted first and made just under 200. In the meantime the sun had been drying out the pitch and by the time we took the field it was much firmer and I reckoned it would both turn and bounce. Opening the bowling I went round the wicket with off spinners. The ball turned at right angles and bounced off the pitch at varying heights. I finished with eight wickets for 31 runs only to be called a cheat by the opposition captain. I pointed out that I had bowled three and the others had been caught by my short-leg fielders and I had no leg before wickets. He replied, 'It's not that, but we had no idea you bowled off spinners, otherwise we would not have prepared that sort of pitch.'

My cricket school had become very busy on Saturdays and now required my full attention so I refused all offers of further contacts in the League.

THE GOVER CRICKET SCHOOL

The Cricket School was built in Wandsworth, South London, in 1928 by W. H. (Bill) Brooke, who took into partnership the two Surrey and England cricketers, Herbert 'Struddy' Strudwick and Andrew Sandham. The business was known as Sandham, Strudwick and Brooke. Bill Brooke (my father-in-law) died in 1937 and the business became Sandham and Strudwick. In 1938 Strudwick retired and I took his share of the partnership. In 1946 Sandham retired and in 1954 I bought the Cricket School premises from the trustees of the estate of my wife and her sister.

So from 1946 I spent the next 44 years working with cricket clubs using the nets in the evenings, making many friends and meeting the varied and assorted types of players who booked private coaching lessons. They came not only from the London and Surrey areas, but from all parts of England, and indeed from all parts of the globe. In my Easter coaching lessons for schoolboys I made some firm friends; when they grew up they, in turn, sent their sons to me. Towards the finish of my years in the School I was even teaching their grandsons.

I recollect one little chap, aged about eight, whose grandfather had requested that I teach him personally. The little boy was suitably impressed until halfway through the lesson when he looked at my England sweater and said, 'Do you play on the telly, sir?' I confessed that I had done, but that it was a long time ago. The little chap's face fell and, disillusioned, he appeared to lose interest in my words of wisdom so I passed him on to a younger member of the staff.

In November 1945 the School was still full of furniture. The space had been let to families moved out of London at the commencement of the war. We wanted the building back for its proper purpose, but first we had to find alternative accommodation for those people not yet in a position to set up house again. I travelled miles around London by bus and on foot until I found suitable places for all the families. They vacated the school in time for me to open on 2 March 1946.

The School building was in a sorry state, although it had escaped any direct hit in the bombing. There were shrapnel holes in the roof, so we erected a tarpaulin cover over the whole area tied down with ropes at the side of the School building. The canvas stayed up for twelve months, flapping up and down when the wind blew, causing much amusement among the pupils as the coaches had to use sign language when they couldn't be heard. We had a sympathetic official in our claim of funds for war damage and at the end of the year we could afford a roof over our heads.

The nets, white canvas sheets, and artificial pitches had been stored in the dressing room for the six years of war and we crossed our fingers when we unpacked them. There were sighs of relief all round when we found all the equipment undamaged by its long incarceration.

We were soon back in the swing of things welcoming the many

cricketers who had survived the horrors of the war. They now looked forward to getting back to normal life and on to the field of play. Some had been through a rough time. Wilf Wooller, the burly Welsh rugby international and Glamorgan all-rounder called in for a net. Wilf had been a prisoner-of-war for four years and he had lost so much weight that, at first and to my embarrassment, I failed to recognize him. It was the same when Freddie Brown, my old Surrey colleague, came in for a net, he too had been 'in the bag' for four years.

Several pupils had been in the Services but were back at University to take up their interrupted studies and they now enrolled for cricket coaching. One was Hugh Griffith, hoping to get his Blue at Cambridge. I was able to help him attain both his ambition and selection to play for Glamorgan in the summer vacation. In later years we often played golf together with the County Cricketer Golf Society. Hugh is now Lord Hugh Griffith, a Lord of Appeal and President of MCC 1990/91.

The Prime Minister, John Major, told me that when he was a young schoolboy, he used to walk, pocket money in hand, the two miles from Clapham Common to the School to take a batting lesson from me. Unfortunately an injury a few years later put a full stop to his cricket, but he still retains his enthusiasm for the game and is patron of the Surrey Cricket Youth Trust.

Mark Thatcher came for two years in the Easter holidays and I was able to help him to gain his place in the Harrow School XI. Father Denis reminded me recently that he also had taken coaching at 'the Academy' previously and that I had repeatedly called out, 'Get that front foot closer to the ball', when he was attempting an off drive.

The young Colin Cowdrey came for intensive coaching. His talent was so outstanding for a fourteen-year-old that, when his first summer term at Tonbridge School was coming up, I wrote to the master in charge of cricket drawing his attention to the young cricket prodigy at his school. Colin played for his first eleven that summer and in the subsequent three years of his stay at Tonbridge. A rare feat, as the normal period in a public school side is one or two years.

In the immediate post-war years MCC decided to launch a coaching scheme. This was to be similar to that run for many years by the Football Association, a method of teaching common to all soccer coaches who had attended an FA coaching course. Those who passed the 'exams' at the end of the course were issued with an FA coaching certificate.

MCC commenced their own scheme by inviting many past Test cricketers to Lilleshall. Here we tried out the techniques of batting and bowling, etc., that would form the basis of the MCC course. The counties also sent their coaches and representatives. I went along at the invitation of MCC and acted in an honorary capacity, working with Harry Altham and Gubby Allen, the MCC representatives. Subsequently MCC decided to issue a coaching manual. Gubby Allen came to the School seeking advice on the basic bowling action because this was something I was teaching every day. We spent several hours together whilst I showed Gubby the breakdown of the action, commencing with the step with the front foot towards the bowling crease and the various co-ordinating movements, right up to the final delivery of the ball. I then wrote a chapter on the basic action for Gubby to use in the coaching manual. I was happy to have made a contribution alongside that of other ex-players.

I had an interesting session one winter's evening when Stuart Surridge had dined with me in my house, next door to the School. We had been discussing his bowling action and I pointed out that his habit of swinging his right leg to bring the back foot behind the front leg as he landed at the crease stopped the flow of his action and lost him pace. If he landed in the orthodox manner taking off with the left foot and letting the right leg swing forward past it he would gain extra rhythm in the delivery. I said that there is 'no time like the present' and so at midnight the School was opened up, the net lights switched on and we got to work. At 1.00 a.m. a perspiring Stuart had 'danced' his feet into position at the crease and it 'did the trick'. Stuart in a short career claimed over 500 wickets and, of course, skippered Surrey to the first five of their seven successive County Championships.

The rhythm of the run up is of paramount importance to the fast bowler, as once this goes he is struggling. This happened to Ken Shuttleworth, the Lancashire fast bowler, in 1975. Ken had been on the 1970/71 tour of Australia playing in two Test matches. He found that he was constantly stepping over the line (back foot in those days) and this was in turn affecting the rhythm of his delivery. Ken had a good physique for fast bowling – broad shoulders and strong legs. I took him to my outdoor nets and we tried all the permutations – shorter strides at the beginning of the run up, lengthening as he approached the bowling crease; short strides all the way and longer strides from start to finish; but the length of run we settled on was a fifteen-yard approach with short strides for the first eight paces and then immediately into the longer strides. After four days' hard slog this seemed to work. Ken played in the next Lancashire game taking four wickets. But, within a week, his rhythm had gone again and he was being 'called' up to ten times per innings. This finished his career and I was sorry for Ken because to drop out of the game after tasting the heights must have been hard to take.

Another time, Sussex asked me to look at John Barclay's off spinners. The old Etonian, who worked in the City in the winter, lacked the jerk of the right shoulder and bowling hand in the delivery of the ball (Jim Laker was the perfect example of this method of imparting off spin). John worked on this for several weeks. He improved his flight and accuracy and did obtain more right to left revolutions on the ball. Although taking many useful wickets for Sussex he never quite developed that bit of 'devil' off the pitch. He skippered Sussex for several years before retiring to run the Arundel Indoor Sports Centre.

Arthur Wellard, the Somerset and England fast bowler and mighty hitter of the ball, assisted me for over twenty years. Arthur was a strongly built man who could put in long spells in the nets and his enthusiasm for the game rubbed off on the pupils he taught. He played club cricket for the Gaeties Cricket Club until he was 70 years of age, bowling through the innings if possible. There is a story told of Arthur when, after two hours bowling and only six wickets down, three to Arthur, the captain suggested that he would like to give a young bowler a chance at Arthur's end. 'That's alright,' said the old warrior, 'I will go on at the other end.' He changed over and took the last four wickets!

When David Sydenham, an ex-pupil of mine from his schoolboy days, and now on the Surrey staff, came to me to develop his outswinger, we could not get it going and for the first time I had to admit a failure on my part. Arthur suggested that he had 'a crack' at David and after a month he called me to the nets and there David demonstrated his outswinger with control of width and length. This 'made' David and, during the many years when I saw him opening the bowling for Surrey and troubling top batsmen with his outswinger, I always mentally said, 'Well done Arthur!'

Apart from helping young players on their way into county cricket I got lots of pleasure in helping the enthusiastic club player – the chap in the third or fourth eleven who suddenly finds he is now capable of hitting 20 or 30 runs or taking two or three wickets in his weekend game.

We also had our funny moments. One pupil of mine was Ben Cross, the star of the film 'Chariots of Fire'. He had recently become a Lord's Taverner and was to play in a Sunday fund-raising match. Two days later an old mate of mine, Colin Welland a fellow Lord's Taverner of Ben, brought his son in for coaching and I mentioned Ben to Colin, saying that he had starred in 'Chariots of Fire'. I asked Colin if he had ever met Ben. Colin replied with one or two expletives, '. . . Know him in 'Chariots of Fire'?! I wrote the b . . . story for the film!'

I was fortunate to have the help of many fine professional coaches. Frank Chester, the famous Test umpire, would come along in the Christmas and Easter holiday periods to take the very small boys. On one occasion he was trying to teach a little lad who was wearing thick pebble glasses and Frank was having difficulty holding the lad's concentration. At last Frank walked down the wicket and addressed the lad, 'Sonny, don't you want to learn how to play cricket?'

'No, sir,' came the reply, 'I would much rather play my violin.'

Other assistants over the years included: Jim Workman (South Australia and Australian Services); John McMahon (South Australia and Surrey); David Gibson (Surrey); Chris Waller (Sussex); Leslie Todd (Kent); Bill Lawton (Lancashire League); Geoff Howarth (New Zealand and Surrey); Frank Lee (Somerset); Lofty Herman (Hants); Neil D'Arcy (South Australia); Joe Skelton (Harrow School coach); and David Sydenham (Surrey). Chris Waller was a product from a Colts coaching scheme of mine. At the age of 15 he was trying to bowl seamers without any sort of pace. I made him concentrate on leg spin and eventually recommended him to the Oval. He was taken on the staff, but his chances were limited since Intikhab Alam, the Pakistan Test leg spinner was in the Surrey side. Although given his county cap, Chris migrated to Sussex and became a regular wicket-taker for several seasons. He is now back at the Oval, looking after the development of Youth Cricket.

We often had pupils whose keenness outweighed their prowess. One chap was so bad that the coaches had a job to hit his bat, even if they threw the ball from halfway down the pitch. He insisted on attending nets and arrived one day with his video camera with the idea of having his off drive filmed. This of course was ludicrous, he had never been within a foot of the ball in all his previous attempts. However, my son John, who also assisted with coaching, said that he would aim the ball very carefully while I operated the camera – at least it would show that he could go through the motions of the shot. I duly stood three yards away on the off side and on the signal to 'go' started the camera whirring. For the first time in his life our luckless pupil connected with a full swing right in the middle of the bat and 'bang' the ball hit my shin with a terrible whack. To say the least, I was 'hopping mad' especially as all my staff were laughing their heads off. The pupil was delighted with his success in hitting his off drive so hard even though he had laid low the 'principal of the Academy'!

It was not all smooth running. The famous cellist, T. William Primrose, was having a net one day prior to going off to engagements in America. A member of the staff bowled a full toss and hit William smack on his left hand. 'Oh no, that's the hand that "twiddles" the strings,' I said and rushed down the wicket.

'Are you all right?' I asked him, but when William took off his batting glove he showed me an unmarked left hand. 'Yes, bowl up, I don't want to miss any more of my lesson time!'

Phew! What a relief.

We often had model agencies hiring the nets for photographic sessions. One cold winter's day an agency brought down six girls to model the next summer's very brief bikinis. A clergyman was having a lesson in one of the nets and was finding it hard to concentrate. I walked down the net and asked him, 'Are you all right?'

'I am finding the presence of these briefly-clad girls very disturbing,' he said. To which I replied, 'Don't worry you are not the only one – I am having a job with my young staff who are also having trouble.'

Some years ago my nets diary showed an appointment for a Mr W. Althorp. He turned out to be a tall, fair headed six-footer, who told me that he was due to play in a Sunday charity match. He had played as a batsman in his public school eleven and also as a fast bowler, but a back injury now prevented him bowling and he would like some batting coaching.

He had obviously played a good class of cricket and was soon meeting the ball in the middle of the bat. He booked further lessons and came into my office to pay the account. I noticed the name Lord Althorp on the cheque and suggested that he should still be addressed as 'Mister' in case one of my staff mentioned him outside. He was often in the news at the time and if the media knew he was attending the School the press might worry him with photographers.

After one of his net sessions he struck up a conversation with a taxi driver client of mine, whose son had booked lessons at the same time as Lord Althorp. The conversation went on for sometime. When Lord Althorp eventually left I disclosed to the taxi driver the identity of his new found friend. He exclaimed, 'I would never have known, he did not act like a Lord, he was so friendly!' I explained that all cricketers talked the same language, and instanced Sir Robert Menzies who, when prime minister of Australia, would always favour sitting on the players' balcony talking to the boys instead of being feted with the rest of the VIPs.

One of my young pupils who has succeeded in county cricket is Mark Feltham, the tall Surrey all-rounder, who was awarded his county cap in the 1990 season. With his right-arm fast-medium bowling and his batting, he is an ideal one-day cricketer, and has also proved himself in the Championship competition.

Mark Benson was appointed captain of Kent for the 1991 season and is well established in the Kent batting line up. A studious type of cricketer, his batting has improved progressively since his days at the School. He showed captaincy potential when he took over the Kent side for a few games towards the end of the 1990 season.

Mark Nicholas, the Hampshire captain, spent many hours in the School nets in his early days. Apart from his middle-order batting prowess, he has proved his powers of leadership, both with Hampshire and when leading England 'B' touring teams. A year or so back he was being strongly tipped for the England captaincy, but unfortunately did not have enough runs under his belt to warrant Test status.

The School was run as a family business. My wife Marjorie ran the office, looked after the accounts and school bookings, assisted by my daughter Elisabeth until she moved away. My son John built up and looked after the retail shop, which became the largest specialist cricket shop in England. He also coached in the nets and became a partner in the business. His wife, Janie, did all the secretarial work.

In September 1989, both myself and John decided to retire and The Gover Cricket School finally closed down, after 60 years. It had been a wonderful way to earn a living, made more so because it had been a family business.

My coaching life started in 1945 and, sadly, finished in 1989 on medical advice. I say 'sadly' because coaching was something that I enjoyed to the full, helping Test players, county and club cricketers and the schoolboys. I made many friends from all parts of the globe and when I finally closed the School many letters came from pupils who were kind enough to write sending their good wishes and recalling the fun they had at The Gover Cricket School.

9
Coaching England Players

IMMEDIATELY AFTER the war Jim Laker and Arthur Phebey, the Kent batsman, attended the School two or three times a week and, like any other professional players, they were given the courtesy of the nets. At the same time I was on hand to advise them. I would stand behind Jim and say, 'I want to see the back of your bowling hand when it gets to the top of the arc of your bowling arm. From that position you can then relax the wrist, making it easier to use the fingers to put maximum spin on the ball.' Originally Jim had been a seamer so I made him check slightly at the wicket and, with a high left arm and braced left side and left leg, then jerk his right hip forward, which in turn gave a snap to the right arm and hand coming across and against his braced left side. Arthur Phebey had a weakness on the leg stump and, working together, we cured this fault. Arthur eventually became one of the country's leading opening batsmen.

Don Bennett was a regular winter pupil for two years for his batting and bowling. His batting improved with a sound technique and all-round stroke play, but he rarely had a chance to prove himself as Middlesex kept sending him in low in the batting order, preferring to use him for his fast bowling.

Fred Titmus started life with Middlesex as a right-arm medium-pace bowler. They asked me to turn him into an off spinner, an easy task for this natural cricketer. Fred once told me that during his career, even in Test matches, if he went slightly 'off song' he would remind himself of the basics for his action that we had worked out together.

I coached two young Surrey fast bowlers in the early 1950s –

Peter Loader and Dave Halfyard. The Surrey committee decided they could only keep one of them on the playing staff and asked my opinion on who was the best prospect. I recommended Peter who, being taller than Dave, could extract more bounce off the pitch and would eventually prove the faster bowler. Peter justified this by playing Test cricket and touring Australia with Len Hutton's team in 1954. Dave moved to Kent and gave them yeoman service.

I had the fast left-arm bowler, David Thomas under my wing for several years in the late 1970s, eventually recommending him to the Oval. David developed both his inswinger and outswinger with me. He started his first-class cricket career in sensational fashion, opening the bowling in a Sunday League match and taking the first four wickets without conceding a run. Unfortunately, injuries cut short his career and his potential was never realized.

Frank Tyson came to me for the whole of the winter of 1953/54. Although a graduate of Durham University, Frank was prepared to join Stuart Surridge and his firm's tree-felling gang in the winter months. This was in order to strengthen his leg and back muscles and on Saturdays he would spend the whole day with me at the School. Frank had a habit of landing at the bowling crease with his left (front) foot pointing toward first slip's left hand, but I decided not to stress this fault because he was still able to make a full turn of the shoulders to get himself side on at the crease. He was soon co-ordinating the swing of both arms and my only other instruction was to make sure he kept his hand upright and behind the ball at the moment of release. All these combined to help him improve his accuracy and to add a yard or so to the great pace he already possessed.

During the following summer, when Northants were due to play Middlesex at Lord's, Frank 'phoned me to say that rain had made the pitch very slow and he thought he would cut down his pace and try to do more with the ball. I told him I could not be at Lord's that day but I was quite sure Gubby Allen, the chairman of selectors, would be there to have a look at him. If he took cheap wickets bowling below his normal great pace, Gubby would not be impressed, but if Frank went flat out and took, say, only one wicket, that would be what Gubby wanted to see – a really fast bowler to operate in Australia. Frank bowled flat out and nearly knocked Denis Compton over the stumps when he was late

93

trying to hook a short delivery. When he returned to the pavilion, Denis told Gubby, 'You must send Frank to Australia, he is the quickest I have faced for years.' I saw Frank on his triumphant tour the following winter in Australia and when asked the inevitable question, 'How does he compare in speed with Harold Larwood?', I replied, 'Just as fast as the old maestro!'

Left-arm bowler John Lever was an early pupil of mine before he went to Essex. He had a loss of form midway through his career, so Essex sent him along to me. John had lost his stock delivery – the inswinger. We had this movement back in a matter of minutes. John's right (front) arm was swinging towards leg slip instead of down the wicket towards the batsman. This caused his bowling hand to be out of position, with the seam of the ball directed at the stumps and staying in that position at the moment of release. By swinging the front arm down the wicket, letting it follow through past the right-hand side of the body, John kept the seam in its correct position towards leg slip at the moment of release.

Gary Sobers came to my nets prior to the 1959/60 Test series in the West Indies. Gary had just recovered from an injury received in a car crash at the end of the summer, when his fellow West Indian Test player, Collie Smith, received fatal injuries. Gary asked the bowlers to bowl short of a length on his middle and leg stump so that he could practise his 'flip' shot. To do this he balanced on his left (back) leg as he swung the bat left-handed and pulled the right leg across himself giving the bat room to swing freely at the ball. The shot required perfect timing. The normal left-hander would be satisfied with a defensive push, but Gary, one of the all-time greats, would invariably crack it to the leg-side boundary.

Peter May, who had just recovered from illness, batted side-by-side with Gary in the next net. All Peter wanted was the ball pitched on half-volley length in order to get his feet moving. This was fine until he played himself in and commenced to hit the straight half-volley back towards the bowler. The powerful Peter hit the ball so hard that after a few narrow escapes I retired and left it to the younger members of my coaching staff.

I saw a nice illustration of the charm of the game in the dressing room after net practice. A schoolboy pupil was discussing the coming winter tour and the particular players he thought should be in the respective Test sides, and the two great players, Sobers and May, were quite happy to discuss the pros and cons with the young fellow.

When Jonathan Agnew came to me as an Uppingham school-boy in the Easter holiday he was full of promise as a fast bowler – tall and with the basics of a good action. I knew he was keen to get into first-class cricket and I immediately suggested nets with Surrey at the nearby Oval. This was arranged with my recom-mendation that he be given a chance to join the professional staff during his six-weeks summer holiday. He then joined the Surrey staff as a full-time professional after another season. The pitches at the Oval were notoriously slow, giving no encouragement whatever to fast bowling, so eventually Jonathan moved to Leic-estershire whose pitches were much firmer. He gave his adopted county yeoman service and there are many critics, myself included, who could not understand why he was not given more opportunities than the few that came his way to stake a claim to a regular place in England's Test team.

I saw Ted Dexter twice at the School – first in his Cambridge days when, at Gubby Allen's request, I looked at his batting. There was nothing I could tell this natural striker of the ball except to say, 'Don't hit the ball back. If I happen to dodge the wrong way they will carry me out!' Though he hit the ball like a horse kicking, Ted used only a superlight bat, which weighed a couple of pounds. His second visit to the School came about before he was due to go on the West Indies tour in 1959/60. I was asked to run the rule over his bowling and together we improved his outswinger.

Midway through his career Micky Stewart struck a bad patch with the bat. He tried hard but without success to analyse the reason for his struggle to score runs in his usual fluent way. So in the winter he came to consult me in my nets. After ten minutes I walked down the net and said, 'If you could mirror your batting to see it from my point at the bowling crease you would have analysed your own fault.'

'Come on then, what is your opinion?' he asked.

'You have no idea where you are in relation to the stumps behind you, so it's not possible for you to judge the width of the line of the ball coming down from the bowler's hand.' We worked on the straight ball and then the swinging deliveries and within a month he was back to normal, judging the line of the ball early in its flight and moving his feet into the correct position to play his shot either side of the wicket. He was 'on song' once again the following summer season.

Early in his Test career Tom Graveney was brought down to the School by Gubby Allen. Tom had the reputation of being a good off-side player, especially off the front foot, his off drives being hit with such ease and grace that he had earned the nickname 'Elegant' Tom. But his off-side play had deteriorated to such an extent that he was working towards the on side even those deliveries pitched on his off stump.

Tom told me that, batting the previous year against the Australian fast bowlers, Lindwall and Miller, he had been told he was not sufficiently behind the line of the ball. He was advised to always play this pair of bowlers by covering his off stump on both front and back foot. He had obeyed these instructions to such an extent that he rarely had room to manoeuvre himself into position to play his off-side shots and had lost the ability to score in his old style, on the off side to any type of bowler.

To bowl at Tom I enlisted the aid of Peter Loader to bowl fast, plus the fast-medium of Arthur Wellard and myself. I suggested to Tom that he took middle-and-leg guard, we would bowl away-swinging half-volleys just outside the off stump, and he would make a firm effort to hit them off the front foot through the off-side covers. I noticed Tom was 'shortening' his hands, resulting in a minimal follow through in the direction of the hit. This was because he was using the right (bottom) hand to control the swing of the bat and the hit at the ball. This was obviously caused through the use of the right hand which had to be predominant in working the ball towards the on side. I now advised Tom to concentrate on the top (left) hand, holding the bat firmly and relaxing the grip slightly with the bottom hand, letting the left hand control the swing of the bat at the ball in the downswing and taking it on in the direction of the shot. We then progressed to gripping the bat handle in Tom's normal way and hitting through the away-swinging half-volley in the direction of the hit and swinging the bat on to a high finish. This long follow through had always been a feature of Tom's front foot off drive, so I was simply asking Tom to go back to his old and successful style of off-side play.

Having done the trick, Tom was soon delighting his fans again, especially in a game against Derbyshire at Chesterfield. The press, reporting his innings of 222 runs, commented on the feature of his innings being his 'magnificent' display of front foot off-side stroke play.

Look around the Oval today and on the Harleyford Road side you will see the Surrey Club's latest building – the Ken Barrington Memorial Sports Centre. It has facilities for indoor cricket and other games, seating for 1,300 people and a members' executive dining room. The Centre also includes new dressing rooms for the players, plus a modern scoreboard and, arguably, the finest press box on any Test match ground. It is a fitting tribute to one of Surrey's most famous and dedicated sons.

Ken Barrington came to me as a youngster to practise his leg-break bowling. He looked promising but nothing special, until one day when I was taking a fast bowler from a minor county and Ken asked me if he could bat against him. I warned him that the fellow was a bit quick and asked was he sure he could handle him. 'I will be all right,' Ken assured me and, taking guard, kept his word. My pupil had just got the hang of the late inswinger, a nasty delivery in the enclosure of a net, but Ken dealt with it easily, moving his feet correctly to defend or hit it away to the on side. When the bowler let go a short pitched bouncer Ken hooked it viciously into the side netting. When the bowler over-pitched outside the off stump, he whacked the ball hard in front of the wicket. Even at that young age he already had strong hands and forearms.

My partner in those days was Andrew Sandham, the Surrey coach, a player with 107 first-class hundreds behind him. At the end of the session he walked over to my net and said to Ken, 'You are wasting your time trying to be a leg spinner. You concentrate on your batting – in future you will be given lessons in batting.'

County cricket during most of Ken's career was played on pitches of variable bounce, so he collected runs, being content to push the straight ball and the short of a length delivery for singles. But if the ball was off line or length he gave it the necessary treatment. On overseas pitches, when he could judge the height of bounce off the pitch, he was a different player. At Melbourne in 1965, he hit the fastest century of the series, needing only 122 balls for his hundred, and only two-and-a-half hours for his total of 115. He hit two 6's, one for his 50 and the other to reach his hundred, plus eight 4's.

During his Test career, whenever the early batsmen had failed to deliver the goods, Ken would invariably stop the rot. He never played any 'fancy' strokes, his approach to the bowling being, 'You will have to get me out, you won't get any help from me.' The Australians often said that, if England were in crises, you could almost see the Union Jack behind Barrington as he walked to the wicket, giving the impression that this nonsense must stop. I know his fellow players appreciated his professional approach to the game.

Although to the spectator Ken may have looked a dour character, off the field he was full of fun and a great leg puller. We had become firm friends over the years and one of his tricks was to mimic my speech. I had a habit of calling people 'Old Boy' and this Ken played to its fullest limits. This nearly got me into trouble during the 1963/64 England tour of Australia. I had just arrived in Sydney to cover the tour for the *Sunday Mirror* newspaper, in time for the game against New South Wales, the last state match prior to the opening of the Test series. The visitors' dressing room was divided into two parts, from the back half you could not see directly into the front half. I saw Fred Titmus in the pavilion and asked him to tell Ken that I would be calling on him in the dressing room to say 'Hello'. A little later, on my way to the dressing room, I ran into Billy Griffith, manager of the England team. After greeting me, Billy said, 'Alfred, I don't mind you coming into our dressing room but I would appreciate it if you would have the courtesy to ask me first.' I protested that I had not yet been into the dressing room. 'Yes, you have,' said Billy, 'I heard your voice a little while ago in the back room.'

Having obtained formal permission from Billy, I then went to the dressing room and, as I entered, Fred called out to Ken, 'Alf's here, Ken'. From the back dressing room I heard my own voice with all it's usual phrases giving me a welcome to Australia. Billy came in a few minutes later and I persuaded Ken to do an encore for Billy's benefit, restoring my good name with the manager.

During the tour, Ken telephoned Geoff Boycott using his 'Alf Gover' voice asking for a *Sunday Mirror* interview, Geoff never suspecting that it was anybody else but myself!

When Ken finished cricket he took up golf seriously and, typical of his character, worked and practised hard at the game. With his strong hands he became a long hitter of the ball and within two years was down to a handicap of 4. He was much in demand as a partner in Pro-Am tournaments.

Ken suffered a heart attack while playing in an invitation One Day series in Australia. He eventually made a complete recovery and said how much he owed to Bobby Simpson, then the Australian captain, who did so much for him in the early part of his illness. After a period of convalescence he returned to England, thankfully to be passed fully fit. As I knew Ken would be keen to get back on the golf course, I arranged to play a few holes to get him back in the swing.

Ken was somewhat rusty, hitting the ball off the tee anywhere but the fairway. He improved as we went along but found it difficult to get back into his old 'groove'. We sat in the clubhouse discussing his golf. 'I never imagined that I would forget how to hit a golf ball,' Ken said. A few minutes later Sean Connery, recognizing Ken, came across and invited him to take part in the charity Pro-Am that he ran in Scotland just prior to the Open Championship. Ken demurred at first, but I pointed out that the tournament was two months away and he should accept. He thought it over for a few minutes, thanked Sean, and accepted.

With his usual thoroughness, Ken put in hours of practise and his swing and timing came back on the day of the tournament. He helped his professional partner to concentrate on his own game without having to worry about Ken, who was busy himself burning up the course and only dropping four shots by the end of the round.

Apart from his keen cricket brain Ken also had a nose for business. As a young player he had worked in the garage trade during the winter months. As his cricket career progressed, Ken wisely thought well ahead to the day when his cricketing days would be over and purchased a small garage in Surrey. With the help of his devoted wife, Anne, who ran the office, the business rapidly expanded taking on various agencies for the leading car manufacturers. Stickers displaying the sign, 'Supplied by Ken Barrington Motors', soon became a familiar sign on the back window of cars cruising around the roads and lanes of the county.

It was Ken's approach to everything he tackled that may have helped to cause his sudden death in the West Indies in 1980. As assistant manager to the England team, one of his duties was to be in charge of net practice and coaching. The team was having a lean time and Ken put in a great deal of hard work to effect improvements. I remember Alec Bedser, who was in the West Indies at the time, telling me, 'Ken spent up to three hours in the hot sun bowling in the nets at the batsmen in an effort to show them how to tackle the West Indies attack.'

The Ken Barrington Memorial Sports Centre will provide for the cricketing youth of the county encouragement and coaching to play the game that Ken so loved. With his Test record of 6,800 runs, Ken's name has already become a legend in the history of Surrey cricket. Like most great players he was full of confidence in his own ability but nevertheless a modest man. 'Alfred,' he would say, 'I always remember the runs in the last match and look forward to the next game as a challenge, whether it's a Test match or county game, knowing that there are bowlers waiting to cut me down to size, so it's up to me to make sure I am the first to dish it out.'

10
Coaching Overseas Players

ONE OF MY early pupils was Dattu Phadkar who had played for India in a Test series against Australia. In Australia he had become an admirer of the Australian fast bowler, Ray Lindwall, so much so that he tried to copy him and lost his form. So the Indian Board sent him to me the following summer.

Dattu's natural run up was entirely different from Ray's, whose approach was made with the minimum effort. Dattu's natural approach was more of a gallop. Ray dragged his back foot before delivery and Dattu was a 'leaper', so I simply had to get Dattu back to his original run up and action, which had already claimed many Test wickets. It was a matter of coaxing as well as coaching to get him back to his natural 'groove'.

Ramesh Divecha was another bowler sent over from India. He had pace but lacked accuracy. He had to get his act of co-ordinating his arms and legs together. Within a month he began to look a fine prospect, moving the ball away at speed and with accuracy. He was keen to get into Oxford University but places were at a premium. I spoke to Martin Donnelly, the New Zealand Test player, then in residence at Worcester College, and after I had assured him that Ramesh was good enough to gain a Blue, a meeting was arranged with the head of the College. His academic qualifications were satisfactory and he was duly admitted. Ramesh gained his Blue and went on to play many Tests for India and, in turn, served Northants for many years.

From South Africa, 'Father' Smith sent over son Chris, the Hampshire and England batsman, when he was only sixteen years-of-age. He looked to have natural talent and we went through

101

the basics of all the shots, so that when he got in the middle he would find out his best scoring shots and develop his batting around them.

John Fellows-Smith, a big-built South African, came to see me when up at Oxford University. His bowling lacked any hip movement and lateral turn of the shoulders essential for left-arm swing. I stressed this at every session until he was moving rhythmically. John is now resident in England, and whenever I see him he raises his left arm high above his head. He won his Blue for both cricket and rugby, and played Test cricket for South Africa. He was also a familiar figure in the Northants side for several years.

I had a long association with cricketers from the Caribbean. Rohan Kanhai, one of the West Indies greatest Test batsman, came to me early in his career when he was the professional to a Scottish League club. Part of his duties was a midweek coaching session, so his club sent him to me for a crash course of two weeks to learn something about the art of coaching. Rohan was a natural cricketer who had never received coaching of any kind. His one idea of coaching was telling the batsman to hit every delivery, but he forgot to show his pupil how the hit could be executed. Rohan worked alongside me when I gave lessons and soon saw the way to pick out pupils' faults, as seen from the bowler's end. He made rapid progress and I was able to allow him to give lessons with me, keeping a 'fatherly' eye on him.

Other players from the Caribbean followed, including batsman Linton Lewis, who subsequently played for Glamorgan; Bob Allan, a wicketkeeper-batsman who, although included in the squad on overseas tours, never made the Test team; and off spinner Derek Perry, who came with the West Indies side in 1980.

Viv Richards and fast bowler Andy Roberts came as club cricketers and members of the same club in Antigua. Viv showed the hallmarks of a class player. He always played right forward or right back and he picked up the length of the ball very early in its flight. I suggested a slight alteration to his top hand but decided after a while that this did not work so I told him to go back to his normal grip. He was suspect to the away-swinger which he had not seen much before. He played at the original line of the ball and consequently played away from the body and across the line of the ball as it swung away. He was playing too early so his left foot was out of position. I made him play later and quicker so that his left foot was alongside the ball when he struck it. To help him play the spinners I put him against John McMahon, the Surrey and Somerset left arm 'Chinaman' bowler. This helped Viv both to use his feet and to pick out the ball from the bowler's hand.

Andy Roberts had pace but his fault was a tendency to fall away towards the off-side field. This resulted in too many deliveries going down the leg side. I first checked with his team-mate Viv, who confirmed this fault. To cure it I placed two high stools on Andy's left-hand side at his delivery point, warning Andy that he could do himself harm if he continued to fall away. A couple of hard knocks did the trick and the good-humoured Andy soon had his body balance going over the front leg towards the batsman. Accuracy and away-swing were his rewards and his potential had improved 100 per cent.

I recommended both players to my own county, Surrey, saying that Richards was destined to become a great batsman and Roberts a deadly spearhead of any attack. They had a trial in the Crystal Palace Indoor School but, although they impressed, Surrey decided to keep their two overseas Test players, Geoff Howarth the New Zealander and Intikhab Alam from Pakistan.

Winston Davis had already played inter-island cricket in the Caribbean before he came under my wing. He had pace, but lacked body swing. He had a high left arm on arriving at the crease and I made him swing it forward and let it go on past the left side of the body in the follow through. This helped him to jerk the right hip and accelerate the swing of the bowling arm. I then took him to my outdoor nets; here I stood by the bowling crease and sent him to bowl off his full run. He went so far back I thought he was going home! He set off from the far distance approaching the crease like a four-minute miler but had no acceleration towards the crease. I gently pointed out to him that, although a fast bowler required an appreciable length of approach to the bowling crease, he was over-doing it by doubling the required length. I also pointed out that I could hardly recommend him to a county because with his inordinate length of run up he would not last the course in three-day matches. A suitable and sensible run up was therefore practised and adjusted and, of course, Winston achieved both his ambitions, to play county cricket (for Northants) and Test cricket (for the West Indies).

In recent years two other pace bowlers made the West Indies

Test side: Tony Gray and Ian Bishop. Tony was slimly built and stood well over six feet, but he lacked a right hip action through his tendency to throw his right leg out and away towards the on side early in the delivery of the ball. Once this was cured his control of away-swing improved, and I recommended him to Surrey. In his first two years, 1987/88, he took over seventy wickets each season and also made the West Indies Test side.

Ian Bishop, reputedly the fastest bowler in Test cricket at the time of writing, came over in 1987. Ian had the type of action that precludes the necessity to turn full side-on at the bowling crease, getting pace into the action with a powerful right shoulder. He owed much to Derbyshire who 'nursed' him through his early days with them and to Michael Holding, the great West Indies fast bowler, who was finishing his career with Derby.

Opening batsman Phil Simmonds was unusual for a West Indies player, most of whom are mainly stroke players. Phil was a solid defensive type and I had to coach him into taking greater advantage of the odd loose delivery. Being a tall man, he could also look for runs off the front foot. We succeeded, and he graduated into the West Indies Test side making many useful scores until a blow on the face in the Lord's Test in 1980 put him out of cricket for the rest of the series.

Bryan Lara came when he was eighteen. His batting and leg-break bowling were good enough for me to recommend him as a pro to a Northern League club. He is regarded by the West Indies authorities as a future Test captain and he already has several hundreds to his credit. He played for the West Indies in their tour of Pakistan in 1990.

In coaching bowlers one is generally working on what is already there – improving an existing action. A real problem does arise, however, when the very action itself is questioned. The legality or otherwise of certain bowling actions is a fascinating subject and one that has always caused controversy.

In 1955, Dudley Nourse, the manager of the South African touring team, asked me to give special coaching to Geoff Griffin, the team's fast bowler, who had been 'called' eight times for throwing in the match the tourists had just concluded against Notts. Geoff had also been 'called' two weeks earlier in the tourists' game against MCC. He was under the scrutiny of the umpires because he had been previously no-balled twice for throwing when playing in South Africa for Natal.

Geoff was sent to me for seven days. I first looked at his action off a shortened run up in my indoor school. He was very square-on when landing on the bowling crease and, with his left foot pointing towards first slip, he delivered the ball with his chest square-on to the batsman. I pointed out to Geoff that from this square-on position at delivery it was possible to throw the ball because his bowling arm would have gone out towards the on side and away from himself. Therefore, when he made the effort to bring his arm back high and closer to himself, ready to deliver the ball, this action could encourage a bent arm and a throw.

I made Geoff change his delivery by getting him to, first, stand at the bowling crease and go through the exercise of this new action and then, second, deliver a ball from the same position. From here we progressed to delivering from a three steps approach to the crease. Once Geoff had passed these 'exams' we went off to my outdoor nets. We always had lunch in my house next door to the School and on the fourth day he fell asleep whilst waiting for his second course. My wife was full of sympathy for the young South African and said, 'You are working the poor boy much too hard.' I had told Geoff at the start of the coaching that given the circumstances I would be a hard taskmaster!

When he had completed seven days' 'hard labour' we were both satisfied he could now deliver with a legitimate action. He had lost about a yard of pace but to compensate he was now consistently moving the ball away from the batsman, as I stressed in my report to the South African management. To help Geoff 'keep in the grove' I wrote the salient points of the new action on a postcard and he took this with him when fielding and referred to it as a reminder.

Geoff came back into the South African team for the first Test match at Edgbaston. He passed the scrutiny of the umpires in the first innings as Jackie McGlew, his captain, gave him four overs at each end so that both the umpires, John Langridge and Eddie Phillipson, could have the opportunity to judge him. John Langridge had already 'called' Griffin for throwing during the MCC match at Lord's.

In England's first innings, Griffin moved the ball away but lacked accuracy in length and line, taking only the wicket of Subba Row in 21 overs for 61 runs. In the second innings, he kept the ball on a length round the off stump with the reward of three wickets for only 44 runs in 21 overs. I was happy with the result and felt that, if the South Africans would allow him to carry on despite his loss of pace, he could still be an integral part of the South African Test attack. But, before the second Test at Lord's, John Waite, the South African Test 'keeper, told me that Griffin would not follow the coaching I had given him and which had seen him through the Edgbaston Test. Apparently he insisted he would be going 'flat out' in order to extract extra bounce from the Lord's pitch.

England won the match by an innings and 73 runs. In the England innings, Griffin sent down 30 overs and took four wickets for 87 runs including a hat-trick, the first South African to achieve this in a Test match, and the first man of any country to do so at Lord's. Although he was 'called' for throwing eleven times by Frank Lee from square leg, I have no doubt Geoff was on 'cloud nine' with his hat-trick and four wickets.

However, Geoff came down with a bump in the exhibition game following the finish of the match just before lunch on the fourth day. It had been noticeable that Griffin had not bowled when Sid Buller was at square leg and, when McGlew put Geoff on with Sid in that position, it was probably thought no action would be taken in an exhibition game. They reckoned without the gutsy Sid, who 'called' Griffin four times in his first over. Griffin completed the over bowling underarm. He was finished, never again to play in first-class cricket.

The South Africans, in my opinion to their shame, objected to Sid Buller standing in the next Test and it was to MCC's credit that the fee Sid lost was paid to him. (In 1965 the visiting South African team made no objection to Sid Buller standing in two out of the three Test match series.)

I was sorry for Griffin. I firmly believe that had he built up his bowling on his performance in the Edgbaston Test he could have stayed at Test level as a fast-medium swing bowler.

Peter May's 1958/59 team to Australia went out with high hopes of success, but they lost the Test series by four matches to one. One of the principal reasons for the failure of the England side was the bowling of Australia's Ian Meckiff in the second Test at Melbourne, which brought a second victory for Australia. After the loss of the first Test, it was vital for England to square the series in this game. Meckiff dashed England's hopes with match figures of three wickets for 69 runs in 24 overs in England's first innings, and six wickets for 38 runs in 15 overs in the second innings. He clean bowled Peter May when the England captain had scored 113. May admitted to me afterwards that he had completely lost sight of the ball from Meckiff's hand. Meckiff accounted for May again in the second innings for only 17 runs.

My first glimpse of Meckiff's bowling had been in the first Test at Brisbane when, in a total of 46 overs in the match, he had taken five wickets for 63 runs. From the press box I could only see him from a side-on view and although his action looked suspicious I deferred judgement. At Melbourne I saw him from all angles when I walked round the stadium and was then convinced he was throwing every delivery. I watched him closely when he was fielding on the off side and it was uncanny to see the similarity to his bowling action when he threw the ball in overarm to the 'keeper.

Meckiff's action had been unchanged from his schooldays through club and state cricket up to his elevation to Test cricket. He was, if one can use the phrase, an honest 'chucker', unlike others who knew when they decided to unleash their throw. Meckiff knew no other way to deliver the ball.

Don Bradman was chairman of the Australian selectors and in my newspaper column a week after the Melbourne Test I wrote that Bradman should not pick Meckiff, a bowler with a suspect action. My comments were of course quoted throughout Australia, which did not endear me to my Australian colleagues in the press box. One of their ex-Test players, turned writer, told me off the record that it was essential that Australia won the series having lost in England in 1953 and again in 1954/55.

Meckiff was 'called' the following season by umpire Eggar when playing for Victoria. He made attempts to smooth his action but on the subsequent tour in the West Indies his effectiveness as a wicket-taker had gone and he dropped out of the game.

England's left-arm spinner Tony Lock had been under suspicion for some time, especially when he sent down his faster ball. This was probably two yards faster than his normal delivery. I had personal experience several years after retiring when I turned out in a Sunday benefit match and stood at first slip to Tony's bowling. Without warning he let go his faster delivery, it hit the edge of the bat and flew past my head before I could move. I hurriedly gave up my 'observation post' and changed to the safety of the covers.

In the 1953 Ashes series against Australia I was working for the

BBC in the commentary box at the Oval for the last and deciding Test match of the series. In Australia's second innings, with their score at 59 for two wickets, Neil Harvey, having taken a single off the last ball of the over, found himself facing Lock. Lock unleashed his faster delivery and bowled the Australian left-hander whilst his bat was still at the top of his pick up. I was asked to give my opinion on Harvey's dismissal. Not wishing to start a controversy I simply said, 'Neil missed a straight delivery.' Tony's five wickets for 45 runs was a prime factor in England winning the match by eight wickets and regaining the Ashes.

When MCC visited the West Indies in 1953/54 Tony was 'no balled' for throwing once in the first Test at Kingston. Tony realized he had a problem with his normal action, over and above his quicker ball. He sought my advice which was to keep his left wrist cocked back for as long as possible before releasing the ball. However, he worked on it in his own way and, knowing he would lose a certain amount of finger spin, concentrated on flight and accuracy. He went on to become a prolific wicket-taker for Western Australia in Sheffield Shield games.

'Locky' was one of the 'gutsiest' players I have known. I remember him taking the field for Surrey in spite of chronic knee trouble at a time when other players would have asked for a wheelchair to get out to the middle!

The intricacies of what does or does not constitute an illegal action is, of course, not confined to bowling. Similarly, faults, problems, questions arise in every aspect of playing cricket and at some time or another every cricketer will need advice. The variety of questions is boundless as I discovered when I wrote for the magazine *Cricketer International*. For twenty-three years my coaching column consisted of replies to readers who had written in. They wanted advice: on faults that had crept into their fielding; on how to play the fast swinging delivery or slow spinners; on the action for the different types of delivery; and wicket-keepers would send their problems too.

I had letters from all over the world, the majority asking interesting and intelligent questions, but I sometimes received the odd 'nut case' letter. Like the chap who wrote to tell me he could bowl fast-medium inswingers and outswingers, also off-cutters and leg-cutters, plus off spin. He said he could also bowl leg spin, a googly and a top spinner. I was wondering if I had tumbled upon a genius, but he rather spoilt it when he said that if he pressed his forefinger hard on the seam as he released the ball he could make it shoot along the ground. He finished by asking me if I could suggest anything to improve his bowling and I wrote back to say that if he cared to come to my nets and show me that he could bowl all the deliveries he claimed, plus bowling a 'shooter', I would recommend him to the chairman of the England selectors. Sadly, my 'genius' failed to take up my offer so I never learned the secret of bowling a controlled 'shooter'.

I once received a question that was impossible to answer. The questioner wrote at some length on his inability to cut the off spinner – he capped this by saying that he played in the hills of northern Pakistan on a matting pitch. I imagined the prodigious turn the matting would produce and replied that I could not help him in any way to cut off spin.

I had many letters from Pakistan and India. Sunil Bhatia wrote from B.M. Das Road, Patna 4, India:

I am a fast bowler, seventeen years of age. Lately I have been having trouble with action which is a little suspect. Would you kindly advise me what I should do to make it fair? Also, what should I do to make my outswinger late in its flight? At present it swings all the way, making it easy for the batsman to play it.

My reply to him was:

If Mr Bhatia is a genuine outswinger, it will be difficult for him to throw and have a suspect action. Normally, bowlers with a jerky arm action are inswingers, for the simple reason that the away-swing action requires the right arm to come up from behind, keeping the hand upright at the moment of release, to steady the seam in the upright position, and to finish with the bowling arm around the right-hand side of the body. The thrower or jerker necessarily drops the wrist at the moment of release, which is more or less following the pattern of inswing. If Mr Bhatia keeps the hand of the bowling arm upright or extended throughout the backward and upward swing, he should eradicate any jerkiness there may be in his action. On the point of swinging early throughout the flight down the wicket, the certain cure is to alter the angle of the ball's flight. Do this by bowling from the edge of the bowling crease and aiming at the leg stump. The ball is asked to do more from this angle, and the tendency is for the flight to straighten itself from a line towards the leg stump in to the direction of the middle and off stumps.

The last *Cricket Clinic* appeared in the *Cricketer Magazine* in January 1990. It was headed 'Use the Hands to Hit'. Clive Burton, of Birches Banns Road, Peanfields, Worcestershire, wrote to say that he was having trouble with his hands when batting. He had had the chance to play for his local club, but after a few games he was left out because of his very slow scoring rate. He went on to say that he never scored quickly at school, getting runs by pushing the ball for ones and twos. The captain of his club side told him he thought his left-hand grip appeared to be wrong, and that he was trying to hit the ball without following through. Clive was taught to grip the bat handle with both hands behind the handle of the bat and had always batted with his hands in this position. He wanted to know what the correct position of the top hand was, and how he could obtain follow through to enable him to hit the ball harder.

This was my reply:

Clive has, I am afraid, been given the wrong advice in his formative years. The grip with the right hand is correct, the palm behind the handle. The left-hand grip is wrong. At the stance position, the top hand should grip the bat with fingers and thumb, with the back of the hand facing the direction of mid-off. If the palm of the hand is facing the bowler, follow through of the bat is not possible. A look at the way batting gloves are designed should convince Clive on that point. All the protective padding is designed to protect the back of the hand. Some first-class players turn the top hand slightly when reaching forward at full stretch on a defensive stroke, in an effort to angle the bat and play the ball down, but never at any other time. The hands must play the most important part in any attacking shot. Any hit is made by swinging the bat with the top hand, hitting (putting the power in the shot) with the bottom hand, and going on to a full follow through, the wrists breaking (or uncocking) at the moment of making the actual hit. With the top hand at the back of the handle this is a physical impossibility.

The attacking shots off the front foot on either side of the wicket call for a full follow through, the bat swinging on through the pitch of the ball in the direction of the shot. With the top hand at the back of the handle, the shot would have to be made with the elbows bent plus a hard push with the bottom hand, with consequent loss of power in the hit.

The hook or pull shot can only be made by swinging and hitting, the bottom hand turning the bat over when the actual hit is made. If the top hand is in the wrong position to start with, then no wrist roll will be possible, the wrong position of the hand will simply 'block' any wrist roll.

The cut stroke, too, will be difficult to make. This shot is made with a whipping action of the hands, the right hand rolling over the left to bring the face of the bat on to the ball. The hands and arms then carry on their momentum to achieve a full follow through. Again, the bad starting position of the top hand would effectively block any whipping action. When playing the leg glide, the top hand is the steerer, turning the bat blade, at the same time keeping the bat angled to play the ball down and away on the leg side. Although the forcing shots off the back foot in front of the wicket do not always require a turning of the wrists, the right hand must uncock as late as possible to get the power into the shot. An incorrect hand grip will inhibit this movement.

Clive will find the correct grip awkward at first. I advise him to practise holding the bat with the top hand only, swinging it to and fro. It will then soon become second nature to him.

I I

Golf

THE PROFESSIONAL GAMES player usually turns to golf as a hobby, and the majority of first-class cricketers are no exception. Their normal approach is to regard hitting a golf ball as being a simple operation compared to hitting a moving, swinging or spinning cricket ball. They are quickly disillusioned.

I well remember Arthur Wellard making a first attempt at golf when we were touring India with Lord Tennyson's team. Arthur arrived on the first tee with a set of borrowed clubs. He watched the first three players in his four-ball match all hit their tee shots well up the fairway. Then he looked at his ball sitting on a tee peg, waiting to be hit, took hold of his club, gripping it the same way he gripped a cricket bat handle, and swung the club as fast as he could at the ball, only to have an 'air shot', the club head passing at least six inches above the ball. In spite of our advice to slow down he thrashed away until, after five more 'air shots', all followed by some fruity language, he picked up his bag of clubs and departed, declaring golf to be a 'bloody silly game and a waste of time'!

Mind you, Arthur was no exception. We all played the occasional air shots on the course when we first started playing the game. We then sought the advice of a 'pro' who would initiate us into the mysteries and art of the golf swing. We would then bash ourselves silly hitting dozens of balls on the practice range and, with our natural ball games ability, would get down to a handicap of around 14 within a space of twelve months. If we had the ambition and spare time to improve, we were soon down to single figures.

I took the game seriously when I retired from first-class cricket. My tutor, Dick Burton, Open Champion in 1939 and pro at my club at Coombe Hill, was a great believer in the full swing of the club being the principal factor in sending the ball on its way. On the other hand, many teaching pros concentrated on the hands to impart the hit. With my height of six feet two inches I found it comparatively easy to cultivate the long swing taking the hands high above the left shoulder. After many hours of work on the practice ground, within twelve months I reduced my handicap to 6.

One of Britain's greatest golfers, Henry Cotton, who won three Open Championships, had always taken a keen interest in Surrey cricket ever since the days when as a small boy he paid his 'threepence' to get into the Oval. In later years he was a frequent visitor to the Oval as a guest in our committee room and we eventually elected him an honorary life member of the Surrey club.

I had played golf with Henry many times long before we met at the Oval once again when he asked me, 'Alfred, have you still got that lovely long swing?' I had to confess that it had become progressively shorter as the years went by and now I could only take the club back to shoulder height.

'In that case,' he said, 'you cannot be any good because you never did make enough use of your hands.'

'You're quite right, Henry. I've lost my length off the tee and now play off a 16 handicap and when I play at my club in Jersey, La Moye, they even give me an extra two shots.'

Henry had a dry sense of humour. Whenever guests were being invited to mid-morning drinks at the Oval he would always say, 'If anybody is opening a bottle of champagne I will be delighted to join them.' He was so popular that a bottle of 'fizz' would appear, to be shared with either a fellow guest or a willing volunteer from the committee.

First-class cricketers have their own golfing body, the County Cricketers' Golf Society (CCGS), and membership is restricted to past and present first-class and Test cricketers. The Society has many low-handicap golfers, including Ted Dexter, Colin Cowdrey, Brian Close, Tom Graveney and his brother Ken, Arthur Milton, Don Bennett, Peter Richardson, Stuart Surridge and John Murray. The Society plays regular matches throughout the year including games against the Universities. For several years I ran a game at Worplesdon (the CCGS home course) against a side of professionals raised by Alf Padgham, a past Open Champion. The pros always played off plus 1 and the cricketers off their normal handicaps. My team would include Colin Cowdrey, Peter May, Fred Titmus, Don Bennett, Godfrey Evans, Stuart Surridge, Bernie Constable, Ken Graveney, Eddie Watts, Gubby Allen, Laurie Fishlock and myself. Alf's team would include many top-class golfers. Max Faulkner always played, including the year he won the Open Championship. Ex-Open champions, apart from Alf, were Dick Burton and Alf Perry, plus Ryder Cup players including Dai Rees.

We normally played foursomes but we never got the better of the pros. One year I persuaded Alf to make it a four-ball, better-ball match. With that format my team had two chances, especially when both players were receiving strokes. We turned the tables by one match. My partner was Australian Test cricketer Ray Lindwall, and we were playing against Alf Padgham and the Ryder Cup player Alan Dailey. Ray and I won the morning round by two holes with one to play. I must admit we had all the luck with the kicks of the ball on the fairway and even when it was bound for a sand bunker 'Lady Luck' was also on our side. Our long putts dropped with great regularity while Alf and Alan missed several holeable ones. We normally mixed the teams up in the afternoon, changing pairs and matches, but Alf and Alan insisted that our match remained intact. Ray and I had hit the ball well in the morning, and so inspired by our performance were we that we hit the ball even better in the afternoon. Even so, we won only by a whisker on the eighteenth green.

Alf, however, had his own back at the end of the day when I was driving him home. Coming down West Hill, Putney, about a mile from my Cricket School, I was caught in a speed trap. When the police sergeant asked for my address, I gave him the address of the school in a very clear tone of voice. He did not bat an eyelid, proceeding to take it all down in his notebook. At this point Alf said to me, 'A pity this has to happen when we have had such a lovely day's golf.' The officer looked across at Alf, and after a close scrutiny, said, 'You must be Alf Padgham,' and proceeded to explain that he played for the Metropolitan Police Representative Golf Team. It transpired that the policeman was having trouble with his tee shot, continually hooking the ball. Alf got out of the car and pulled out a club and set the officer up on the grass verge at the side of the road. 'Let me see you grip the club and then take a few swings,' Alf said. A slight alteration to the grip and a little more pivot of the shoulders on the back swing was advised and, after a few practice swings, Alf told the officer, 'You will now be able to keep the club head square to the ball and this will stop the hooking.'

The officer was profuse in his thanks, adding that it had been, 'An honour to meet Mr Padgham.' I had been watching with amazement at the lesson given under the street lamps and when the officer came round to me he tore his notes up and said, 'And you watch your step in future.'

We drove off to the School and in the bar Alf started chuckling. 'What's the joke?' I asked. In between his chuckles Alf said, 'They all know Alf Padgham but have never heard of Alf Gover, only one mile from his famous Cricket School. I bet my members at Sundridge Park (where Alf was their pro) will enjoy this one!'

I have had the opportunity to play golf in various parts of the world, South Africa, Pakistan, India and Australia. During the MCC tour of Australia in 1964 I was playing in Canberra with Fred Titmus. Fred had just taken up the game and had the typical cricketing novices' way of slicing the ball from left to right. The Canberra course was very narrow with gum trees on either side and though Fred allowed for his slice, too often the ball would finish in the rough. It was fortunate that Fred was even-tempered and full of fun as I am sure that any other player under these circumstances would have 'blown his top'. Since those days Fred has cured the 'bend' in the flight of the ball and plays to a single figure handicap.

Golf can be a lot of fun. I was playing in a Croydon Alliance meeting five days before Christmas. The rules of the competition required every competitor to bring a prize, these were given out at the end of the day in 'order of merit' with the best gifts given to the winners and then down the list until the last pair, with the worst return of the day, came to the table to collect the last two solitary prizes. I had flown overnight from India and played like an idiot. My partner, Ted Ray (not the comedian), played well over the first nine holes but then his golf gradually deteriorated under the pressure of playing the course single-handed. Ted and I finished last by a big margin and when we two low handicap golfers strolled up to collect the 'dunces' prize – two small ashtrays – we were greeted with ironical cheers.

Worse was to follow later in the evening. As we left the warmth of the clubhouse it was pouring with rain. In the car park stood my car with a flat tyre. Out came the jack and spare wheel which I handed to Ted saying, 'You know I am useless at this sort of job.' 'I know,' he said, 'like your ruddy golf!'

I tried to protect him from the rain with my golf umbrella but it still managed to trickle over the edge and down his neck. The job finished, a drenched Ted said, 'And keeping the rain off your mechanic is also something else you can't do. Give me the keys and I will drive to my place as you can't do anything right today!'

In 1965 I organized a golf tour of Scotland. I arranged overnight train reservations, booked sleeping compartments and was also responsible for arranging play on the various courses, paying green fees, bar bills, lunches and teas. My 'duties' also included having to report what the 'flogger' came to at the end of each day, when each of us paid our share.

We decided to call ourselves the 'Honorable Eight' having agreed that no putts, however short, were to be conceded except of course 'tap ins'. There were eight players plus myself and we made teams from Colin Cowdrey, Peter May, Ted Drake, Stuart Surridge, Les Ames, Eddie Watts, Joe Davis (the snooker champion), myself and Barry Woolf, the well-known Jersey golfer. We were tough and keen golfers.

Our tour began at the North Forland course (just behind our hotel) but even after the overnight journey we still teed off, both in the morning and the afternoon despite the rain. We played different courses every day, the three Gullane courses, Dunbar, Darren and Gosford House.

The tour was so successful that I arranged them for the next few years. One year we went to the home of golf, St Andrews. We were lucky to receive the courtesy of the course and clubhouse through the introduction of the reigning captain of St Andrews, John Blackwell, who was also a member of Kent County Cricket Club and a personal friend of Colin Cowdrey.

It was a calm sunny October day when we teed off with only two caddies, one for each foursome. Colin's four were first off. Colin was resplendent in a new red jersey. We soon sought the wisdom of local knowledge from our caddie. At the first hole, on being asked the line off the tee, he replied, 'Follow the laddie in the red jersey.' This worked well for the first three holes until slow play, on our part, left us well behind and the 'laddie' in the red jersey was out of sight. On being requested to give us a line at the fourth hole he confessed that it was the first time he had caddied at St Andrews and we must make our own decisions. We hit the ball in the right direction at the majority of holes and all was going well until we reached a double green serving two holes. Our foursome had given the caddy for the round to carry for Joe Davis, who had early on formed a poor opinion of the advice given by his bag carrier. Joe's ball was on the edge of the green, the flag many yards away, and jokingly Joe said to the caddie, 'I should think I want my driver for this putt.' The caddie pulled out the driver and offered it to Joe. He looked at the club and said, 'You stupid man, I can't putt with that.' The caddie fixed Joe with his eyes and replied, 'Well make up your mind which club you want.' We waited for the expected explosion from Joe but it didn't come. Instead he walked a few yards away, stroking his chin in that familiar way known to television viewers when he was faced with a difficult shot on the snooker table. Finally he took out his putter and struck the ball as hard as possible, finishing close to the hole. He knocked it down and on the way to the next tee I asked him, 'What was the nonsense keeping us waiting to putt while you went for a short walk?'

'Alfred,' he replied, 'I was so fed up with that useless caddie I could have wrapped that driver round his neck, but I calmed down when I realized that the poor little blighter was having a struggle to carry my heavy bag, all for the chance to earn a few bob.'

The next year our base was at Muirfield, which had been the venue for several Open Championships, and was the home of the Honorable Company of Edinburgh Golfers. I had written to the club secretary seeking permission to play the course. When he replied in the affirmative, he revealed that he was an ex-club cricketer and a member of the famous cricket body, The Forty Club. He said he would look forward to seeing our 'illustrious' eight.

On our first visit to Muirfield we pulled up at the Caddie Master's Office to book our 'bag carriers'. I told him that we had been given permission to play the course but he regarded the bunch of Sassenachs in front of him with grave suspicion and turned away to use his 'phone, we presumed to ring someone in authority in the clubhouse to confirm our respectability. But it became clear that all caddies were on the course carrying in the annual foursomes Club Championship.

Up at the clubhouse we were welcomed by the friendly secretary who explained that the tees were not numbered and that there were no directions as to the whereabouts of each tee for the next hole and the foursomes had already reached the last nine holes, so we were in solitary state over the opening holes. How we found our way around was a miracle and so was Barry Woolf's amazing round. We were playing off medal tees and Barry was playing from a handicap of 10 but he went round Muirfield in a gross 76. Joe Davis, who had lost a bet with Barry on their best net scores, paid up and then promptly proposed that Barry's handicap should be reduced by two shots. This was carried unanimously despite Barry's protestations.

When Joe Davis played with Ted Drake against Peter May and Eddie Watts, he enquired if they would like a small wager on the result. The offer was declined and Peter, then playing off a 10 handicap, smacked the ball about 240 yards up the fairway. 'Good Lord,' said Joe, 'does he always hit them like that? And to think that I wanted a sidestake!' Peter had one of his very good days when all went right for him, and with Eddie nipping in occasionally, Joe and Ted were well beaten. Congratulating Peter on his golf round, Joe added, 'Am I glad you are not a betting man!'

Our golf at the weekend was enjoyable, not only in the pleasure of playing the famous course, but also because the club had an exclusive membership, so the course was never crowded on Saturdays or Sundays. This was a pleasant change from our home clubs where starting times off the first tee had to be booked well in advance, normally during the preceding mid-week. Preferment was only given to the captain of the club who would always be fitted in on the first tee, a tradition always acknowledged by the members and I confess that I always made use of this privilege when I captained the Wimbledon Park Golf Club.

After two days at Muirfield we journeyed out to the many fine courses around the Edinburgh area. Longniddery with a high wind blowing got the better of us all except two of our low handicap players, footballer Ted Drake and cricketer Leslie Ames. Leslie was used to playing in the wind on his local links courses in Kent at Sandwich and the Royal St Georges. Ted had a flattish swing and a slight adjustment to his grip enabled him to keep the ball low into the wind.

The following year we journeyed to the West of Scotland where our headquarters was at Troon. On our opening day (Saturday as usual after our all-night journey from London) we were asked to play at Troon Portland in the morning. This, we were assured, was the easy course, the one to play before tackling the Old Troon Championship course in the afternoon. Half-way through the morning round Joe Davis was having doubts about the wisdom of tackling Old Troon in the afternoon. He was finding difficulty off the tee driving over the rough in front at several holes. However, he played the last three holes level par and, like all club golfers in similar circumstances, immediately looked forward to his afternoon round. Strangely enough he managed to play the tougher course only one shot above his 12 handicap. This became the main topic of his after-dinner conversation for several nights, until one evening when the saga was about to start once again and we all put cottonwool in our ears! 'All right you lot, point taken,' said Joe.

Early in the day when I booked the caddies at Troon I asked the caddie master for his best carrier for my bag. He gave me a medium-height chap who, he assured me, was a top-class caddie who carried in all pro tournaments north of the border. 'Angus,' he said, 'will look after you!' And for 16 holes Angus and I were a happy partnership. Unlike the majority of caddies who carry for the pros, he did not bore me with tales of famous victories. He gave me advice on distances, the hazards ahead and with his local knowledge helped me to 'read' the greens. But we came apart at the seventeenth, a par 3 short hole. I pushed my iron off the tee into the rough on the right-hand side of the green. I asked Angus for my wedge, explaining I would play a draw shot but he handed me my sand iron to play a pitch shot. I explained that I had no intention of pitching, I was going to play a draw shot with my wedge. I addressed the ball and had just commenced my short swing, only to be completely put off by Angus who said in a loud voice, 'You'll noo do it.' My resulting futile stab moved the ball two inches. My next shot, played in silence, sent the ball scuttling across the green six feet past the flag and I carded five.

The eighteenth was played in complete silence. No word of advice came from Angus and no word of thanks when I paid him, adding a generous tip. It is customary at the end of the round for the caddie to carry out his last duty by taking your bag to the clubhouse, but not Angus. He dropped my bag on the ground and walked away without even acknowledging my thanks for his help and advice all day. Puzzled, I went to the caddie master who asked me if I had done anything to upset Angus. I told him about my adventures on the seventeenth. 'That's it,' he said, 'you should not have argued with him. He always gets upset when amateur golfers argue with him.' He added, 'In any case, he was right, you should have pitched with the sand iron.' I beat a hasty retreat with my tail between my legs.

That year, 1965, was the Honorable Eight's last organized trip to Scotland as for various reasons the members found it difficult to fit it into their business schedules. But we all have happy memories of the kindness of the many warm-hearted Scottish folk we met, and the generous hospitality we received from all the golf clubs we visited.

For many years after our Scottish trips were over I would often meet Joe Davis at various sporting functions in London, and on one occasion he came across to me and said, 'I am having my autobiography written for me, and I want to mention our trips to Scotland with the Honorable Eight, and to say that you managed the trips and especially that you were our "chief flogger".'

'Joe,' I said, 'you cannot possibly print that.'

'Why not?' he replied.

'Well,' I said, 'then you must describe me as being "in charge of the kitty" as the word "flogger" could create a wrong impression, especially when eight fellows were staying for two whole weeks!' Joe laughed, and, seeing my point, duly made the alteration.

I did make another trip later to Scotland to Carnoustie to watch the Open Championship won by Gary Player. We had a party of four: myself and my wife, Marjorie, Bruce Donkin and his wife, Mary. The girls came with Bruce and myself to watch the morning's play on the first day but they only lasted six holes. After being bustled about by the moving crowds they deserted the golf course, asking to be excused, and went off to nearby Broughty Ferry where they window shopped and then came home with Scottish woollen garments, which they assured us were absolute bargains.

A well-known personality in the world of snooker, Bruce had been a presenter of the television show 'Pot Black', and was the tournament director when the pros started playing at Bellevue Manchester and Deansgate Manchester. These competitions were sponsored in those days by Park Drive Cigarettes and then moved to the smaller Crucible Theatre in Sheffield. Bruce was tournament director for several years and, as a director of E. J. Riley, he explored the Far East. Tournaments were soon being staged there.

Bruce and I would play eighteen holes in the morning at one of the nearby courses of Monifieth, Barry or Wormiehills, and then watch the golf at Carnoustie in the afternoon. We had an amusing experience after a morning's golf at Monifieth. We met two elderly Scottish golfers who had just returned from watching the morning's play at Carnoustie. We asked them, 'How are they getting on at Carnoustie?', expecting to get the names at the top of the leader board. But, in a broad Scots accent, and with a hint of satisfaction in his voice, one of them replied, 'Aye, they canna beat Carnoustie. Eight of them in the burns at the seventeenth and eighteenth this morning.'

Bruce and I followed Gary Player in the afternoon of the final day's play. It was my choice as Gary is quite interested in cricket and I had met him on several occasions. It was a lucky choice, as the South African played great golf to win the Open Championship.

Back in England, I had always hoped that my sons David and John would take up golf as their winter game and often took them to Wimbledon Park Golf Club. One morning I was standing with the boys on the first tee waiting to go off when Sid Field, then one of England's top comedians, walked down from the car park. I introduced the boys to Mr Field, and John, aged 13, looked up and asked, 'Are you Mr Field the funny man?' Sid smiled and said, 'What a nice intelligent boy you are,' adding, 'and you won't hold me up on the way round the course, will you?'

'Oh no, sir,' said John, 'you can come through our match whenever you like.' Sid caught us up on the sixth hole and when we waved him through he ignored David and myself but thanked John for his courtesy in allowing him to go through our game.

Sid at that time was the star of a play called 'Harvey' at the Prince of Wales Theatre in London. The theme of the play centred around an invisible rabbit called 'Harvey', and the role played by Sid called for long conversations between Sid and 'Harvey'. During the run of the play Sid asked me to play because he found difficulty in getting partners during weekdays. Sid's regular caddy

was a chap called Fred Harvey and on the very first round Sid
startled me when, having had advice from caddie Fred Harvey,
he looked over his left shoulder and held a conversation with the
other 'Harvey'.

'What are you talking about? It's a six iron. Fred says it's a
five, you know nothing about golf. Now. Shut up.'

Sid would then commence his address to the ball but no sooner
had he started his preliminary waggle than he would stop and
address the invisible Harvey again. 'For heaven's sake stop mumbl-
ing about "a six iron".' Sid played his shot and said to me. 'Sorry
about that Alfred, I hope it will not put you off.' I decided to go
along with Sid's gag and assured him not to worry that it would
affect my game.

Caddie Fred carried out his duties in the normal way as if
nothing untoward had happened though Sid went through the
same routine at several holes during the round. At the end of one
particular round I said to Fred, 'He nearly got me at it when he
was having that prolonged argument with "Harvey" on the tee
at the short tenth.'

'I know,' said Fred, 'I have had to put up with that ruddy
rabbit business ever since the Guv (Sid) started in the play.'

A week after the long run of the play ended I was playing with
Sid again at Wimbledon Park and he was back to normal – no
sign of 'Harvey'. 'What's happened to the rabbit, Sid?' I asked.
'Oh' he went out of my mind when the play came off.'

When I asked what he meant by 'out of my mind', Sid explained that during the run of the play he was on stage most of
the time and, 'I had to convince both myself and my audience
that I really was having conversations with "Harvey", so I took
the character home with me.'

Whenever I am asked to describe my greatest thrill in golf I
always have difficulty as it could have been when I drove myself
in as captain of Wimbledon Park Golf Club, or as captain of the
CCGS, or as a winner of the Foursomes Competition at Coombe
Hill Golf Club in partnership with jockey Ken Gethin, or my first
ever 'hole in one' at the short twelfth at Sudbrook Park Golf Club
in a Stage Golfing Society meeting.

Perhaps this last one was my greatest golfing moment as I had
played golf for twenty years before becoming qualified to join
'The Hole in One Club'. It cost me a 'bob or two' in the bar
afterwards but I would cheerfully double that amount to do it

again. Although I have had many near misses since that day I am still patiently waiting for an 'encore'.

Friends often ask me how I came to be a member of the Stage Golfing Society (SGS). I qualified through the medium of my radio and television work. Jim Laker and Danny Blanchflower were members with similar qualifications. The stage golfers were a great bunch to play, people like Terence Alexander, Bill (William) Franklyn, Eric Sykes, Gary Marsh, Dickie Henderson and Sean Connery and they took their golf seriously.

One of my foursomes partners when I was a member at Coombe Hill Golf Club was that great all-round Irish athlete Kevin O'Flanagan. He played soccer on the right wing for Eire and Arsenal and also played rugby union for his country. He was by profession an orthopaedic surgeon and worked in London with one of my friends, Bill Tucker, who was also an ex-rugby international.

Kevin and I had won our quarter final heat in the club foursomes the previous Sunday and were due to play the semi-finals the following Sunday. On the morning after our quarter-final win I went to the practice ground to hit 200 balls but half-way through I pulled up with a strained thumb on the right hand. Now, when Bill Tucker first set up in practice I was one of his first six patients so whenever I had an injury and 'phoned to see Bill I was always fitted in, even if he had a very busy schedule. I went straight off the practice ground and rang Bill's clinic in Grosvenor Square asking for an appointment in the afternoon saying that it was most urgent because I had a serious injury. I was duly fitted in and when I walked into Bill's surgery he asked, 'What's your serious injury?' I started to explain that I had strained my thumb and was due to play in an important game the coming Sunday. Bill exploded, 'Alfred, I am busy with badly-injured jockeys and rugby players and you come in with a strained thumb!' At that moment Kevin, who had been told I was in the surgery, came into the room and asked me, 'What's the matter with you Alfred?' After I had explained, Kevin turned to Bill and said, 'You have to cure that thumb before Sunday, Alfred is my partner in the semi-final round of the foursome at Coombe Hill.' Bill reluctantly agreed and daily treatment cured my 'serious injury'. A win into the final would have been a happy ending, but alas we lost the match at the eighteenth hole.

The SGS used to hold their annual dinner at the Savoy Hotel,

London, and in the year when Clifford Mollinson was captain of
the society Maurice Chevalier was our principal guest. The dinner
had been overbooked and, to accommodate all the diners, additional seating had been arranged on the inside of the top table.
Clifford Mollinson was a keen cricket follower and a very close
friend of mine and no doubt this was why I found myself seated
on the inside of the top table, directly opposite Maurice Chevalier.
It was a great thrill for me as I had been a fan of the great
Frenchman for many years. During the course of dinner he asked
me if I was working. Thinking of my busy schedule at the School
I replied, 'Yes, in fact I have too much work at present.' Maurice
raised his hand and shrugged his shoulders in his own inimitable
way and said, 'We cannot have too much work' and then went
on about the dangers of turning work away. I realized that he
thought I was in show business and I thought of explaining my
particular line as a cricket coach but decided it would be too
difficult for him to understand. So having agreed with him on the
subject of work the conversation turned to other channels.

The Society always provided its after-dinner entertainment
from the ranks of its members, who performed on the stage at one
end of the banqueting suite. After the opening 'acts' had been on
stage, Clifford announced Maurice Chevalier, and the five-piece
orchestra on the stage immediately struck up the tune of 'Louise',
one of Maurice's greatest hits. Putting the familiar straw hat on
his head, he performed from his place at the dinner table. The
force of his personality and performance was sheer magic, and I
felt privileged to have been there that night.

During a short leave from Army duties in 1943 I had arranged
a round of golf at Swinley Forest Golf Club near Ascot with the
headmaster of my sons' prep school, Sydney Beckwith. I arrived
in civilian clothes on my bicycle with my clubs over my shoulders
to find, what appeared to be, an empty clubhouse. I was suddenly
challenged by an oldish man of military bearing, the secretary of
the club, who barked out, 'What are you doing here?'

'I am playing with Sydney Beckwith' I replied.

'Are you serving?'

'Yes,' I said, and back came another bark, 'And what, might I
ask, is your rank?' When I gave him my commissioned rank of
Captain, a smile broke out on his face and his right hand was out in
greeting. 'My dear fellow,' he said, 'I am delighted to see you here. I
am sure you will enjoy your golf, the course is in splendid condition.'

I repeated this conversation to Sydney when he arrived, and asked, 'I wonder what he would have said if I had replied that I was only a sergeant?'

'Oh,' said Sydney, 'in that case I would not have asked you.'

'Doesn't that old chap realize there is a war on?' I asked.

'Yes,' said Sydney, 'but he is still "living" the First World War of twenty years ago.'

The Sunday after the arrival of Bobby Simpson's Australian side in 1964 I arranged a day's golf for them at the St George's Hill Golf Club, Weybridge, Surrey. I invited sixteen friends to play with the tourists. The day was not to be a contest between the tourists and my side – an Australian cricketer and one of my side were to make a partnership in each match.

At the top, Aussie captain Bobby Simpson was paired with England's captain Ted Dexter against Aussie Neil Hawke and Stuart Surridge. All four were low-handicap golfers and renowned long hitters off the tee. After the morning round, Neil flopped down onto his seat in the locker room declaring that he was exhausted, adding, 'We all tried to out distance each other off the tee and through the green.'

'Who won the match?' I asked.

'Don't know,' said Neil, 'but I reckon Ted and Bobby just got their noses in front by two hits off the tee.'

During pre-lunch drinks I introduced Neil to the club secretary, Brigadier Thorne-Thorne. Neil looked a little perplexed, 'What did you say?' The brigadier confirmed that his name was indeed Thorne-Thorne. Neil said, 'You must be joking, you can't have two ruddy names!' But further confirmation assured Neil, who went off to tell his team-mates of the strange habits of the 'Poms' who could not be satisfied with just one name.

12

Evening News Colts

IN THE IMMEDIATE post-war years, Surrey were lucky. They had newcomers Alec Bedser, Arthur McIntyre, David Fletcher, Eric Bedser and Jim Laker, all of whom were beginning to make their mark for the county. Godfrey Evans had taken over the mantle of wicketkeeper from Les Ames for Kent, but the majority of counties were still being served by players nearing the end of their cricketing careers, and I was worried that as they finished very few new recruits were coming into the game.

I was prepared to look for, and give free cricket coaching to, any promising young cricketers I could find. But where to find them? I decided to approach E. M. (Lyn) Wellings, a pre-war Oxford University and Surrey cricketer turned journalist. He was now cricket correspondent of the London *Evening News*, and he agreed to help me find my young cricketers by publicising this in his weekly column 'Talking Cricket'. However, he called me into the press box at Lord's a week later to say that he had discussed this with his editor, John Marshall a cricket lover, who had suggested it was hardly fair that I should bear all this expense. Marshall proposed that I allow the paper to sponsor a scheme, naming it the *Evening News* Colts Cricket Coaching Scheme. This would help me to find talent to recommend to county clubs for trials, and it would also help the boys go into good club cricket, all part of helping the game keep healthy and alive with new talent. Lyn Wellings's first piece about our scheme brought 600 applicants. We saw every boy, but of course we could not coach all of them. I thought sixty would be the limit as I had other commitments in my nets with lessons and schools.

So we probably missed one or two good players when the 'sorting out' had to be done. We made a reserve list from the 'drop outs', in case any of our chosen sixty failed to come up to the mark after six weeks' coaching. The boys were attending weekly, so we reckoned in six coaching sessions of one hour each, we could give the boys a good 'examination', but inevitably some had to fall out. One who failed after six weeks was David Evans who, later by his own efforts, got himself onto the Warwickshire staff, playing in their second team as wicketkeeper-batsman. At the same time he was on the books of the Aston Villa Football Club. After two years in the Midlands, he went west, joining Gloucestershire and signing for Bristol Rovers. After a stay there of two years he was told by both clubs his services were no longer required, and, seeing no future in professional sport, David turned to the commercial world, becoming a very successful business man. He kept his links with sport, and in turn played for Edmonton Cricket Club, a prominent North London side, and later became chairman of Luton Town Football Club. Elected chairman of the Lord's Taverners in 1982, he directed his considerable energies into sponsoring and raising money for the Taverners' charities.

So, when I decided some years later to run a scheme at my indoor school to find a fast bowler, I found a willing sponsor in David Evans. He paid the coaching fees, the fares of those travelling a long distance, and presented them all with a souvenir of their attendance on the course at a dinner he gave for them in a London hotel.

The *Evening News* Colts went on for five years. Apart from the winter coaching we ran a Sunday side playing against top club teams. All the boys' expenses were paid for by the paper, and Lyn Wellings or myself would captain the side. We had some fun, especially on one occasion in a game at Wickford in Essex. We had a late cancellation on Saturday night, so I persuaded Stuart Surridge, the famous Surrey captain, to join us and make up the number. We batted first on a pitch where the ball came through very fast and low. Under these pitch conditions we told the boys, 'You must play everything off the front foot.' The opening bat played back and lost his off stump, and received a stern lecture from Stuart and myself on his return to the pavilion. With the score at around 70 for five wickets I decided the score required respectability, and promoted Stuart and myself in the batting order and soon we were in partnership together. We played off the front foot for the next 30 runs when – crash! – I played back to a long hop and lost my off stump. In the same over Stuart made a similar mistake, going in likewise fashion. Our senior boy, Alan Moss, who had already made his initial appearance in the Middlesex side as a fast bowler, took the lead for the boys.

'Now, gentlemen,' he said to Stuart and myself, quoting Stuart word for word, 'on this pitch you must play everything off the front foot, and by that I mean every single ball and don't you forget it!' With a smile Alan added, 'I suppose when you are an old player you are allowed a mental aberration.'

In the five years the scheme ran it produced two Test Match players in fast bowler Alan Moss of Middlesex and Essex wicket-keeper Brian Taylor. In addition, several of the Colts had long county careers: fast bowler Ken Biddulph with Somerset, batsman Clive Dring, and off spinner Alan Dixon of Kent. The 'scheme' discovered a promising fast left-arm bowler in Simon Dennis, who played for Yorkshire for several years and later moved on to Glamorgan. Malcolm Heath, a fast bowler spearheaded the Hants attack for many years, and Alan Gibson, an all-rounder, played out his career for Surrey and then continued as county coach for several years. Surrey also had Bill Smith, a left-handed batsman, and David Sydenham a left-arm fast bowler who enjoyed many triumphant days. Henry Tilly at medium pace served Middlesex for several seasons.

Many boys joined the top Surrey and Middlesex clubs and played for the counties' second elevens. One was Norman Parks, a prolific run scorer in club cricket for Beddington and a regular in the Surrey second eleven. There were many like him who just failed to make first-class grade, but the coaching they received enabled them to enjoy many years in club cricket and made them many friends. That, of course, is one of the charms of the game – the opportunity to make lifelong friendships. Even after all these years I still receive Christmas cards from many parts of the world from my old '*Evening News* Colts'.

13
Writing for a Living

I TOOK OFF to a great start in the 1936 season taking wickets in both innings of every match. I was on top of the world when I unexpectedly came down to earth with a bump – I had a sudden attack of lumbago.

I told Sandy Tait, our trainer, that he must get me out on the field as I was on a run of wickets and wanted to 'ride' my good fortune. Sandy gave me heat treatment, massage and physiotherapy. He stuck a belladonna plaster over my lower back, strapped it up with elastoplast and told the skipper that I would be OK to bowl but must not make any sudden bending movements to pick up the ball. I had a good day with the ball, picking up six wickets before close of play.

I was shown reports of the day's play written by Bill Evans, cricket correspondent of the *Star* (the now defunct evening newspaper), in which he had a real go at my sloppy fielding. Bill came to see me in our dressing room the following morning.

'Alfred,' he said, 'I have only just heard that you were playing yesterday in spite of an attack of lumbago, so I apologize for my report of yesterday.' I replied, 'Bill, you gave an honest report of what you saw in the middle; your report did not bother me, having taken six wickets in the innings.'

The majority of the Surrey players were only sensitive to criticism when it was written by a first-class cricketer turned press man. Some years later when I 'crossed the floor' to join the media I always remembered my own playing days and that any criticism I made would be constructive.

My entry into journalism came in 1952. Robin Needham, the

chief writer in the London office, of the D. C. Thompson Scottish newspaper group, asked me to write a weekly commentary on cricket. This was published in *Thompson's Weekly*, which had a circulation covering Scotland, Wales, the Midlands and the West Country.

I was willing to have a crack at journalism because, although I had previously only written brief articles in various sporting magazines, Thompson's was a good grounding for an aspiring journalist. Robin was a kindly advisor in my first few weeks, then he told me that I was now quite capable of standing on my own two feet.

I had two years with Thompson's before the *Sunday Mirror* sport's editor, George Casey, offered me the job of cricket columnist and reporter. The policy of the paper was to only employ writers capable of writing their own copy, ghost writers were not allowed. George had looked into my journalistic background before making the initial approach to me. I got on very well with George, a straightforward man whose word was his bond. George had worked his way up from office boy, through to the sports editor's desk and was one of the most experienced in Fleet Street. I served the paper for thirteen happy years, making three trips to cover Test series in Australia.

I always quote the story of George and Jim Wicks, who was Henry Cooper's manager, when the *Sunday Mirror* was proposing to publish Henry's life story. George, with Henry and the editor of the paper, held a meeting to discuss the financial arrangements. When the terms had been agreed the editor said he would draw up a contract and send it on to Jim for signature. 'Contract,' said Jim, 'I don't want any b . . . contract, I have already shaken hands with George and that's good enough for me.' With a large amount of money at stake the bewildered editor found it hard to believe that business could be done in such a bizarre way, but with Henry concurring, he agreed to go along with these two 'cockney gentlemen'.

My first summer with the *Sunday Mirror* coincided with the first ever tour of England by Pakistan. I was interested in the tourists, having coached many of their players in the summer of 1953. Their first three-day match, a Saturday start, was against Worcester and I covered the match. I was also engaged by the BBC to give summaries and comments during the day's play.

When George gave me his requirements for copy times I was

completely bewildered. I had never reported a match before, and I was totally in the dark when he said he wanted a forward-looking piece for the Scottish edition at 1.30 p.m., a report on the day's play to date at 4.30 p.m. for the London and West of England (including Wales) editions, and a piece for the Northern editions at 4.00 p.m. Arriving at Worcester I sought out Lyn Wellings of the London *Evening News* to solve the puzzle for me. He explained that at that time the Mirror Group printed only in London, so the provincial papers had to go from London to reach the provinces and Scotland in time for distribution to the news-agents.

I had no difficulty in reporting the play to date, but, at 1.05 p.m., with the tourists on 65 for two, I stuck my neck out by writing that Pakistan batted in depth and should be capable of recovering to make a respectable score. It was a lucky forecast – Pakistan finished the day all out 428.

Their fortunes turned with the advent of Maqsood Ahmed, who came in at the fall of the second wicket. Having had Maqsood at my Cricket School – where he was known as Merry Mac because of his approach to the business of run-getting – I informed my colleagues in the press box that they were about to see some-thing special. Maqsood would not trouble to play himself in; he always attacked the bowling as soon as he took guard. However, twenty-five minutes later, Maqsood was exactly 1 not out. During the lunch break my colleagues in the press box pulled my leg and said they presumed my 'Mighty smiter of the ball' would be 15 not out at the tea interval. However, they changed their tune as, in the two-hour session, 'Merry Mac' hit up 111, including two 6's and seventeen 4's, and with Alimuddin put on 181 runs.

I wrote my London office piece on the events of the day, my pre-lunch prediction about Maqsood's prowess as a mighty hitter of the ball, and went on to describe his innings in detail, then I filed my copy. After a brief interval, my telephonist came to me with a message from the London sport's desk which said 'Story stands in all editions.' I took it along to Lyn Wellings in the press box and asked him what it meant. 'Let me see your copy,' he said. 'That's a good story as only you could write it from that angle, owing to your close relationship with the Pakistan team.' I then asked Lyn about the close of play details, but he said, 'Don't worry about that – the subs (sub-editors) will see to that.'

I became a member of the London freelance branch of the

National Union of Journalists (NUJ) before the beginning of the 1954 season because I would be writing match reports under my own by-line. Union membership was not necessary for contributing a column or for the ex-cricketer using the help of a 'ghost' writer.

At the end of the 1954 season the *Sunday Mirror* editor offered me the job of covering the forthcoming winter tour of the MCC team in Australia under Len Hutton. The team went with high hopes. Australia had held the Ashes for nineteen years, the longest period on record, but England under Len Hutton in the 1953 series after four drawn Tests had beaten Australia in the fifth Test at the Oval by eight wickets.

England's defeat in the first Test at Brisbane shook the pundits who now took a gloomy view of England's chances of retaining the Ashes. I took a more optimistic view of the situation and in my cabled report to London pointed out that Alec Bedser had had four catches dropped off his bowling all in the deep. I had never before seen Alec lofted to the deep field. A fully-fit Bedser would never have suffered this indignity. He should not have been playing as he had not fully recovered from a bout of shingles and was lacking the energy, the pace and movement off the pitch which had made him one of the all-time great fast-medium bowlers.

Frank Tyson, the spearhead of the England attack, had been given a great build-up by the Australian press prior to the Brisbane Test. But in the match he was failing to live up to his reputation, rarely troubling the Australian batsmen. I had coached Frank the previous winter at my School, but I now saw that the cause of his failure was lack of rhythm in his delivery of the ball. This was caused by lack of rhythm in his run up; in his last few strides he was straining – lengthening his strides in an effort to reach the bowling crease. This, of course, caused lack of balance and timing in his delivery and also lost him height at the moment of release.

I met Len Hutton late on the Saturday evening and it was obvious that he was disappointed at the way the match was going and with Frank's lack of success. I suggested to Len that Frank made an alteration to his run up, it was far too long and this distance was mitigated when, after the first eight paces, his feet 'stuttered', the right foot dragging on the ground. I suggested that Frank cut down his run and started from the 'check point' in his run up.

Frank practised this approach in the nets and looked a different bowler in the second Test at Sydney. Len Hutton, in his book, acknowledges my suggestions on Frank cutting down his run up and the success that followed in the third Test in Melbourne. Frank, of course, shattered the Australians. The 20,000 people at the ground saw Australia all out in the two hours before the lunch interval, and Frank's figures now hold pride of place in the cricket history books.

Len Hutton's dry sense of humour came to the fore when we were discussing events later that day. 'Alfred,' he said, 'there is one thing I am sorry about.'

'What's that?' I enquired, thinking it would be appertaining to the cricket. Len replied with a twinkle in his eye, 'The poor caterers now have 20,000 pies and sausage rolls left over on their hands!'

Between the Sydney and Melbourne Tests I covered the Davis Cup Tennis Match between Australia and the United States in Sydney. The MCC team were having a six-day 'mid-term' break from cricket and I had a 'phone call from my sport's editor in London wanting a full report on the tennis.

Although I had played tennis in a friendly way, I knew very little of the finer points of the game, but once again Lady Luck was on my side. I had previously met Harry Hopman, the manager of the Australian tennis team at the Wimbledon Park Golf Club which runs alongside the All England Tennis Club. I met Harry during the practice day before the match and he talked in general terms about the match and the technique of his players Ken Rosewall and Lew Hoad.

Unhappily for Australia I had to describe the defeat of the Australians: Bill Trabert and Vic Seixas beat Lew Hoad and Ken Rosewall 3 sets to 1 in the doubles; and, in the singles, Bill Trabert beat Lew Hoad 3 sets to 1, and Vic Seixas beat Ken Rosewall 3 sets to 1. Tennis fans will of course know that the Australians reversed the result the next year when they beat the United States in the quarter finals.

When in Sydney I always stayed at the Astra Hotel at Bondi Beach. The Oldfield brothers (no relation to Bert, the Australian Test 'keeper) were friends of Keith Miller and Keith told them of my ambition to ride a surf board. The hotel's situation allowed me to attempt to 'crack a wave' early in the morning before going off to comment on the day's play on the Sydney cricket ground.

I made friends with lots of surfers, all of them sympathetic to my numerous tumbles when I attempted to stand on the surf board. At times, of course, my language was a bit rough. Later, I had an embarrassing moment when I met a fellow surfer, whom I only knew as George, in Collins Street, Sydney, and he was wearing the 'cloth' of a clergyman.

'George,' I said, 'I had no idea that you were in the church, I would not have used that rough language in front of you had I known.'

'That's alright, Alfred, I can hardly wear my collar when I am in bathers, but if you swear in my presence when I am "dressed" that would be a different matter.'

There often occurs a period during the latter half of a cricket tour when news for the weekly column is 'thin on the ground'. However, I was lucky that during such a period Len Hutton gave me an 'exclusive' on his future plans and ambitions in the game. The story 'wrote itself' and my piece on the 'Captain Looks Ahead' brought a rare 'well done' cable from my editor.

During the 1954 season I covered the Yorkshire versus Surrey game at Sheffield. I left London late on Friday and by 1.00 a.m. I had only motored as far as Chesterfield in Derbyshire. This, I thought, is far enough. The hotel in the station yard was in complete darkness but eventually the door opened in response to my repeated knocking and a sleepy-looking night porter appeared. I requested a room for the night. I signed the register and the porter said, 'I suppose you are not the same Gover who used to play for Surrey?' I admitted this was so and he roared with laughter saying, 'I have heard about you when the old days are mentioned – how you jumped on the pool table and it collapsed under your weight!' This incident had happened in 1938 at the end of the Derby versus Surrey game. Eddie Watts, Laurie Fishlock and myself had stopped for a drink in the hotel bar with the Derby players Stan Worthington and Tommy Mitchell. The conversation turned to physical fitness, with Eddie and Laurie backing me as the fittest man in the party, quoting my winter training on the Dulwich Hamlet football ground. This training included jumping over the fence surrounding the pitch, and Tommy Mitchell challenged me to prove it by doing a standing jump onto the pool table. I accepted with the proviso of being allowed one forward step. Up I went and landed on the top which immediately split apart. The lads roared with laughter which soon subsided when the manager rushed in. He was placated by Stan Worthington, a local hero, who promised full compensation for the repairs and any loss of income. We all shared the cost when we met later in the season. I had forgotten this episode of my younger days but, 'be sure your sins will find you out' even after a lapse of sixteen years!

In 1955, Surrey were playing Middlesex at the Oval when rain stopped play for the day at 12.30 p.m. so Gubby Allen, then chairman of selectors, Stuart Surridge and myself decided to play golf in the afternoon at Wimbledon Park. I rang George Casey to tell him that there was no more play at the Oval that day and that I would be going off to play golf with Gubby and Stuart.

'Golf will be OK,' said George 'but not at Wimbledon Park. You will go to Wentworth and cover the last round of the Daks Tournament. I will want your story when play is finished for the day.' I protested that I was his cricket writer not a golf reporter, only to be told that a journalist with a low handicap should find reporting golf a piece of cake. So 'bang' went my chance of taking a 'bob or two' from Gubby and Stuart on my home course.

On arriving at Wentworth, luck as so often in my career came to my aid again. I had envisaged difficulty in getting on to the course but the official in charge of the gate recognized me and arranged car parking for me. I then bumped into Maurice Hart, an old friend who was the London *Evening News* golf correspondent, and he obtained the press pass for me to go on the course, and then showed me the 'ropes' in the press tent.

I had a look at the leader board and went off to find Bobby Locke, ex-Open Champion, whom I had met several times, but when the South African golfer dropped shots to put himself out of contention I looked around for another promising match. I met Henry Cotton, there in his role as golf writer for the *News of the World*. 'Come with me, Alfred, I have an idea that young Wilkes from South Africa is going to win.' Henry's instinct and experience proved correct, with Wilkes topping the list and pocketing the winner's cheque. I was able to report the winner's play over the last eight holes and also get quotes from Bobby Locke on his young fellow-countryman winning the tournament – his first entry in competitive golf in the United Kingdom.

I 'phoned my report through to my paper and then, after the customary fifteen-minute interval, 'phoned George in case he wanted any additional information. His first words were, 'Good story – I told you it would be a piece of cake for you!' I took the compliment, but kept quiet about my help from Henry Cotton and my acquaintance with Bobby Locke.

I made my second tour to Australia in 1958/59 with Peter May's side. The team had travelled by ship to Ceylon (Sri Lanka) and then by air for the rest of the journey. During the stop in Ceylon at Colombo, Peter May, Peter Richardson, Tom Graveney and Jim Laker had been invited to visit the recently built Cricket School managed by Vijay Bihar. Three years previously Vijay had been sent to me at my School to undergo a three-month course to learn the art of coaching and Cricket School management. When Peter May's party had made a full inspection of the facility Vijay said that they must meet Son number One, and proudly presented two-year-old Alfred Gover Bihar. This was a nice compliment but the touring players said, 'Alf gets around a bit,' and pulled my leg saying that the child had some of my features.

Peter May's side was strong on paper but, surprisingly, they were beaten in Australia by four matches to one. This was due to a combination of circumstances. England's opening pair failed to give the side a good start. The figures for the total runs in successive tests were Richardson and Milton 16 and 28, Richardson and Bailey 7 and 3, Bailey and Milton 19 and 20, Richardson and Watson 89 and Richardson and Bailey 0 and 0.

The other factor in England's failure was the questionable actions of the Australian attack: Meckiff, Rorke and Slater.

One pleasant aspect of the tour was the off-spin bowling of Jim Laker. After his magnificent bowling in the 1956 Ashes series in England when he performed his historic 19 wickets feat at Old Trafford and took 46 wickets in the series, the Australians declared that he would have little success on the hard Australian pitches. But Jim confounded his critics by heading the Test averages with 15 wickets for an average of 21.20 runs per wicket. This was in spite of missing the fourth Test at Adelaide with an injured spinning (fore) finger.

During the second Test at Melbourne, played over the New Year holiday, the team relaxed with a game of seven-a-side football on the beach in front of their hotel. They invited me to make up the number, putting me at wing-half, but facing international soccer players Arthur Milton and Willie Watson. Against these characters I was completely out of my depth. I never put a foot to the ball until ten minutes before the end of the game when they listened to my plea to let me have a kick.

We also had Bill Edrich and South African Test star Hugh Tayfield reporting Peter May's tour and they both used the same ghost writer, Clive Taylor. During the Adelaide Test they sat on either side of Clive, each one in turn giving his views on the play. A couple of minutes after they had both left I saw Clive's hands resting on his typewriter and looking rather blank. I was seated directly behind him and asked, 'Anything I can do, Clive?', assuming that he wanted details of the scores of the play.

'Thank you, Alf, actually I can't remember who I am supposed to be just now.'

I missed the 1962/63 tour of Australia with Ted Dexter's team as all Fleet Street Sunday newspapers decided not to send their own correspondents. A pity, as it was the coldest British winter ever recorded and I envied the team out in sunny Australia. I was on holiday in Spain when the paper 'phoned from London to say they would not be sending me on the winter tour. This created a complication as I had agreed to commentate on the state and Test Matches for the Australian Broadcasting Commission (ABC). To give them adequate notice I 'phoned Bernie Kerr, the head of ABC Sport, to let him know I would not be able to take the engagement. The broadcasting contract alone would not have been sufficient reimbursement to pay for my air travel to Australia, plus the internal travel and accommodation, as it was always going to be only a subsidiary to my newspaper employment.

Bernie was understandably upset and said, 'Alfred, what am I going to do for an English voice in the commentary box?' I suggested that he ask Frank Tyson who was teaching at a Melbourne school. Bill duly approached Frank who accepted and was such a success that Bill used him in the commentary box for several years.

I did go to Australia again, in 1965/66 with Mike Smith's team. Although the Test series was drawn the team enjoyed a measure of popularity owing to their refreshing approach to run scoring. They were always willing to attack. In the second Test at Sydney, Geoff Boycott and Bob Barber, opening the innings, put up 98 runs in seventy-six minutes. In the third Test at Sydney Boycott and Barber put on 234 runs for the first wicket before Boycott was out for 86, and Barber finished with 185.

The Christmas break for the team came before the start of the Melbourne Test on 30 December. Mike had invited me to join the team at their motel on Christmas Day and golf had been arranged for the afternoon at Don Bradman's home club. It was thanks to his influence that the course, which would normally have been closed, was opened up especially for the tourists. I discovered that I had left my shoes back in my hotel and, with little chance of getting a taxi, Ritchie Benaud, who was covering the tour as a journalist, offered me the loan of his car, an open sports MG. I asked Ritchie how he had managed to get the car up from Sydney, his home town. He replied that, as a player, all he had known about his own country was the view from an aeroplane, the journey from the airport to the hotel and hotel to the cricket ground, but now that he was following the tour by car he said that he was really getting to know the country and the people who live away from the cities.

Ken Barrington was at his best in the final Test at Melbourne when he hit the fastest hundred of the series, scoring 115 inside two-and-a-half hours, including two 6's and eight 4's.

Whilst the match was in progress Sir Robert Menzies, Australia's prime minister and a past-president of the Lord's Taverners (1962), accompanied by myself and Ian Johnson, ex-Australian captain and now secretary of Melbourne Cricket Ground, presented Ken Barrington with a Lord's Taverners tie (which I had brought out with me from England). Ken had been elected the Lord's Taverner's cricketer of the year.

Sir Robert was a cricket lover and when his eleven played Mike Smith's side at Canberra he threw a dinner party for all the many ex-Australian players working in the press box and covering the tour. He was kind enough to invite me too – the only 'Pom' amongst the gathering. Every guest had to sing for his supper. When it came to my turn Sir Robert insisted on my telling the story of opening the batting with Jack Hobbs at Northampton, a tale he had heard on his visits as a guest to the Master's Luncheon Club in London. Sir Robert prompted me several times, much to the amusement of the Aussies, who were enjoying the story of the 'opening' partnership between number 11 and the legendary master batsman. They roared with laughter when I came to the part in the story when Jack said to me, 'Will you do me a favour and get out, there are a lot of good players waiting to come in.'

In 1967 George Casey 'phoned me one Saturday morning at

the ungodly hour of 6.00 a.m. to tell me to go to Sandwich in Kent to cover the Walker Cup golf. I told him it would be difficult for me to get in without a press pass or car park permit and reminded him he had sent me to cover golf at Wentworth in 1955 minus the necessary passes, but George must have had great faith in my ability as a gatecrasher as he simply said, 'You will manage alright!'

Arriving at Sandwich I was refused entry to the car park and not even a rustling of bank notes in my pocket had any effect. Fortunately, Leonard Crawley, the international amateur golfer and an old golfing 'mate' of mine, and the golf correspondent of the *Daily Telegraph*, drove up and explained to the 'guardian of the gate' that I was a bona fide journalist, and the gates were opened. Leonard helped me to obtain a press pass and offered me the facilities of the *Daily Telegraph* 'phone booth. Sadly I had to report the familiar story of a win for the United States by 13 matches to 7.

Great Britain's team included a school boy prodigy, Peter Oosterhuis from Dulwich College. Peter made a great impression with his power golf and soon after leaving school turned professional and achieved the rare double of playing for Great Britain in the Walker and Ryder Cup matches. I asked Peter if he had also played cricket at Dulwich, a school famous for the tradition of producing Test players, such as Billy Griffiths and Hugh Bartlett. Peter said he liked cricket but found using different muscles a problem plus the 'opposites' in the swinging of the golf club and the cricket bat.

The sacking of Brian Close from the England captaincy on the Saturday of the Oval Test against Pakistan in 1967 caught the cricketing public by surprise. In a twin-tour season, he had led England to victory over India, winning all three Tests. He followed by leading England to victory over Pakistan by two Test matches to one. I was told in the very strictest confidence that Brian was being relieved of the England captaincy in favour of Colin Cowdrey, my information being so confidential I could not give this sensational piece of news to my paper.

Brian was a particular friend of mine and due to dine with me at home that night. When he arrived with Vivian, his wife, it was obvious from their demeanour that the selectors had given him the news of his dismissal. Shortly after his arrival Richie Benaud, who apart from television commentaries reported the Tests for the *News of the World*, 'phoned me to ask if Brian Close was with me. It was obvious that Ritchie had heard a whisper on the captaincy and wished to check the story. I had to tell Ritchie that Brian was not with me, and to be on the safe side Brian went to Stuart Surridge's house just ten minutes away. He had only been there a matter of minutes before Ritchie rang Stuart asking the same questions. Stuart gave a negative reply. Ken Barrington, who was playing in the Test and had called in on Stuart on his way home to Mitcham, suggested that Brian and Viv stay the night with him. All went well until 1.00 a.m. when Ken was rudely disturbed by a reporter and photographer who knocked on his door and said that they understood that Brian was staying with them and could they talk to him and have a picture. Ken, who had always had a good relationship with the press, told the reporter that he appreciated that they were only doing their jobs but they must get off his premises.

Ken asked me the next day how the reporter could have known that Brian would be staying with him. 'For a good newspaper man', I told him 'it is a process of elimination – from my place, to Stuart's, and then to the only member of the Test team living in the London area.'

At the end of the 1967 season I retired from the *Sunday Mirror*. I had enjoyed my thirteen years in the service of the paper and the camaraderie of the press box that exists among cricket writers. I had established a firm friendship with my editor, George Casey. He was a legend in his own lifetime, the longest serving sport's editor in Fleet Street – thirty-nine years. I called him the 'Vicar of Bray', since he'd served under thirteen editors in his fifty years with the paper.

I would not be going to the West Indies for the forthcoming winter tour so I suggested Brian Close as my replacement. As the ex-England captain, his comments on the cricket would be interesting and attract the attention not only of regular readers to the paper, but all cricket followers. Brian was accompanied by Peter Smith, who was subsequently cricket correspondent for the *Daily Mail*, until appointed to the staff of the Test and County Cricket Board as press officer.

It was possible that a touch of 'sour grapes' could have crept into Brian's ideas on the performance of Cowdrey's team, especially in the Test matches, but to his credit the reports were fair and any criticism was constructive. Nobody was more pleased

---

than Brian that the team went unbeaten in all first-class matches played and the Test series was won.

In the early 1950s the *Daily Mirror* had staged an annual cavalcade of sport at the White City, London. They presented showjumping, athletics, five-a-side soccer, rugby sevens, speedway and five-a-side cricket.

The five-a-side cricket was played with a soft baseball-type of ball; the players used normal bats but batting gloves and pads were not necessary. The batsman could only be out caught or run out at the batting end. The pitch was 15 yards long with a single wicket and the bowler was not allowed to deliver the ball above shoulder height. Boundary hits did not count and every hit had to be run. The batsman had to run 12 yards to a point on the right side of backward-leg position and then back to the batting crease to make their runs. All the fielders had one 8 ball over in turn and also kept wicket for one over.

I stood at backward short-leg with a hand mike, commentating through the public address system. I first introduced the fielding side and then named the batsman at the wicket. After making a hit all the batsmen, without exception, would start running in the normal way up the wicket towards the bowler's end. I would call out, 'Come back – this way.' The batsman would then put the brakes on and tear across to the leg-side position and endeavour to return in time to the stumps at the batting crease. Because of his early loss of direction he would struggle to beat the throw in. I would then invite crowd participation in the game and involve them in run out decisions saying, 'Was that out?' If the run out was obvious I would accept their decision, but if it was close I often gave the verdict to the batsman, especially if he had only just come in. This would bring 'boos' (in good fun) from the crowd and occasionally I would then reverse my decision and the 'boos' would change to 'cheers'.

My teams were normally made up of Surrey players and from the visiting team to the Oval. One year when Surrey were playing away from the Oval, Essex provided the opposition for a team of Lancashire League 'pros' including Frank Worrell, Gary Sobers, Rohan Kanhai, Sonny Ramadhin and Manny Martindale. The game came under fire from the cricket purists and ardent fans calling it a travesty of cricket. As far as I was concerned, apart from it's entertainment value, I was happy that it was considered necessary to have cricket in some form as part of the programme.

14

My Involvement with Films, Radio and Television

IN 1947, I was first introduced to the mysteries of film production, when I was invited to act as technical adviser to 'Badgers
Green'. The outdoor scenes were filmed at Littlewick Green, near
Maidenhead in Berkshire. The plot of the film centred around the
village cricket team, the squire and a villain. The squire was
heavily in debt and the villain had his eye on the squire's lovely
daughter so he challenged the squire to put up his village team
against one raised by himself. If the squire won, his indebtedness
to the villain would be scrapped, but if the villain won, the
squire would have the choice of selling up the manor house and
grounds to pay his debts or to give his daughter's hand in marriage to the villain.

The squire first consulted his daughter and after assuring her
that his village team, who had gone undefeated for three years
could not possibly lose, she reluctantly consented, and the deal
was agreed with the villain. To strengthen his side the squire
persuaded a first-class cricketer to join the team, a left-handed
batsman, who was played by Gary Marsh. At the time Gary,
who was a star of theatre and films, was the reigning captain of the
Stage Cricket Club and, coincidentally, was a left-handed batsman.

As the film's technical adviser it was my job to see that all
cricket details were correct. I discovered that most actors playing
the parts of cricketers knew very little about the game and I had
to put them through the correct movements when batting, bowling or fielding. The two actors playing the more passive role of
the umpires were shown how to make the signals required by the
film's script. To film the close up of Gary's strokes the camera
men would take their trolley half-way down the pitch and I

142

would take up position alongside them, out of camera range, and throw the ball to Gary the length and line required for the various strokes. The director rarely needed more than two takes for each scene. As a pro cricketer my throwing from that distance was extremely accurate and this made it easy for Gary to play his strokes for the cameras.

For the long-distance shots I would advise the director on the placing of the field. I had already rehearsed an actor in the bowling action – he would take two steps to the bowling crease and with a full swing of the bowling arm release the ball. The cameras would pick him up in his last stride to the bowling crease and as the ball left his hand the cameras would stop filming. The results of the day's filming seen later in the viewing room showed the long shots 'married' to the close-ups of Gary playing his shot. It was my first experience of the 'cheating' done by the camera.

One mid-morning we were busy filming long shots when down came the rain. The director decreed that the unit would have it's lunch break (food is always provided when on outside locations). Gary told me he had a friend called Sydney Frazer who had been in show business and who now ran a café/restaurant some fifteen minutes away by car. Gary also told me that Sydney had promised him a big steak if he could drop in to see him during the daytime. Food rationing was still on at the time, and so, when Gary said, 'This is too good a chance to miss. Come on, Alfred', off we went.

Sydney was delighted to see his old mate, and he immediately showed us two luscious-looking pieces of meat, which, having received our approval, were taken back to the kitchen to await the order to start the grill. Sydney soon had Gary reminiscing about old times, Sydney doing most of the talking while they celebrated each story with a drink – getting rather the worse for wear. In the meantime my stomach was rumbling at the thought of attacking that large and juicy steak. At last they finished talking, and Sydney turned to go into the kitchen, but, at that very moment, there came a screech of car brakes outside the café door, and the assistant director rushed in to tell us that the sun had been out for the last fifteen minutes and that they were waiting to start filming. The café's windows were heavily curtained, so we had been blissfully unaware of the change in the weather. We not only missed our steaks but were not very popular on our late return, as 'time is money' when a film is on a small budget.

To make matters worse I pointed out that the clock on the village hall, which had come into shot during the morning filming now stood at 2.15 p.m., whereas when we shot in the morning it showed 11.50 a.m. The action being filmed called for continuous play and a time lag of over two hours would have looked most peculiar to a discerning cinema audience. The hold up before the clock was set back held up the start of filming for another ten minutes. Fortunately, however, Gary's stand-in, Dick, who was similar in build, had in our absence done his job of rehearsing Gary's movements to help the camera operators line up their lens ready to 'shoot' Gary when the director called 'action'. Considering Gary's 'condition' I was amazed at his polished performance.

It is normal for a director to call for at least two takes before declaring himself satisfied. However, the first shot went so well that harmony was restored and the rest of the afternoon went smoothly, with even the necessary changes of camera angles slotting into place without a hitch. At the end of the day's work, I drove off to London with Gary and of course our first topic of conversation was the steaks and how they had slipped from our grasp. 'It was my fault,' said Gary. 'I should have stopped him as I knew Sydney suffered from verbal diarrhoea!' Then he added, 'Our only chance is to pray for rain tomorrow.' But the Fates conspired against us, and filming went uninterrupted for the next five days until the conclusion of all the outdoor filming on Littlewick Green.

My next venture into films was in 1955 when the famous director, Anthony Asquith, asked me to assist him as technical adviser in the making of the film 'The Final Test' written by Terence Rattigan. The film told the story of a famous England opening bat playing in his final Test match at the Oval. This role was played by Jack Warner with Len Hutton playing himself as captain of England and with a supporting cast including Cyril Washbrook, Denis Compton, Godfrey Evans and Jim Laker. Robert Morley was also in the film.

As Jack Warner had to be fitted out with an England cap, slipover, sweater and blazer, I wrote to MCC who gave me an introduction to Simpsons of Piccadilly, the official suppliers of all the England regalia. Simpsons agreed to supply our requirements only after both Jack and I signed a document to the effect that the clothing must in no circumstances be worn outside the studio and at the finish of the making of the film all the equipment would be returned to them. This requirement is because the crown surmounting the three lions on the England badge is the prerogative of the Home Office acting on behalf of the Queen, although no permission is necessary for the wearing of the three lions.

Jack had no idea of how to handle a bat and my first job was to take him in my nets at the School and teach him the basics – stance at the wicket, backlift and how to bring the bat down to play at the ball, head kept steady with the correct eye line to follow an imaginary ball coming down the pitch from 22 yards away. Then the back foot playing at and missing the ball. The plot called for him to be out leg-before-wicket for a duck in the first over.

I also took him through the facial expressions of a batsman when he has been hit on the pad and the bowler has appealed for an lbw decision; how he looks up at the umpire, awaiting his decision, and then the expression of disappointment on being given out, especially for nought in a batsman's final Test innings.

Jack, of course, had no trouble 'acting' the facial expressions, but he found the technique of batting harder to assimilate and it took ten days' intensive coaching and hard work before he felt satisfied. He had now mastered even the smallest details of each stroke that he had to play and I was amazed that Jack, who had started as a complete novice with the bat, could now look and act like a professional batsman.

'The Final Test' was filmed at Pinewood and the main action of the production centred around the England dressing room. The producers had gone into the smallest detail when building the set of the 'England dressing room', with the exact number of clothes hooks and lockers. They had even put in the screw top which protruded from the floor where it lead onto the balcony. (Whenever complaints were made by players at the Oval who tripped up on the screw top it was explained that to move the offending object the floor around the area close to the door would have to be pulled up.)

Viewed from the dressing room balcony were two huge canvases painted for the film to give the illusion that you were looking at the playing area with the seated spectators in the background. When Anthony Asquith asked for my opinion of the 'Pinewood' Oval I could only say 'Ruddy marvellous!' He also had one query – was the clock on the wall of the dressing room electric or manual? I had to admit that, although I was familiar with the clock's presence, I had never noticed what type it was but I would 'phone the Oval to find out. They were in the same boat as myself but promised to go and find out and came back amazed that after many years of going in and out they only now noticed for the first time that it was a manual timekeeper.

The front of the pavilion was also amazingly realistic. It consisted of the concrete steps used by the players going to and from the dressing room and the perimeter fencing and gate leading onto the field on either side of the steps, plus seven rows of seating which had been built five each side, enough for the cameras to show movement on the steps and for the members to applaud players coming off the field. The facia of the pavilion looked exactly the same to me as it did in my playing days when coming off the field and then trudging up those steps. The door leading into the main pavilion had on its right the members' reading room and the set even showed the daily newspapers. To complete the illusion the pavilion brick wall showed the two different shades of brick which had been a feature of the building for as long as I could remember.

Anthony Asquith's 'Number One' was called 'Blackie', I never did find out his real name. Among his various duties was to be in charge of the extras and he usually worked from a stand mike. One day when a scene of members applauding a batsman coming off the field was about to be taken, I noticed that all the older extras had been placed along one side of the gangway where they would be 'in camera' all the time and the younger extras were placed three or four places in from the gangway where they would only occasionally come into shot. I thought the age groups should be mixed up so I went to Blackie's stand mike to issue my instructions to the extras. I had only said 'Gentlemen', when Blackie pushed me away from the mike saying, 'For heavens' sake, you must not direct the extras or we will have a strike on our hands.'

'Why?' I asked.

'Because it's my job and you are not a Union member.' He then asked me what was wrong and when I told him he had the extras duly shuffled around.

Three days later the cameras were stationed on the balcony shooting into the dressing room when I noticed Cyril Washbrook's heavy winter overcoat hanging on a peg in the room. Having learned my lesson I made no attempt to take it down but pointed out to Blackie that the overcoat would be entirely out of place on a warm sunny day.

'That is "Harry Props" job', he said and called for 'Harry Props'. The studio was a long rambling building and we could hear Blackie's message being relayed by studio hands until it reached 'Harry Props' who duly arrived ten minutes later to solemnly take the coat down. Having handed it over to Blackie he then went on his slow walk back to whence he had come.

Although the cricketers in the cast were playing themselves, at times they found it difficult to be natural when facing the cameras and when speaking their lines, usually no more than a sentence. For example: the batsman coming into the dressing room just after getting out might have to say, 'I played a bad shot.' If Anthony was unhappy with the intonation he would take me to his studio 'office' and ask me to take him over the correct intonation. Anthony was a kind man and fully realized the players' difficulties in front of the cameras, so after talking to me he would then take the player concerned on one side and very patiently guide him into the natural way of putting over his lines. Len Hutton had the advantage of early rehearsals with the director before each day's filming and both his lines and his deportment as the 'England captain' came across in a natural and relaxed manner.

Anthony asked me to find him another cricketer, quite apart from those already engaged in the film. He wanted a fast bowler with a good action who could both be filmed from back and front camera angles when delivering the ball and also speak four lines of dialogue. I invited Bill (William) Franklyn, a useful fast bowler with the Stage Cricket Club, to take on this role. He was able to accept because he was currently acting as understudy to Peter Ustinov in the production of 'The Love of Two Colonels' which was showing in a London theatre. Bill was on the threshold of his career which later lead to fame and stardom in the theatre and on television.

The fast bowler played by Bill had been named Linder – a mixture of the names of the great Australian Test fast bowlers of that period, Lindwall and Miller. Anthony was delighted when Bill gave such a smooth and professional performance. (At the time of writing Bill is still playing and taking wickets at the age of 60. He runs his own side of actors called 'The Sergeants'; they do not keep their score sheets because Bill says that actors have enough of bad notices.)

When 'The Final Test' was released it proved to be quite popular in the cinema and it has since been shown several times on television.

Some four years later I was invited to act as technical adviser again, this time for a film entitled 'Two Gentlemen Sharing', a film telling the story of two young law students both in love with the same girl. The law students were supposed to be a West Indian who was a good cricketer and a young non-cricketing Englishman.

A very handsome coloured American actor had been engaged to play the character of the West Indian left-handed batsman. The American actor had never seen or heard of cricket before and my first job was to take him to my School nets. For the first three days I asked him to take a passive role, by watching the coach at work with other pupils. Then, after the coaching session was over, I would take him into the club bar with its walls entirely covered with pictures showing contemporary and great players of the past in action. Here he could listen to the pupils and coaches and their conversations in cricket 'jargon'. My idea was for him to assimilate the atmosphere, both in the nets and the bar, so that he would get an appreciation of the cricketing character he had to portray.

When we commenced our work in the nets it was apparent that he had little ball sense. The script required him to play some flowing strokes off the back foot on the off side. I had to start with the very basics, throwing underarm from three or four yards away and gradually extending the yardage until I stood several yards back and could make the ball bounce high enough for him to play the back foot shot. He was somewhat apprehensive when I switched from the tennis ball to a hard cricket ball but soon overcame this and gave signs of being able to play the shot. I explained to him that he would be filmed playing the back foot shots following the same routine as in the School. For the long shots a ball would be sent down well wide of his left-hand side outside the off stump. All he had to do would be to go through the motions of the shot ignoring the ball which would go harmlessly past him. He could then retire from the crease and his place would be taken by Gary Sobers who played the flowing strokes, filmed in long shot and with his face not discernible, thus completing the illusion.

The outdoor scenes were filmed on the Westminster School Ground in Vincent Square, London. John Snow, the Sussex and England fast bowler, renowned for the accuracy of the line and length of his deliveries, had been engaged to do the bowling sequences. He was to bowl to the American at the crease and later on to Gary. The sun was shining, the London University Cricket Team providing the slip fielders and the wicketkeeper were standing well back, the umpire at the bowler's end was resplendent in white coat, and the American actor was taking his stance at the batting crease. Everything in the garden was rosy.

The director, looking pleased with life, called 'roll them' and the cameras started to whirl. John commenced his long run, wicketkeeper and slips crouched, the batsman, with bat raised, waited to complete his days of learning and long rehearsals of his back foot shot. John reached the crease and released the ball, the batsman had his bat half-way down when the ball, which had been directed to well outside the off stump, swung in towards the batsman and carried on when it hit the seam. It struck the poor unfortunate actor a frightful blow on the most vulnerable and painful part on the inside at the top of the left leg. He collapsed in a heap holding his leg and yelping with pain. When we eventually got him to his feet he refused to go through the scene again and although John Snow and I assured him it would not happen again he was adamant in his refusal. The director left the actor in the hands of his agent and in the meantime filled in time shooting a love scene between the rival suitor and the girl. I watched for a while but found it was much less exciting than our abortive cricket scene. The American was persuaded back the following morning after much hot water and physiotherapy treatment overnight.

Some years later I made my first and last appearance as a film extra in the television series 'Bergerac'. I was on a golfing trip to Jersey where the series is filmed. The friend I was staying with told me he had accepted an invitation to be an extra for the next day's shooting and had also put my name down. He persuaded me to go along with him pleading that it was just a 'bit of fun'. We duly turned up on location the next day – a village hall where the character called 'Charlie', played by Terence Alexander, was supposed to be addressing the local electorate in an effort to claim their votes in his attempt to be elected as a member of the local ward (council).

Terry and I were old mates from our Stage Golfing Society days and after a giggle about my appearance as an extra he told me he was worried about the way things were going. I presumed that he was referring to the filming of that particular episode. 'Not a bit of it', he said, 'my worry is about the second Test Match at Lords where England are staging a fight back against the West Indies.' He went on, 'Please let me know how the score is going when we break between takes.'

Between 1949 and 1955 I served spells with the BBC Sound Radio Team covering the Test matches. At that time the expert gave the summaries of play at lunch and tea intervals and also at close of play, and in addition he did commentaries during the day's play.

The job brought many amusing incidents. At Lord's one day, Alan Moss, the Middlesex fast bowler, was operating from the pavilion end. It was 5.30 p.m. in late August, and the sun was directly behind the pavilion. As Alan set off on his long run up, I said 'And Alan Moss is chasing his own shadow up to the bowling crease . . .' I was quite chuffed with my comment, an original remark. It must have made an impression, because under similar circumstances I heard the same expression used by one of the regular and very famous broadcasters a few days later, and I thought to myself, 'That is a spot of plagiarism.'

When India were playing England at the Oval in 1952 Rex Alston was commentating on the play when he said, 'Alfred you know this ground well enough, is it going to rain?' He turned and pointed to the black clouds gathering over the gas-holder side of the ground. 'No', I replied, 'it never rains from that quarter only from the back over the pavilion.' Ten minutes later the ground was under water. 'That', said Rex 'is the last time I will ever ask you to forecast the weather.'

I was in the commentary box at the Oval in 1953 when England, under Len Hutton, won back the Ashes. When the match began to go England's way, the BBC decided to cancel all the regular programmes in favour of the story from the Oval. England went on to win the Ashes for the first time since 1926. During the closing hours of play we greeted all the cricket-playing countries in the world, such was the interest in this Ashes contest. After Denis Compton hit the winning run and the players and umpires had made the safety of the pavilion, a vast crowd of excited fans covered the ground in front of the pavilion, facing the balcony, cheering whenever they spotted an England player and continually calling out for Len Hutton. It was a great day for English cricket, and for the fans who in years to come would be able to say: 'I was at the Oval in 1953.'

In the after-match commentaries describing the scenes I was able to boast, 'I was here in 1926 as a youngster of 18.' I described to the listeners my emotions then, when finally the game was won and my mad dash across the field to be in the forefront to get a close-up of England's heroes. I was one of the last to leave and then only because the ground was being cleared of all spectators and reluctantly I obeyed the officials' request to leave the ground.

The BBC made a tape recording to celebrate the 70th birthday of Jack Hobbs, and John Bridges, the producer, asked me to act as link man introducing all the great players as they gave their thoughts on Jack's personality and his ability as a player. From Australia, Don Bradman, Arthur Mailey, Jack Gregory and Berty Oldfield all paid tribute, as did a host of English Test contemporaries. I remember bringing in England's great left-hander, Frank Woolley, who gave Jack a back-handed compliment: he said Jack Hobbs was undoubtedly the greatest right-hand batsman of his time.

It is easy to make a slip up when working in the commentary box. I once said, 'A brilliant piece of fielding by Tony Lock at third man' when in fact the bowler was Tony himself. In those circumstances I found it best to make a joke and say, 'I know Tony is quick on his feet, but even he could not have travelled that distance so fast. In fact it was "so and so" fielding down at third man.'

In 1956 ATV launched a new series called 'Seeing Sport', an instructional series covering all the major sports. It ran for thirteen years, becoming the longest running show ever of its kind, and it engaged the top coaches in their particular sports. The coaches were: Alf Gover (cricket); Tommy Docherty, the famous Scottish international player who went into club management with Chelsea in 1959 (soccer); Gerwyn Williams, the Welsh International with thirteen caps (rugby); Tony Mottram, the Davis Cup star (tennis); Johnny Leach, twice winner of the World Championship (table tennis); Geoff Dyson, England coach in the 1948, 1952, 1956 and 1960 Olympic Games and Chief National Coach of the Amateur Athletic Association (athletics); John Disley, Olympic star and winner of several international events (climbing). The first-ever broadcast was made from The Gover Indoor Cricket School in October 1954.

As I was to appear on camera I was curious about the procedure of getting the programme 'on the air'. The producer sat at the scanner machine with his assistant and sound engineer and his microphone allowed him to talk direct to the floor manager and camera man. The producer had a mixer controlling the four pictures that we could see on his monitor screen, he then selected the picture for the viewers to see.

We would make the School area ready for the camera positions by rolling the side netting of all four nets up onto the roof netting. At the bowler's end was erected a wide-angle camera with zoom lens able to take in the whole of the playing area. At the batsman's end there were two cameras on the off side, one at point and another on point's right-hand side, one used for close-ups and one for me to look at when putting over my coaching points. At the bowler's end I had to be in a position to be within range of the zoom camera, usually from around two yards down the wicket.

The floor manager, who was always out of camera, would point me in the right direction, should I be working to the wrong camera (I am pleased to say that he never had occasion to do this). He was also the timekeeper – giving us the passing of the minutes with his fingers from three minutes down and then a final roll of the hands over each other indicating thirty seconds.

The programme, lasting thirty-five minutes, went out to the viewers at 5.00 p.m. and we started the rehearsal at 2.00 p.m., checking sound effects and camera angles. This was followed by a dry-run, a rehearsal on closed circuit camera, allowing both the producer and 'performers' to see the 'forecast' of the programme and to make any last-minute alterations – usually the producer's brainwave.

For my programme I would have engaged a 'star' Test cricket player to demonstrate the batting, bowling and wicket-keeping techniques. We would only cover one batting stroke on each broadcast, first demonstrating the details and finer points of the stroke without using the ball, then on to the stroke playing the ball.

The initial programme was on batting, showing the grip, pick up of the bat and the forward defensive shots. My first rehearsal lasted fifty minutes. My wife, Marjorie, heard the producer say to the floor manager, 'This is a shambles, I thought Alfred would be the ideal man for this programme – he is a journalist, has experience in radio and television and is a coach.' He then turned and saw Marjorie standing nearby and said, 'I am so sorry, I did not know you were here.'

'That's alright,' she said, 'don't worry it will be alright on the night!'

I was blissfully unaware of the conversation but realized I was well over the time in rehearsal. I gave it some thought and talked it over with Don Bennett, the Middlesex player and a pupil of mine who was doing the batting stint. I then walked across to my producer Tony Flanagan and said, 'I can "tighten" it up if I can work in close-up, holding Don's hands when he picks the bat up, cocking the wrist early in the pick up, relaxing the right hand at the top of the backlift and taking the bat back in line with the middle and off stumps. Then, guiding Don's hands when the bat swings down to meet the ball, to show the left foot having gone out alongside the line of the ball. In the meantime, I can make a running commentary on all the movements leading up to the bat coming down to meet the ball.'

Don then demonstrated the complete stroke from the stance position, this gave me time to walk to the bowler's end and bowl a series of half-volleys for Don to push away.

The 'dry run' satisfied the producer, both for camera angles and timing. For this initial programme of 'Seeing Sport' I asked Don to act as demonstrator knowing he would not 'freeze' in front of the cameras. Don, having been a pupil of mine was familiar with the routine. The 'live' broadcast went well. Everybody was happy, including the producer and, of course, myself. Having got over the first hurdle, the following three broadcasts went so well that Tony suggested I let him know in advance what part of the game I proposed to cover – batting, bowling, wicket-keeping or fielding and the name of my star guest. On the day of the broadcast I would tell him how I proposed to work with my stars, on the instructions and what they would be demonstrating. I would of course then be directed by Tony in the presentation of the programme.

I had many of the top Test stars as my guests including Peter May, Richie Benaud, Frank Worrell, Gary Sobers, (Lord) Learie Constantine, Ken Barrington, Mike Smith, Jim Laker, Tony Lock, Alec Bedser, Bill Edrich, Len Hutton, Willie Watson, Tom

Graveney, Arthur Wellard, Joe Hardstaff, junior, Fred Titmus, Alan Moss and Brian Close.

The programme had its amusing moments. When Peter May demonstrated the forcing shot off the back foot on the off side he nearly decapitated the camera man stationed at silly mid-off. Peter's back foot shots were renowned for their power and in this demonstration he was slightly off line in the intended direction of his hit, missing the camera man by no more than one or two inches. This was during the 'dry run' and a hurried adjustment of position was necessary to placate the apprehensive camera man. When the programme was broadcast Peter missed the camera man but came close to hitting his wife Virginia, who was watching the 'action' and who was pregnant with their first child at the time.

When the programme had been running for three years I had the second 'black out' in my 'performing' career reminiscent of my first with ENSA during the war. We were transmitting the programme from the School. Don Bennett was demonstrating batting and I said, 'I am now going to bowl a long hop, pitched on the off stump and Don will demonstrate the pull shot – note how he gets his feet into position.' I turned round to look at the zoom camera lens when I had a complete 'black'. I thought, 'What am I doing here looking into a camera lens, am I supposed to say something?' I knew from the whites I was wearing that it was something to do with cricket but my mind was blank, so I told the story of my first meeting with Patsy Hendren, the Middlesex and England batsman, before the start of the MCC versus Surrey match at Lords. Before I had got to the end of the story my memory had been jogged and I was 'down to earth' again and went on to finish the Hendren story before looking into the camera and saying, 'If you look down to the batting end you will see another Middlesex batsman, Don Bennett, waiting to demonstrate the full power of the hook shot against the short of a length "long hop" delivery.'

At the end of the programme Tony came up to me saying, 'You had me scared when I saw that blank look come over your face, but you got out of it OK and I liked the funny Hendren story. Do you think we should include an anecdote every week?' However, I did not agree and the idea was dropped.

The summer programmes came from an outdoor location, the Masonic Boys School at Bushey in Hertfordshire. The setting was

19 and **20**. Frank Tyson above and myself below in 1936. In spite of the distance in years the similarity of our style was often remarked upon. We both had a natural style. The similarity was in our method of 'setting ourselves up' at the crease in order to deliver a ball.

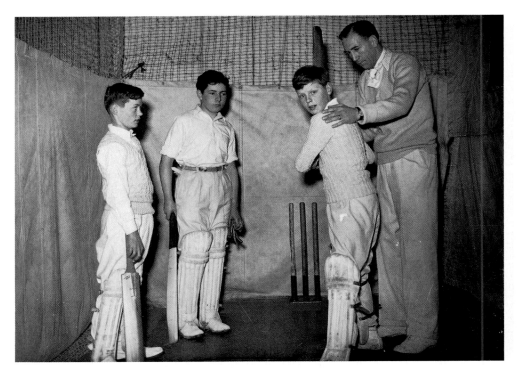

21. Coaching youngsters at the Cricket School. I coached hundreds of youngsters during my years at the cricket school. Here I am taking the boy's bat up, making sure his wrists are fully cocked, and getting him side on.

22. At the Cricket School with, from left: Ken Barrington, Fred Titmus, myself, Colin Cowdrey. This was a practice session prior to the tour of the West Indies in 1960.

23. Here's Colin Cowdrey and myself playing Golf at the Royal Calcutta Club with our hosts, two members of the club. We won our foursomes match. Colin was at his best that day playing a stroke or so below his six handicap.

24. At the Cricket School with two captains of England, Peter May and Ted Dexter. Ted came down for a practice session and for me to run the rule over his bowling action and Peter, then Captain of our Test team, came in to have a net himself.

25. At the Cricket School trying to correct Geoff Griffin's suspect bowling action. This picture was taken on the first day of Geoff's course with me. Note how his left foot points towards first slip, his front knee is bent, the left side has collapsed and the left shoulder has dropped all helping to throw the right arm out of line and make it bend. It was the complete chuck.

26. The BBC Commentary Team in 1960 from left: Bernie Kerr, Arthur Wigley (Scorer), John Arlott, myself, Rex Alston, and with earphones Max Muller our producer and then head of outside sports broadcasts. This was the Test Match Special team of the day.

27. Commonwealth Touring Team to Pakistan in 1963. Back row from left: J Murray, C Watson B D'Oliviera, C Griffith, K Palmer, S Nurse, D Slade, K Ibadullah. Sitting from left: W Alley, T Graveney, myself, P Richardson, R Kanhai, K Andrews, B Butcher.

28. Lunching with the Master. From left: Sir Jack Hobbs, myself, John Arlott, Leo Harrison. We met on the Master's birthday, the Lord's and Oval Tests and also at the pre-season lunch. Can you see our tie? Green, with the motif of a cricket bat, with crossed knife and fork with a knights helmet above the handle.

29. In Australia in 1966 with Prime Minister Bob Menzies, myself, Ian Johnson (ex Australian Captain and Secretary of Melbourne Cricket Club) and Ken Barrington receiving his Lord's Taverners tie. I was deputed by the Taverners to take Ken's tie on his being elected the Taverners Cricketer of the Year, and to invite Sir Robert Menzies a Past President of the Taverners to make the presentation at Melbourne on the morning of the second Test Match.

30. When I wanted to put on a demonstration of batting and bowling in my nets for the local schools, Ken Barrington, Fred Titmus and Brian Close came along and demonstrated their skills to the delight of all the lads. Here Ken is explaining the grain on a cricket bat to the obvious enjoyment of the boys at being so close to the great players.

31. With the Commonwealth team in India 1965. Back row from left: Keith Andrews, Camey Smith, John Mortimore, Lance Gibbs, Mushtaqu Mohammad, Barry Knight, Bill Coldwell, Basil Butcher. Sitting from left: Colin Cowdrey, Peter Richardson, myself, Gary Sobers, Brian Close.

32. In my Presidential Year of the Lord's Taverners, 1974, we invited Sir Donald Bradman over from Australia as our guest of honour on the occasion of a night at an Anglo-American Sports Club Dinner with boxing contests, all in aid of the Taverners Funds, at the Hilton Hotel. Supporting Sir Don, from left: Alan Watkins, Doug Wright, myself, Denis Compton, Reg Simpson, Alec Bedser, Jim Laker, John Dewes, Ted Dexter, Jack Young. Middle row, from left: Sir George (Gubby) Allan, Norman Yardley, 'The Don', Sir Len Hutton, Keith Miller. Seated from left: Bill Edrich, Billy (S. C.) Griffiths, Godfrey Evans.

33. April 1975. H.R.H. The Prince of Wales takes over the Presidency of the Taverners from myself. In the picture: John Snagg, myself, Peter Palmer (Chairman), the chap with the bald head is Billy Cotton Jnr.

34. A Lord's Taverners dinner in 1981 with Harry Secombe as President. Also, amongst others, Sir John Mills, H.R.H. The Duke of Edinburgh, John Snagg, myself, Eric Morecambe, Sir Brian Rix. The dinner at the Dukes Hotel, London, celebrated the Taverners Thirtieth Anniversary.

ideal, with a good firm pitch. For òne programme I had invited ex-Australian captain Richie Benaud. I told him I would pick him up, as he might find difficulty in finding Bushey and the Masonic School, but Richie assured me he knew the way and would report to the location at 2.00 p.m. However, by 4.00 p.m. there was no sign of him and I began to get worried, fearing he could be involved in an accident. At 4.30 p.m. Tony Flanagan asked me tc think up ideas to work on camera by myself for the scheduled programme time, but that daunting prospect was solved at 4.50 p.m. when Richie arrived – having changed into whites in the car – explaining that his driver had lost the way.

In the few minutes available before going 'live', I briefed Richie on the programme. I wanted him to do, first, his leg-spin bowling and, then, some batting; he could pad up during the commercial break. Richie is such a natural in front of the cameras that the programme proved to be one of the best transmissions in the whole of the thirteen-year run, though we nearly had one hiccup. We had first shown Richie's grip for his leg break, the method of finger spin, the use of the floppy wrist in delivery and finally Richie bowling, with the camera showing the turn off the pitch. I then said, 'Now Richie will demonstrate his googly.' Only for him to say, 'I can't do that because of a bad shoulder.' He added, 'Not that I ever said anything about it, your chaps in the England team were still looking for it.' This admission was of course a novel and interesting piece of news for the viewers, which all helped to 'make' the programme. Richie followed up by offering to demonstrate the delivery that had brought him many Test wickets – the 'flipper', bowled at a quicker pace with a shade of top spin.

Another slight hiccup occurred when Ken Barrington came to Bushey to demonstrate the art of the late cut. We had gone through all the usual shadow batting and the time arrived for the demonstration with the ball. Don Bennett was the bowler and I stationed myself by the stumps on the leg side to make my running commentary. Ken stood in the stance position at the crease and, as Don ran up to the bowling crease, I commenced my 'chat' by saying, 'Don will now bowl this ball short outside the off stump and I want you (the viewers) to take particular note of the way the batsman (Ken) rolls his wrists over to send the ball down and away.' Up came Don and down came the ball – a short-length delivery at well over medium pace and coming straight towards me just outside the leg stump. Ken looked up rather nonplussed, so looking into my 'commentary' camera I said, 'Don's had a mental aberration, he thinks Ken is a left-hander!' Don was back bowling next delivery on the spot and allowing Ken to show his full skills.

The world's greatest all-rounder, Gary Sobers, came to Bushey to show his skill as batsman and bowler. I well remember that in rehearsal time he asked me, 'Do you want me to pick up the bat towards the stumps?' It was a good question because I was able to explain to the viewers that Gary had very flexible wrists which enabled him to commence the pick up taking the bat up away from himself on the off side, and then bring the bat in at the top of the backlift to point in the direction of the stumps. So he was back to 'square one' in my teaching of the pick up.

We did not have time to go through Gary's repertoire of bowling – fast left-arm, in and outswing, Chinaman (the left-hander's off break) and the googly. We chose to show the 'mysteries' of his spin bowling.

There was one batsman who at my request changed his grip. This was Joe Hardstaff, the Nottingham and England batsman. (I had been rude to his father as a young player.) Joe held the bat at the extreme top of the handle. He was a fine all-round stroke player and, surprisingly for his grip, one of the best hookers of short-pitched bowling in the business. Joe willingly obliged although he said that even the matter of changing his grip by an inch made it feel very strange to him.

I took Arthur Wellard, the Somerset and England all-rounder and renowned hitter of sixes, to Bushey, with its wide open space, so that he could show the way to send the ball over the boundary fence, or, as Arthur always described it, to give the ball a little 'heave-ho'. He demonstrated his straight pick up stressing the importance of a full follow through when going for the big hit.

Jim Laker appeared on a programme sent out from my School. Although he had just retired from the first-class game he was still able to impart a huge degree of turn on an indoor pitch. His forefinger bent inwards and was swollen in size through years of working on the ball. This all made good television. Jim was a natural – to show his methods I engaged him in conversation letting him do most of the talking and the demonstration of grip and how to impart spin. Along the way I brought up his historic nineteen Australian wickets at Old Trafford in 1956 and got him to tell us some hitherto unknown secrets on his success that day.

When the television series started I had to use a roving hand mike on a long lead. This would occasionally catch in the ends of the artificial pitch in the bowlers' run up area. To save me stopping in my tracks the floor manager would scurry across on hands and knees to loosen the cable, so it was a relief when the radio mike arrived. I was the second person to use this type of mike, Bruce Forsyth having used one the night before at the Sunday Palladium. The lead on these early radio mikes was attached over the shoulders and resting on the chest, then travelled inside the sweater and down the inside of the trouser leg.

Thirteen years after 'Seeing Sport' was first transmitted, ATV moved to the Midlands and the series was finished. It had had consistent good ratings and I was happy that cricket had been an integral part of the series.

15
Coaching and Touring Pakistan

I HAVE ALWAYS had an interest in Pakistan cricket since their fledgling days on the international scene. In 1952 the Board of Control for cricket in Pakistan sent me four players to be at my indoor cricket school for two months' intensive coaching: batsman Imtiaz Ahmed, fast bowler Khan Mohammad, and all-rounders Rosidinhshaw and Agasadat.

Imtiaz was already an established batsman and many critics in Pakistan said, 'You can't teach an old dog new tricks.' I had to tighten up the loose strokes that might get him out and not make any drastic changes in his basic technique. One of his favourite shots was to sweep to leg, but too often the ball was hit into the air, the right hand not always coming in at the correct time in the hitting of the ball, the face of the bat being closed too early. His off drive was good, but against the ball swinging away he checked his follow through, his right hand came into the stroke too early so that the necessary swing of the bat with his left hand, taking the bat out and away through the ball in the direction of the shot was mitigated. This in turn led to both loss of power and the possibility of an outside edge as the ball was moving away from the bat. Imtiaz, a modest and likeable character, willingly applied himself to these slight changes in his technique, and on his return to Pakistan hit 400 runs in the annual Quadrancular Tournament.

Khan Mohammad was ideally built for a fast bowler, standing six feet three inches. He had broad shoulders and good strong legs, a lot of natural ability and, most important, liked bowling fast. Without this enthusiasm it is difficult to coach a 'quickie' owing to the hard physical grind involved. I had to find Khan another two yards of pace, which meant quicker acceleration of the bowling arm from up behind himself ready to deliver the ball. To do this Khan required a bigger turn of the shoulders on landing at the crease, and a full swing with the left arm forward, co-ordinating this with a jerk of the right hip to bring the trunk round from side-on towards the batsman just before the moment of release of the ball. With adjustments to the grip and position of the hand at the moment of release, Khan was able to make the ball swing away from the batsman and with his extra pace was, to his delight, a much improved performer.

In 1953 the Pakistan Board sent me seventeen players for a three-month trip, two months' coaching and one month playing matches. They were managed by an old opponent of mine, Saeed Mohammad, who had played for All India against Tennyson's team in 1938, and who had just captained Pakistan in an unofficial Test series against India.

This team was captained by Fazal Mahmood, a right-arm fast-medium bowler sending down off- and leg-cutters mixed up with a very late inswinger. Fazal was already an established bowler with many impressive performances to his credit. My approach to coaching Fazal was one of caution. He had an unorthodox action: when his bowling arm was about to begin its upward swing from behind himself he would check and do a twirl with his hand and wrist and then go on with the upward swing ready to deliver the ball. Any alterations to his action would have ruined him, so I decided to improve his repertoire by teaching him away-swing. This meant a different moment of release of the ball in comparison with his other deliveries, having been accustomed to turning his hand to impart inswing and leg-cut he found it difficult to keep the bowling hand upright and behind the ball at the moment of release, in order to bowl outswing. We started by standing at the bowling crease and going through the motions of pushing the ball down the pitch. This gave Fazal the feel of away-swing release and we gradually progressed until he could bowl it from 22 yards.

The other players of the squad included Zulfiquar Ahmed, Hanif Mohammad, Alimuddin, Maqsood Ahmed, M. E. Ghazali, Maque Mohammad, Mahmood Hussain and Mohammad Aslam.

These eight players all came as part of the first ever Pakistan team to play Test cricket in England. They won a memorable final Test at the Oval by 27 runs. I was one of the few people not surprised at Pakistan's unlikely win.

When the Pakistan players came over for coaching in 1953, it was obvious to me they had an abundance of talent, especially Hanif Mohammad who looked outstanding. It was after the first three days' coaching that manager Saeed Mohammad told me Hanif was very worried. He thought he had done something wrong because I had not given him any coaching. I called Hanif over and told him he was a natural player and there was nothing I could tell him, I simply promised to advise him how to build an innings once we started playing matches. But that was not necessary. I soon discovered that opening bat Hanif was quite content to occupy the crease for as long as possible, building his score up according to the quality of the bowling. The following year, when Pakistan came over, he scored 1,623 runs with a top score of 142 not out. Later in his career, in Karachi in 1959, he occupied the crease for ten hours and thirty-five minutes to score a massive 499 runs, the highest individual score in first-class cricket.

Zulfiquar Ahmed, one of the side's all-rounders, had batting that required encouragement more than work on the mechanics of the strokes: this gave him confidence in his own ability. He was also an off spinner who spun the ball but lacked depth in flight and top spin. 'Zulfi' was quick to learn, and had an extremely successful tour in 1954.

Alimuddin, a strongly-built right-hand batsman had obvious talent and a good range of shots on both sides of the wicket and off his front and back foot. He simply required a little tightening up on his defensive shots. He was another success in the 1954 team, scoring 1,083 runs. Maqsood Ahmed gave English spectators much entertainment. In 41 innings he hit 1,314 runs.

Fast bowler Mahmood Hussain arrived as very raw material. A big chap with plenty of pace but little accuracy, he was ever willing to learn. We tightened up his action and gave him a quieter approach to the wicket off his 15 yard run in order to give him time to deliver the ball. Going too fast when he arrived at the crease meant he had no time to get properly balanced. I gave him a higher left arm and a braced front leg on landing just prior to delivering the ball, which gave him accuracy and extra pace plus the ability to swing the ball away from the bat. He used these to good effect the following year taking 72 wickets at an average of 21 runs apiece.

Two of the players who had attended the School in 1952 also came in 1953. Imtiaz Ahmed had an outstanding tour, scoring 1,105 runs and, as wicketkeeper, catching 65 and stumping 21. Khan Mohammad was unfortunate with injury, his one outstanding performance being five for 61 in the first Test at Lords, when he and Fazal (four for 54) bowled out England for 117.

Pakistan continued sending parties over for coaching, but now under the name of the 'Pakistan Eaglets'. They included players like Mushtaq Mohammad and Majid Jahangir Khan, who went on to play for Glamorgan and scored 1,000 runs a season for several years. Mushtaq became one of Pakistan's most successful Test batsmen and also gave Northants several fine years of service, including the captaincy of the county eleven.

When Pakistan defeated England at the Oval in 1954 by 27 runs my loyalties were so divided I did not know whether to laugh or cry. The breakthrough came early on when Fazal took the important wicket of Len Hutton, caught at the wicket by Imtiaz off an outswinger, the one delivery I had shown to Fazal, who went on to take six for 46. England collapsed to be all out for 143 runs. Pakistan had got off the 'mark' in their first year in international cricket and it was on this side that they built their cricket, eventually becoming the best side in the world next to the West Indies.

Saeed Mohammad was an Anglophile, having been attached to the British Army during the Second World War. In 1958 he spent a summer in England and asked me to arrange some cricket for him. I introduced him to Richmond Cricket Club telling him he would be assured of a warm welcome. They wanted convincing as to his ability but I persuaded them to give him a game in the eleven.

At the age of 43, Saeed had now put on a little weight and the grey hairs were beginning to show. I heard afterwards that the young opposition fast bowlers, on his initial appearance, decided to bowl bouncers at the 'old gentleman'. Much to Saeed's amusement and the bowlers' surprise and dismay, Saeed kept hooking them hard to the square-leg boundary. Saeed made many runs for the club that season and, with his pleasant personality, also made many friends. We occasionally played golf at my club Sudbrook Park Golf Club, Richmond. Saeed had a low single-figure handicap and often said he would like to spend three or four years in England and he could then play golf with me all the year round. However, when I pointed out that our winter golf meant playing in freezing weather with frost bitten grounds and icy cold winds, he had a change of mind. I saw him occasionally during his visits on business for several years. He was always well wrapped up for our inclement weather. He would shudder when I recounted my recent rounds of golf wearing two sweaters and a waterproof jacket, plus gloves, and a woollen hat to keep my head warm, and then with a big smile he would say: 'Alfred, I shall be playing in shirt sleeves next week at my golf club in Lahore.'

In 1963 the Pakistan Board of Control invited me to take a Commonwealth team for a three-month tour starting in October and going on to the end of December. My party consisted of Alfred Gover (manager); Peter Richardson (Kent, captain); Rohan Kanhai, Basil Butcher, Seymour Nurse, Chester Watson and Charlie Griffith (West Indies); Keith Andrew (Northants); John Murray (Middlesex); Tom Graveney and Doug Slade (Worcestershire); Bill Alley (Somerset and NSW); Basil D'Oliveira (Lancashire League); Khalid Ibadullah (Warwickshire and Pakistan); and Ken Palmer (Somerset).

I had asked Basil D'Oliveira to represent the South African 'place' in my Commonwealth team, alongside the West Indian players and Australian Bill Alley. Basil had built up a great reputation in South Africa but being 'Cape Coloured' his prospects of advancement in first-class cricket in his own country were minimal. So a number of South African cricketers recognizing Basil's talent organized a fund to send Basil to England where he joined a Lancashire League club and was an outstanding success with both bat and ball. He was also a great success in my Pakistan team as an all-rounder, so much so that Tom Graveney and myself decided that Basil's obvious class was wasted in League cricket and Tom recommended him to Worcester.

The rest is cricket history, Basil distinguished himself with bat and ball for Worcester and played many Tests for his adopted country.

The team's batting line-up with Peter Richardson, Rohan Kanhai, Seymour Nurse, Tom Graveney and Basil D'Oliveira had much to offer. The all-rounders were Bill Alley, Khalid Ibadullah, Basil D'Oliveira and Ken Palmer. Fast bowler Charlie Griffith led the attack, supported by Chester Watson. Doug Slade provided variation in the attack with his left-arm spin.

We travelled overnight to Karachi from Heathrow arriving at 6.00 a.m. where we were welcomed with the usual garland of flowers placed round each player's neck, a new and amusing experience for those making their first visit to the sub-continent. Before the players went off to their hotel I told the captain that after they had unpacked and taken breakfast I had arranged for transport to take them to the ground for two hours practice. There were a few moans at being asked to practise straight after an all-night journey. But I pointed out that they would surely be expected to put in some practise during the day and surely it would be best if they practised from 9.00 a.m. to 11.00 a.m. in the comparative cool of the morning instead of the heat of the afternoon. The papers reported on the enthusiasm of the players in practising after an all-night journey, so it proved to be a very good public relations exercise.

When the players had left the airport for the hotel I proceeded to customs with all their documents, passports, etc. All went well until I produced Basil D'Oliveira's green South African passport. The uniformed official threw up his hands.

'This man cannot enter our country,' he said. I had to do a bit of quick thinking, so explained at length that Basil had come to England because of his poor treatment in his own country. I went on to say he had proved himself and I had invited him to join my team to Pakistan. 'I know from my cricket association with Pakistan that he will be welcomed with open arms.' The officer listened with a grave look on his face then went into the back of the office and started typing, after a while he came back and laid a piece of paper in front of me, 'You will sign this please.' I read the paper which declared that Basil D'Oliveira was a South African of Indian descent. I asked the officer how he had thought that one up and shrugging his shoulders and with a big smile he said, 'Before partition I was trained by the British.'

However, it was some time before I left the airport. The crates containing the many spare bats, pads and gloves I had brought for the benefit of the Pakistan cricket authorities had in error been carried on to Singapore and this meant a lot of form filling and 'oiling' of palms before I was satisfied the gear would be returned post-haste to Karachi.

MCC had toured Pakistan the previous winter and I was given to understand by players who had been part of that touring side that the management had been persuaded to attend several receptions, in addition to the one official function previously arranged for each match during the tour. I therefore had a strict understanding with the Pakistan authorities to have only one reception per match, including the Test. The Pakistan Board gave the team an official reception at lunchtime on the day of our arrival, and after the function was over I was approached by several local club officials saying they had arranged receptions when we returned to Karachi for the first Test after playing up-country. I told them in no uncertain terms that I had an agreement to only one official reception and could not accept any extra invitations. They all told me that invitations to meet us had already gone out and the receptions must go on. I told them to cancel their invitations or alternatively entertain themselves. My team would not be attending. I found this happening at every match venue and had to be very firm in my refusals of their hospitality.

I also asked the authorities to provide me with three bottles of whisky every day so that my players could drink it as a medicine every night before their evening meal. I took this precaution having learnt from my previous visit to the sub-continent in 1938 with Tennyson's team, when most of that side had suffered from dysentery. We had been advised, though a little late in the day, that a daily tot of whisky kept the complaint at bay. They were quite right: our party had a clean bill of health throughout the tour.

Our first game over three days was at Ahmadabad, the side had some good practice, all the batsmen making runs and the bowlers having their first experience of bowling on a placid Pakistan pitch.

My old pupil and friend Fazal Mahmood had retired from Test cricket and was working in the commentary box. During the game I walked across the field outside the boundary rope to see him. He saw me coming and we met half-way, where we did the usual Pakistan friendly embrace. The fans in the nearby stand were delighted to see this sign of friendship between their great Test bowler and the manager-coach from England.

We were back at Karachi after that game for the first Test. I saw a vast difference since my last visit in 1938. The city had spread its boundaries over what had been desert land and high-rise flats and houses now dominated the skyline. In 1938 the Test match had been played on the gymkhana ground. This had a small members' stand with enclosure, and temporary stands were built of scaffolding to seat the general public. The new ground had been built on the outskirts of the city. It had a large members' stand and enclosure to match. The 'outer' went back eighteen seats and they were fully covered.

I had a local liaison officer for the match, a good worker but very camera conscious. Whenever a picture was taken by the press of a player, or players, he would manage to get himself into the picture. The boys decided to cure him. A poster of a scantily clad female, showing the top half of her body completely nude, was obtained through the help of one of the Pakistan team. This was then pinned just inside our dressing room door. A press photographer entered into the joke and the liaison officer was told the press wanted a picture of him with the captain. He was delighted. He was then carefully led into the dressing room to avoid the poster coming into his view and after the picture was taken led out in a similar fashion. Peter Richardson made sure the liaison officer stood in front of the 'lady'. When our co-operative photographer delivered the print we showed our camera conscious official the revealing picture. This we said would be appearing in the Karachi papers. He was near hysteria and begged me to use my influence to prevent publication. His wife and his wife's family would be disgraced and he would never be forgiven. We kept him on the hook for half-an-hour and then told him it was a put-up-job and our reason for the hoax. It cured him, whenever he saw a camera man with a player he would turn smartly about and scuttle out of camera range.

We won the toss in the first Test and batted on the first day scoring over 440 runs. Rohan Kanhai hit 129 and Basil Butcher, Bill Alley and Ibadullah all topped the half-century mark. On the placid strip Pakistan topped the Commonwealth team's total by 14 runs, Mushtaq hitting 178. The only three bowlers used by the Commonwealth, Griffith, Watson and Slade all conceded over 100 runs. Charlie Griffith got his own back in the Commonwealth's second innings. Going in at number 9 he hit 98 (run out) of the team's 422 for eight.

At the close of play on the first day we were pleased with our opening day's performance, but subsequent events showed that not everybody was in the same frame of mind. As our coach left the ground we were greeted by about 500 spectators. 'That's nice,' I thought, expecting them to give the players a big cheer of appreciation for the runs they had put on during the day. To our astonishment they hurled stones and bricks at the coach, breaking some windows and sending all the boys diving for cover. It was a miracle no one was hurt. I called out to the driver in my best Urdu, 'Juldy, juldy!' (quickly). But I need not have bothered: his foot was hard down and he was turning away from the stone-throwing 'fans'. The team were justifiably upset, and John Murray said, 'I suppose they will shoot us if we bat slowly.'

On reaching our hotel I immediately 'phoned the Pakistan Cricket Board secretary, reporting the incident, and telling him I was not prepared to go to the ground the next day. 'I have a valuable bunch of internationals in my care.'

I was 'phoned within the hour: they could not understand the stone-throwing as there was no anti-British feeling 'at the moment'. I was then assured we would have adequate protection for the rest of the match. The next morning a posse of armed police guarded the coach and shepherded us to the ground. They stayed on guard all day and followed the same procedure for the rest of the match.

We had hoped the pitches for the rest of the tour would give the bowlers some encouragement, only to be disappointed. The second Test match at Lahore produced 1,460 runs for twenty wickets, our side hitting a massive 630 for nine declared. Rohan Kanhai hit 161 and Tom Graveney 164. Pakistan replied with 580, Mushtaq hitting 159. Charlie Griffith at one stage unleashed a barrage of bouncers due to an lbw appeal being turned down and frustration at the hopelessly lifeless character of the wicket. This caused Abdul Hafeez Kardar, an ex-Pakistan captain, and umpire Idris Begg, the radio commentators for the match, to leave the commentary box and make a protest to me about Charlie's use of the bouncer. They wanted me to have a message sent on to the field to have it stopped. I pointed out that Peter Richardson was captain and I would not interfere with his authority on the field; and, in addition, that if the Pakistan batsmen lacked the ability to face bouncers on this placid strip, then they should not be playing. I must stress that no protest came from the Pakistan team. Mushtaq had no complaints: he was quite happy hooking the short-pitched deliveries during his knock of 159.

Fazal Mahmood had joined the police force on his retirement from first-class cricket and risen to the rank of chief inspector. He picked me up in his car on the first day of the Lahore Test, resplendent in his uniform. Approaching the ground, he turned up a one-way street in the last stages of reconstruction and was immediately challenged by a road works official. Fazal pointed to his badge of rank, told them his name, and was waved through. I asked Fazal if it was the badge or his name. 'The badge, old boy. Most useful.'

The third Test at Dhaka told the same story of a drawn game. On a slow pitch devoid of grass, 1,300 runs were scored. Peter Richardson, declared his second innings closed at 344 for six, with the intention of getting a result. This left Pakistan almost three hours to score 261 runs. But they ignored the challenge, making 228 for five after 51 overs. A result in this game, especially for the home side, would have been good for Pakistan cricket. I could never understand why they did not go full out for the runs.

This final match was reduced to four days, owing to the funeral in Dhaka of a former prime minister of West Pakistan. Our hotel was on the funeral route and that day we were using the facilities of the Dhaka Club for swimming and tennis. We had been warned to keep out of sight and cease activities in order not to offend the many hundreds of mourners following the funeral. The coffin was on a coach, covered with flowers to a height of thirty feet. When the funeral procession was about a hundred yards away, we saw to our horror Keith Andrew emerging from our hotel, camera in hand. He stopped in the middle of the road to face the oncoming procession and started clicking away. We wanted to call out and warn him, but the manager of the club advised us against the whole team being in view. We watched anxiously as Keith kept clicking away until the funeral procession was only fifty yards off. Then, with a wave of his hand towards the mourners, Keith joined us in the club. He had been blissfully unaware of the furore he might have caused among the mourners, and the club manager could only surmise that Keith had been mistaken for an official press photographer.

The tour did much to help the development of Pakistan's young players. Leg spinner Intikhab Alam became a regular in Pakistan's Test side and played for Surrey for many years. Asif Iqbal gained fame for Pakistan and later played for Kent finishing as their captain.

The tour also did much to restore confidence in Pakistan cricket, after losing to Dexter's side in 1961 and losing badly in England in 1962. To quote the official Pakistan report on the tour: 'The showing against Gover's Commonwealth side proved the lion still had a switch in his tail. All three Tests were drawn and Charlie Griffith, the West Indies fast bowler, had his teeth drawn.' (I have no doubt Charlie thought it a painful extraction on those placid pitches.) The report went on: 'There were prodigious feats of batting by Saeed and Mushtaq and gradually pessimism gave way to optimism and the worst seemed to have passed.'

My team must have done them a good turn: on their Australasian tour they drew the one Test match against Australia and three against New Zealand the following winter.

During our game in Rawalpindi earlier in the tour, against the Governor's XI, Fida Hussan, the Pakistan Board of Control representative with the team, invited me to a game of golf starting at 6.30 a.m. in order to finish in time to get to the cricket by 10.30 a.m. Fida told me to bring an extra sweater: 'It gets a bit cool early in the morning.' That was the understatement of the whole tour. A bit cool? The frost was on the ground and I could have done with a pair of gloves plus a hat to keep my head warm. We arrived on the first tee for our four-ball game. Fida was playing with a local, a businessman who had a handicap of two. I was given as a partner a chap dressed in Pakistani clothes – the white shirt and blouse with a sweater over the top, and the loose white clothing being pulled under his crotch. This I understand was called a dhoti. I thought to myself: 'Fida has done it on me, giving me this chap as my playing partner', and I refused the offer of a small wager on the match. But my second thoughts were too late. My partner had a first-class golf swing and sent the ball around 240 yards up the middle of the fairway. As we walked up the fairway I asked Fida who my partner was. 'Oh, I forgot to tell you, Alfred, he is the club's marker. In other words, he is the pro.'

A remarkable change in the weather came after we had played eight holes. We shed both sweaters and started perspiring in the hot sun, but not the marker. Still wearing his sweater, his play was immaculate. He kept belting the ball up the middle and sinking his putts from all parts of the green. I was the silent partner, cursing myself for missing the chance to take money in the nicest possible way from Fida.

16

The Lord's Taverners

THE LORD'S TAVERNERS were founded by a group of actors who watched cricket at Lord's Cricket Ground from the (old) tavern. Their objective was to raise money for the good of cricket and they were off to a fine start when His Royal Highness, The Prince Philip, Duke of Edinburgh, consented to be their patron and 'Twelfth' man. Today HRH still gives the Taverners his patronage and retains an interest in their fund-raising activities. Beneficiaries include the English Schools' Cricket Association who receive £60,000 for their programme of representative matches and the staging of the finals of their various competitions. The rest of the money raised buys New Horizon mini-buses for handicapped children and for handicapped people in sport.

I was invited to join them in 1952 as a cricketing member to play in five or six matches, in a team made up of former first-class cricketers and show biz personalities. I gave it some thought before accepting as I had given up active cricket in 1950 after my final season in the Birmingham League. However, bowling at pupils in my School kept me fit and loose and I could still 'turn my arm over' at a little over medium pace, so I decided to accept. And what a good decision I made to be a Taverner! I met lots of my old buddies from my cricketing days and made a host of new friends from the world of show business.

I was soon involved in organizing Sunday games, raising a team and skippering the side. I always enlisted thirteen players, those from show biz were allowed to cancel at the last minute if they were offered a professional engagement. All thirteen players would take the field and after they had been identified by the announcer on the public address system they would then take turns in going off the field to the autograph table, or to the 'Polaroid' camera tent to be photographed with a 'fan'. These activities went on throughout the match and the small charge levied made a considerable contribution to the day's fund raising activities.

On Saturday, 16 June 1962, the Taverners played their first home match – at Lord's against an Old England XI. Billy Griffiths, then secretary of MCC, and myself raised the two sides. The majority of players on both sides had been retired for a few years but were still capable of showing their skills – batting and bowling and scampering around the field. Their past deeds were still fresh in the cricketing public's memory and the game attracted a crowd of 15,000 people. 'A whiff of Valhalla'.

The match was played in the normal way with the only light-heartedness coming from Roy Castle and Norman Wisdom playing for the Taverners. The Taverners won the toss and batted. The Reverend David Sheppard (who later in the year went with Ted Dexter's team to Australia) went for 6, John Pretlove for 1, Eric Bedser for 1, then in strode Keith Miller to save the face of all the fond fathers who, having eulogized on the prowess of the players to their sons, had brought them to Lord's to see the great men in action.

Keith Miller cracked a 4 off his first ball and within the next hour had hit 54, including three mighty 6's. Fellow Australian, left-handed bat, Ben Barnett followed Keith and, with Raman Subba Row, kept the scoreboard going. Raman eventually went for 82 with the score at 186. Ben went at 8 short of his hundred. Soon came a comic interlude between Roy Castle and Norman Wisdom – the first came from Norman. The blade of his bat had been sawn across invisibly and when he came in to bat Denis Compton told him he would bowl a nice half-volley just outside the off stump so that Norman could have a good swing. The half volley duly came along, Norman's swing connected with the ball and the bottom half of the blade flew off. Norman stood with his half of the bat in his hands and then went into his famous act singing, 'Don't laugh at me 'cos I'm a fool.' The crowd loved it and roared with laughter. They had another big laugh in the next over when the two entertainers went for a quick single and met in the middle of the pitch, collided and intertwined arms going through the routine of trying to disentangle without success.

The umpire called 'dead ball' and sanity returned when the two 'wrestlers' eventually reached their respective ends. Roy and Norman then got down to the 'nitty gritty' putting on 26 useful runs – Roy hitting 22. Old England's 321 topped the Taverners by 319 by 2 runs, Cyril Washbrook, Jack Robertson, Jack Ikin and Denis Compton providing the entertainment.

There were repercussions from some of the elderly members of MCC. Two 'denizens' of the Long Room at Lord's stormed into Billy Griffiths's office complaining of the disgraceful behaviour on the middle at Lord's – they said it was an official complaint, and insisted it should go before the MCC committee. It took all Billy's charm and diplomacy to persuade them that such a step was not necessary because he would read the 'riot act' to the Taverners. Billy laughed later on when he relayed the old members' protests about the indignity heaped upon the 'hallowed turf'.

Billy had another awkward situation to deal with later on. Women were never allowed in the Pavilion and, after the game, the teams were invited to the MCC committee room for drinks. The ladies were told by Billy that they could have drinks in the Tavern Bar and their men would meet them later. MCC did not know our girls – we had just filled our glasses when, to our amusement, in walked the girls. 'You cannot come in here,' said Billy, 'ladies are strictly forbidden.' The ladies' spokeswoman, whose name I won't mention, said, 'Billy, there must always be a first time – what have you in the drinks line?' Billy knew when he was beaten and gave the girls his official invitation to join the party.

The Taverners played the first-ever Sunday games at Lord's, and the Oval, in 1965. The day before their game against Middlesex at Lord's in August, they had been engaged in an Old England game on the Warwickshire County Ground, Edgbaston and many of the same players turned out for the Middlesex game. The only non-first-class cricketer in the Taverners' team was Bill Franklyn. Middlesex fielded a full eleven led by Mike Brearley. The old Middlesex stars Jack Robertson, Denis Compton and Alan Moss were in the Taverners' team. The game was played seriously and against the young Middlesex side the Taverners could only muster 278, Middlesex playing out time to score 302 for 7.

The following Sunday at the Oval the Taverners opposed the

Surrey Old Players Association. In spite of a delayed start owing to rain the match attracted a crowd of 5,000 and the Taverners had established that Sunday cricket was a viable proposition, a forecast of Sunday League cricket.

In the meantime I had been taking my mixture of cricketers and celebrities around the club grounds. I had a pool of players on my list of probables: ex-Test players Jack Martin (Kent); Arthur McIntyre (Surrey); Jack Robertson, Denis Compton, Bill Edrich, Alan Moss and Peter Parfitt (Middlesex); Doug Insole (Essex); Frank Worrell (West Indies); Keith Miller and Ben Barnett (Australia); plus Stuart Surridge (Surrey) and Arthur Phebey, John Pretlove and Maurice Fenner (Kent). From the world of show biz came Sir Brian Rix, Bill Franklyn, Peter Dineley, John Alderton, Jack Cardiff, Tony Fayne, David Frost, Johnny Blythe, Richard Hearn ('Mr Pastry'), Tony Britton, Micheal Dennison, Cardew 'the Cad' Robinson, Nicholas Parsons, Roy Castle, and, on odd occasions, Sir Harry Secombe and Eric Sykes.

Ray Lindwall the great Australian Test fast bowler was in England on business for the whole of 1961 and played in all my matches. Ray was given an insight into Old English country customs, on the way home from a match at Hambledon one day. We had stopped at a village for 'light refreshment' when Ray came over and said, 'Alfred, look, outside there are a lot of fairies dancing round with bells on their ankles and arms.' He went on: 'Look at them. Throwing their feet about and waving their arms in the air. Look at the way they're dressed! Light green tight-fitting dresses, with frills down the side of their trousers and on the front of their jackets!' I explained to Ray that the dancers were Morris dancers who were probably recruited from the small villages in the area. However, Ray took a lot of convincing that the dancers were not effeminate, but just men who valued the traditions of the countryside.

In 1974 I was elected president of the Taverners, the only cricketer to have held the office as it is usually filled by someone from the world of show business. When my term of office finished, the Taverners were fortunate when HRH The Prince Charles found time to take the presidency and graced us with his support over the next two years.

We then went back to show biz presidents, who included Eric Morecombe, Sir Harry Secombe, Ronnie Corbett, Terry Wogan,

David Frost and Tim Rice. The presidency of the Taverners is no sinecure; he is expected to be present at all our fund-raising activities (Prince Charles excepted, of course, but he supported us whenever his official duties allowed).

I enjoyed my period in office. Apart from making many new friends it gave me the opportunity to visit Buckingham Palace. The Taverners many years ago provided the cup for the winners of the County Cricket Championship and our Prince Philip always invited the winners to Buckingham Palace where he would present the cup and individual souvenirs. The president of the Taverners always attended this ceremony.

The Taverners hold their annual ball at Grosvenor House on the first Monday in November. In my year of office we were honoured with the presence of HRH The Princess Anne (The Princess Royal). As president I acted as host to Princess Anne and Captain Mark Phillips. The other guests on my table were: Marjorie, my wife and hostess, my son John and his wife Jane, my daughter Elisabeth and Stuart Surridge, junior, Neil Durden-Smith and his wife Judith Chalmers, Tim Brooke-Taylor and his wife Christine. Neil knew Captain Phillips through the world of showjumping and we learnt that Tim Brooke-Taylor's show, 'The Goodies', was one of Princess Anne's favourite programmes. It was my pleasure to start the dancing by partnering Princess Anne. I was on my best behaviour. 'Do not,' warned my wife, 'try any of your fancy "extra" steps!' I kept strictly to the book and to the dance tempo of Victor Sylvester and his band, and received an understanding smile of approbation from the Princess.

In 1980 the Taverners celebrated their 30th year and a celebration dinner was attended by Prince Philip and past-presidents. It was held in Dukes Hotel, London, and the past-presidents were: Sir John Mills, Stephen Mitchell, John Snagg, (Sir) Harry Secombe, (Sir) Brian Rix, Jimmy Edwards, Eric Morecombe, Tommy Trinder, Sir Edward (Ted) Lewis, chairman of Decca Radio, and myself.

Harry Secombe, our reigning president, was in the chair and it was an informal meeting with not even the services of a red-coated toastmaster. After the normal speeches and toasts to 'our guests', 'cricket' and 'the Lord's Taverners', Prince Philip requested that all the ex-presidents tell a story. My fellow ex-presidents from show biz took this in their stride and entertained us with their own particular brand of humour. In this company I was last to speak and was at a distinct disadvantage, so, sticking to my own line of 'business' I told the story of going in first to bat with Jack Hobbs. I embellished the story as I went along and sat down to generous applause. I was not quite sure whether the applause from the show biz ex-presidents was genuine or sympathetic from 'pro' to 'amateur'!

I had the honour of playing cricket with Prince Philip at Arundel against the Duke of Norfolk's team. We had an amusing incident during the after-match buffet in Arundel Castle. Our ladies wanted to 'powder their noses' so I asked the Duke of Norfolk if he could tell me the whereabouts of the toilets for the ladies. He waved a ducal hand towards the wide staircase at the end of the banqueting hall saying, 'Up those stairs, turn left and you will find fifteen ' – in fifteen bedrooms.

In 1965 we made a trip to the Isle of Wight and my team included Jim Laker. The locals batted first on a very green top pitch, ideal for swing bowling. Jack Martin, the ex-Kent and England bowler, and Bill Franklyn opened the bowling. They made the ball swing around but with little impression, taking only one wicket between them for 25 runs, Jack being the wicket-taker. I put myself on to bowl, pitched the ball well up to the bat to take advantage of late swing and in three overs took three wickets for 6 runs. I then took myself off saying, 'I mustn't ruin the game.' I then retired to the deep to the cries of 'Bighead' from my loyal (?) team.

The Taverners often gave displays of big hitting – as on the occasion when they excelled themselves against Sunbury. Australian Ben Barnett, opening the batting, started the run spree hitting seven 4's and two 6's in an innings of 46 runs. Bill Edrich followed with a breezy 28 made up of five 4's and one 6. The pattern for the day having been set, Keith Miller and Stuart Surridge assaulted the bowling and the houses adjoining the boundary. Keith hit 103 including seven 6's and fourteen 4's and Stuart knocked up 49 including nine 4's and two 6's.

Wales had long been starved of representative cricket and gave the Taverners a warm welcome when they played Old England at Swansea. At last the Welsh had a chance to see an England eleven in Wales, albeit an Old England side. They showed their appreciation by raising £1,250 for charity, breaking our previous record for a cricket match.

Peter May skippered the Old England side and made a crowd-pleasing innings of 72 which included four 6's, one of them being a tremendous hit off the back foot over extra cover. Peter was playing with a borrowed bat having discovered that his own required repairing. He sought the help of local match manager, Bill Edwards, in his sports shop. Bill lent Peter a One Star Stuart Surridge bat, the lowest in the Surridge range. He told me some weeks later that he had no chance of getting the bat back from Swansea Cricket Club as all the members wanted to use the same bat that had been wielded to such good effect by the great Peter May.

Harry Secombe, in his home town, played in the Taverners side. We fielded first and it took Harry fifteen minutes to walk down the 72 pavilion steps as all his old 'mates' had reserved the seats next to the gangway and Harry stopped to have a quick word with each individual. When he eventually joined the rest of the side waiting patiently on the field he told us that he had just met many old friends, Dai and company, some of whom he had not seen for twenty years. I think they must have inspired him as, when he went on to bowl his slow-medium leg-cutters he clean bowled Dick Spooner, the ex-Warwickshire 'keeper and left-hand batsman, before he was even off the mark.

In my presidential year with Surrey in 1980 I invited Harry and his brother, the Reverend Fred Secombe, to the Oval during the final Test against the West Indies. They arrived well before play started and Fred, seeing the previous day's runs total on the score board, said, 'That's the number of hymn . . . ' The brothers then immediately sang the first verse in harmony, to the astonishment and delight of distinguished fellow guests.

The Taverners used to stage their own 'event' (which by hook or crook we always won) at the annual ball at the Grosvenor House. One year we had the Boat Race, with the Oxford and Cambridge crews taking the oars on the 'boats', the rate of their strokes being electronically recorded. They were then challenged by the Taverners. HRH The Twelfth Man inspected the Taverners, to each of whom he then gave a whiff of oxygen. While the race was in progress, the recording machine was being pumped up by HRH The Twelfth Man in favour of the Taverners. At the end of the race, His Royal Highness consulted the machine and declared the Taverners 'first past the post'.

In another year we had basketball as the 'event' and the famous

Harlem Globe Trotters played an exhibition and then took on the Taverners. They were thwarted of victory. Whenever they aimed for the basket, the top would suddenly close or become so small that the ball would not fit in, whereas on the other hand whenever the Taverners attempted to score the circumference of the basket would enlarge to enable the ball to go in easily.

Another year the theme was taken from the television programme 'Come Dancing'. Six Taverners lined up, three dressed as the ladies in evening dress, and three in white tie and tails. They chose the most unlikely members to take the parts of the 'ladies': Bill Franklyn was billed as Wilhemina Franklyn; I was described as Alfreda Gover; and Johnny Blythe as Johanna Blythe. We commenced by lining up and dancing the 'Zorba the Greek' dance – unfortunately the rest had no rhythm, I was the only one in time. We then spread out in formation and danced in pairs. My partner was ex-Rugby League player and playwright Colin Welland. I was doing fine until I slipped doing a quick reversing step, and, wearing boots, gave Colin a terrific kick on the shins. He let out a resounding yell, and said in a stage whisper, 'You b . . . fool, Alf' This was greeted by loud laughter from the diners. Tommy Trinder completed the evening when, after I had changed back to black tie, he said, 'That's better, Alfred, you were the ugliest woman I ever saw!'

The following year the Ball again had dancing as part of its 'event'. Henry Cooper, Geoff Milburn and myself, plus actor John Alderton, dressed up as women – we must have looked horrible. Part of the routine had us in a wide circle and in turn changing places with each other; we were supposed to give each other a friendly pat on the cheek as we passed each other. When I changed places with Henry Cooper he waved his left hand and nearly knocked me off my feet. I remonstrated with him afterwards, 'You were only supposed to give me a light tap, Henry.'

'That's all I did,' he replied.

'In that case, I'm glad you were not asked to give me a light slap, because I would have been carried off feet first!'

In 1960 the Taverners took part in a BBC production 'Up Green and at 'Em', a play in which the good squire, Tony Britton, owed money to the wealthy villain, played by Jimmy Edwards, who covets the squire's manor house. The villain challenges the squire to a cricket match between his team and the squire's team:

the stakes being the squire's house if the villain won, but if the squire won his debts would be cancelled.

The local colonel who backed the squire was played by Roger Livesey. Stephanie Voss, the only girl in the play, was the colonel's daughter and the young squire's girl friend. Boris Karloff played the villain's butler and Charlie Chester the crooked bookmaker. John Slater played a plain clothes detective. The play was seen 'off stage' with all the action coming from the cast in front of the pavilion.

The villain had recruited several county and Test cricketers to ensure the winning of the match: Doug Insole, Jack Martin, Godfrey Evans, Arthur Phebey, Stuart Surridge, Jack Robertson and myself. But the young squire had an ace up his sleeve. Unbeknown to the villain, the colonel's nephew, born in Australia, was a great Australian Test batsman and bowler. He had arrived in England and had agreed to play and help defeat the villain's team. The Australian Test star was played by Bill Franklyn. In fact, Bill was born in Australia and came to England at the age of 14, so the Australian accent required for his part came naturally.

During rehearsals one day Bill was involved in an accident with a deck chair, catching his fingers in the arms when it partially collapsed. It was painful enough to make him pass out for a few seconds. The first thing that he saw when he came round was Boris Karloff who said, 'Come on, Bill, there's nothing wrong with you, wrap your fingers up and get on with the play!' Medical attention was, however, needed before poor Bill could carry on.

The play was broadcast on Whit Monday, 1960. All the show biz artists had to be contracted by the BBC and were paid the normal fees which they then all handed over to the Lord's Taverners Fund. Who won the match? The young hero's team with the long lost Australian nephew, who won the match all on his own.

David Frost always played in my teams, in between flying to and from the United States. Playing in a game in North London he took part in an opening partnership of over 100 runs with Len Hutton, 'Frosty' making 50. David's cricket was of minor county standard and he was a useful 'keeper in addition to his batting. I gave David a net at my School on the Saturday morning prior to his greatest triumph, when, at the Oval in 1980 the Lord's Taverners played an Old England XI. Opening with Australian ex-Test star Bobby Simpson, David again took part in a century partnership hitting a chanceless 50. I reckon he walked on air as he came off the field proud of his success on the 'hallowed turf'.

The Taverners rarely turned down any fund-raising opportunity and one came along in 1974 when many of the leading wine dealers and vintners offered us dozens of crates and barrels for sale to the trade. The sale was held in Bond Street and I arrived, as president of the Lord's Taverners, to see eight 'sampling tables' laid out with the wines ready for tasting. I was invited to sample the various vintages, but declined explaining the reason for my presence. We had asked half-a-dozen show biz Taverners to attend to add a little colour to the proceedings: comedian Arthur Askey arrived and was duly escorted along the line of tables with the polished decanters of wine. He paused at the final table and then said, 'No, I can't see my favourite.'

'And what is that?' he was asked.

'Fray Bentos,' came the reply.

The Taverners took cricket to Portugal in 1988. I visit the Algarve twice a year and was asked if I could raise a celebrity team to play on the new cricket ground in the Val de Lobo. I declined but suggested that I ask the Lord's Taverners. They agreed to go if all expenses were paid and the Taverners Fund was given the usual guarantee of £5,000 for the match.

After the game, which was a great success, the local organizer said they were proud to have been the hosts to the Taverners team playing overseas for the first time. After first thanking him for all his hard work I let him know that the Taverners had sent a team to Hong Kong that same weekend – and also played a weekend's cricket in Monaco every year.

Golf, too, figures amongst the fund-raising efforts of the Taverners and the Harry Secombe Golf Classic at Effingham Golf Club in Surrey has become well known on the Pro-Am circuit. One year I played in the same foursome as Harry, who was partnered by the captain of the home club. My partner was ex-Ryder cup player Syd Scott. Syd was, of course, hoping to play well and have a share of the generous prize money on offer to the pros. The many leading pros in the field attracted a following of the real golf enthusiasts, but our four, or should I say, Harry, attracted the following of a mixture of club members loyal to the club captain and lots of women with young children, some of them even in pushchairs. Harry had the honour of first hit off the tee and gave it a good solid crack. He gained the first laugh of the day when the ball burst into coloured pieces after travelling twenty yards. Off he went with the noisy chattering fans in attend-

ance – poor Syd had no chance. He would be about to play a
delicate chip to the green when prams would move noisily around
behind him as the Mums hurried to get a close up of Harry ready
to play his shot, or hopefully to hear him cracking jokes.

I am not a follower of horse racing so it was a new experience
for me to visit Sandown Park Racecourse as a VIP. I was
accorded this privilege because I was attending as president of
the Lord's Taverners and the racecourse authorities had made it
a Lord's Taverners Day with collections during the afternoon in
aid of our funds. In the course of the afternoon I was interviewed
three times in front of the stands; by a television commentator to
talk about the aims of the Taverners; and then of the show biz
and sporting stars who made up the Taverners membership.
Before my first appearance in front of the cameras I had been
given a tip by a racing correspondent friend and had a modest
wager and backed the winner. Near the close of the first interview
I was asked, 'Did you back the winner of the last race?' The
answer being in the affirmative I was then asked what horse I
fancied for the next race. I declined to answer and rushed off to
find my friendly tipster, who duly obliged with the name of a
horse telling me to back it for a win or a place. I took a chance
and had another small wager – and so backed another winner. I
went straight in front of the camera again to be told, 'I bet you
didn't get that winner!'

'Oh yes,' I said, 'and I got odds of eight to one.'

However, my racing correspondent tipster told me that he had
no further firm information the rest of the afternoon, but I was
quite happy to sit back and just watch the racing from the VIP
box. Later, the owner of a horse running in another race told me
that his trainer and jockey fancied the chances of his horse, although he thought they were being optimistic. As I was already
in pocket, I decided to back the horse and my luck held and I
had another winner. Before the next race the chairman of the
Taverners took me on one side and told me he had been told in
the strictest confidence the name of the winner of the next race so
I placed a bet on my way to the television spot. Before we went
on the air I told my interviewer my luck in the last race and told
him the horse I had been given for the next race. He said that
after informing the viewers I had backed yet another winner he
would ask me my fancy for the next race, adding, 'I hope your
information is good because punters in betting shops will be

thinking you have inside information and many will back your fancy.'

Alas, my 'confidential' tip finished fourth and that was the end of my efforts as a punter at a race meeting. My main connection with the 'sport of kings' continued with my encounters on the golf course with my wealthy bookmaking golfing friends.

In 1962 I took the Taverners to play at Ford Motors Sports Club on their Ilford ground. I had an attractive team, including Ray Lindwall, Frank Worrell, Bill Edrich, Ben Barnett, John Warr and Alec Bedser plus ex-world championship racing driver Jackie Stewart who gave us his support – and a surprise – by arriving by helicopter and landing in the 'middle'.

We were delighted with our record-breaking effort in raising funds at Ilford, so when we arrived at Twickenham Green the following Sunday we told our hosts of the Ford 'triumph'. 'We can beat that figure,' they said and kept their promise to the tune of £694. 'That will take some beating,' we said, but how times change – today we only take fixtures guaranteeing £5,000. But now Taverners games often top that figure and cricket makes a valuable contribution to the one million pounds raised every year.

When the Taverners hold their Christmas lunch each year it is customary for the president to send a telegram to the Patron and Twelfth Man, the Duke of Edinburgh. During my term of office I sent the following:

Christmas Lunch 9 December 1974
From President Alf Gover, Lord's Taverners To the Twelfth Man

> T'was Christmas Day in the workhouse,
> The Taverners were full of beer,
> But they never forget their Patron,
> And wish that he were here
>
> Three rousing cheers for the Twelfth Man
> Echo loud and clear
> We wish you a merry Christmas
> And a fast-scoring new year.

President
Alf Gover

I received this reply:

> Twas Boxing Day in the Tavern
> And the morning after for some

Though they might not forget their Patron
They'd forgotten the effects of rum

If you want to stay out of the workhouse
At any time of the year
Take heed of the words of this verse
And keep the Taverners only on beer.

Signed PHILIP.

When the Taverners played at Crawley, Brian Johnston had a great day behind the stumps. The scorecard read: caught Johnston bowled Lindwall, and stumped Johnston bowled Laker. Apart from airing his knowledge of the game on BBC radio, Brian is of minor county standard behind the stumps and was delighted to have his name in tandem with two of the game's greatest bowlers. I had six bowlers who had opened the bowling for their country: Ray Lindwall (Australia); Frank Worrell (West Indies); Jack Martin, John Warr and Alf Gover (England); John Fellows-Smith (South Africa).

To open the bowling, I began with Ray Lindwall and Harry Secombe. In his fifth over, Harry marked out a long run, tore up to the wicket and went through the bowling action without releasing the ball, then made his exit from the field to start a lengthy period in the photographic tent. Harry was always a willing and hard worker for the Taverners cause – he took on the job of president in 1967 and 1968 and again in 1981 and 1982. He is the only Taverner to have had two such periods in office.

The Taverners sometimes came up against tough opposition batting which sorely tested the players' skills. In a match at Windsor, the young opening bat never looked like getting out, so I complimented him on his batting and then said that he would be even better if he picked his bat up high. Up went his bat and down went my yorker and his off stump. After the game he asked me what mistake had he made when he was bowled out and I said, 'You picked the bat up much too high.'

'But, sir,' he said, 'you told me to pick it up.'

I replied, 'That is the only way I could have got you out – so consider that a compliment!'

In 1990 the Taverners membership had risen to over 1,000, including members in the counties and the Channel Islands, known as 'the regions'. Australia has its own 'foundation' with headquarters in Sydney.

The ladies of the Taverners ran the tombola at the annual Ball for many years, their last effort and final tombola raised £18,000. For their efforts the ladies were made honorary Lady Taverners.

Then it started all over again when the director, Anthony Swainson, said, 'What about you girls getting to work and raising money for the Taverners' funds?' The ladies took the challenge and they elected Joan Morecombe (widow of Eric) as their first president, with Anne Subba Row as chairwoman. For the first five years Joan and Anne were supported by many ladies with famous cricketing names: Betty Surridge, Marjorie Gover, Lis (Gover) Donaldson, Margaret Price, Anne Barrington, Susan Embury, plus Myra Secombe, Judith Chalmers and Diana Thomas (wife of Leslie Thomas) who was chairwoman 1989–90.

The ladies have raised over one million pounds in seven years, including over £100,000 in 1990.

17
Cricketing Characters

MY HAPPY PARTNERSHIP with Surrey lasted first as a player for twenty years, then I was elected to the Surrey Committee in 1938. After which I served in turn as Chairman of the Junior Cricket Committee, then the main Cricket Committee and then as a member of the Public Relations Committee, culminating in being elected to the highest office in the Club of President in 1980 – the first professional player to hold this office.

In the summer of 1980 the West Indies came over, and in addition it was the centenary year of Australia and England Tests, the first having been played at the Oval in 1880. Although Surrey had been hosts for that first game the celebrations were organized by the Test and County Cricket Board. Australians who had appeared in Tests against England were flown over and joined their counterparts, the Old England players.

As president of Surrey I was fortunate enough to attend all the lunches, receptions and dinners and to preside over the Surrey box at Lord's in the one-day game between the present teams of England and Australia.

I had a funny experience when going to the first reception in the City of London given for the old players on both sides. As president of Surrey I was due to arrive fifteen minutes before the start of the proceedings and I parked my car in the car park by Southwark Bridge. Getting out of the car, and after walking a few yards, I heard an engine running. I said to my wife, 'Some fool has left his engine running.' I then realized it was mine and dashed back to find that I had pushed the self-locking door button and my keys were still in the ignition. I panicked, but fortunately one of the car-park attendants was passing by and managed to lower a window.

Panic over, I arrived with a few minutes to spare. There I met up with old friends and opponents: Harold Larwood, Bill Voce, Lesley Ames, Billy Griffiths, Colin Cowdrey, Peter May, Alec Bedser, Tom Graveney and many more ex-England Test players. And from Australia, Keith Miller, Bill Ponsford, Stalk Hendry, Jack Fingleton, Ray Lindwall, and Alan McGilvray, to name just a few.

JACK LEE

For most of my playing days I lacked support from my slip fielders. After Percy Fender retired, chances would rarely be taken – you would think I was bowling with a hot potato. But although my slip fielders grassed so many catches I never got annoyed. They were doing their best and losing my temper would not have helped me, but I was tried to the limit during a Surrey versus Somerset game at the Oval. The visitors won the toss and the brothers Lee, Frank and Jack, opened the innings. With an unbroken partnership of 49 on the board Jack edged a ball off my bowling straight to Eddie Watts at first slip. Eddie had dropped five chances off my bowling in the two previous matches but this one he caught and in one movement threw it back to me so quickly that I caught it before I had finished my follow through. Jack stood his ground. I called out that Eddie had caught it and turned to the umpire appealing for the catch to be upheld. He said I had obscured his vision in my follow through; he asked the square-leg umpire for his opinion, which was that the wicketkeeper was blocking a clear view of the slips.

Jack took a single off the next ball, the last of my over and when he came to my end I assured him that Eddie had made a fair catch. Jack, a very honest and likeable man, apologized for not walking, the reason being that the ball had returned so quickly, and then added that he would get himself out. He kept his promise by playing a deliberate miss to a straight ball from Eddie, much to Eddie's delight. To say the least, I was not amused.

TED BROOKS

The wicketkeeper that day was Ted 'Brookie' Brooks, my one reliable ally. Brookie, standing well back, would wave first slip away from his right hand because he said that was his area. A big chap, standing six feet tall, he would throw himself to take catches high or low. I took 100 wickets for the first time in 1932 and much of this breakthrough to the coveted three figures was due to Brookie's skill behind the wicket. 'Caught Brooks bowled Gover' was quite a feature in reports of a day's play.

Brookie became a 'keeper by accident. Taken on to the Surrey staff as a medium-pace bowler, he was playing for the Club and Ground on the famous Mitcham cricket green when the side found themselves one short, the 'keeper having cancelled at short notice. The coach in charge of the side looked around for the best catcher in the side and Brookie was handed the gloves. 'A natural,' said the coach, 'you forget bowling and concentrate on keeping wicket.'

He was also a fair batsman. Full of confidence in his own ability, he batted at number 9, so I often found myself at the wicket with him. When Surrey played Australia at the Oval on the 1934 tour they hit up a big score in the region of 500. The slips were not on their best behaviour and down went seven chances off my bowling. But Brookie came to the rescue, diving to take two catches for me. I finished up five for 147 off 34 overs. This resulted in a call to Lord's for the second Test, but I was relegated to twelfth man, so I missed out at the last minute.

Surrey always played Australia twice at the Oval, mainly for financial reasons. In this match Brookie brought the house down. Australia had such spinners as Clarrie Grimmet, the left-arm Fleetwood Smith and Bill O'Reilly, a redoubtable trio even on a plumb pitch. But, in the early hours of the morning, the pitches were covered only at the bowler's end, and our powerful batting line up failed for once, so when I joined Brookie at the wicket we were in a poor state. Normally Brookie and I would have a bit of fun, especially when it was late in the day, hoping we could pick up a wicket when the opposing team batted out the last half-hour. However, this time Brookie said, 'Now, Alf, no fooling around. We must be serious and get the side out of trouble. You can leave Clarrie Grimmett to me.'

And, to prove his words, he hit Clarrie for six into the members' pavilion. Clarrie gave the next delivery a bit of air. Brookie took two steps up the wicket in an effort to repeat the dose, but he misjudged the flight and the degree of turn on the ball, and this found him threshing the air with his bat. So vigorous was his follow through that he lost balance, then fell backwards and finished with his right arm outstretched, pushing the bat into the batting crease, and at the same time calling, 'I'm in, Ben' to Ben Barnett, the Australian wicketkeeper, whose return to the stumps was late as the ball had turned so much he had had to stretch wide on his right-hand side to retrieve it.

Several overs later, I was playing forward to left-arm spinner Fleetwood-Smith, when I caught my bat in the top of my pads and the bat came out of my hands in the process. The ball went off the edge of the bat past first slip, behind me, and Brookie called, 'Run up!' As we passed he said, 'Hurry, we can get two.' I turned for my second run to see my partner, having picked up my bat on the way down the wicket, holding it aloft. He passed it to me as we crossed. This brought loud laughter from the crowd, who were enjoying the spectacle of two tail-enders making runs on a turning wicket when their more illustrious predecessors had failed. It also brought a classic remark from Don Bradman: 'What's this, a relay race?' We put on 62 valuable runs before Brookie was out lbw – Ted Brooks 33, Alf Gover 29.

In a Surrey versus Middlesex game at Lord's, Brookie was batting at number 10 and got hit on the foot by a ball from fast bowler Jim Smith. He played out the innings and then limped off the field announcing that he would not be able to field. So Laurie Fishlock was given the job. In my third over I bowled a ball with too much swing, firing it outside the leg stump. It carried on down on the leg side. Laurie moved smartly across and at full stretch caught it in his left hand. Someone in the dressing room called out to Brookie, 'Laurie is a natural behind the stumps.' That cured Brookie: within two overs he ran out and literally tore the gloves off Laurie saying, 'Give me my gloves, this is my job.'

Brookie had a quick turn of wit which surfaced when Surrey played South Africa at the Oval in 1935. The visitors won the toss and decided to bat on a plumb, easy-paced pitch. We got an early wicket and in came the number 3 batsman – with the number 4 in the order padded up and sitting out on the visitors' balcony. He was summing up the bowling and getting his eyes accustomed to the light. By mid-afternoon he was still sitting there, thinking, no doubt, 'These two don't want anyone else to bat on this lovely strip.' The crowd had gone very quiet, having tired of instructing the Surrey bowlers how to do their jobs, when a lorry passing the ground on the Harleyford Road side backfired. Quick as a flash Brookie said, 'Blimey, number 4 has shot himself.'

Brookie was a magnificent 'keeper standing back, but just failed to keep this high standard standing up to the spinners. Playing against Leicestershire at the Oval he missed two chances off leg spinner Freddie Brown's bowling in the space of two overs. He followed this by taking a great diving catch to a ball edged low to his right-hand side towards a normal first slip position off my bowling. He then turned to Freddie Brown and said, 'If I can't stump them I can catch them.' Freddie was not amused.

A great boost to morale was listening to Brookie in the dressing room when the side were struggling. He was a supreme optimist and if we batted badly in the first innings he would often say, 'Good job for you batsmen that it's a two innings match so you have a second chance to get yourselves and the side out of trouble.' He could entertain us with a succession of card tricks. His three-card 'find the Lady' was always a great success and over the years we never caught him out. He would perform this trick for the visiting team but he never allowed anyone to bet on their effort to 'find the Lady'. He had another trick where he used three thimble-like containers and into one of these he would place a small hard round nut. He would show the thimble containing the nut and then, waving both hands, he would place the thimbles face down on the table and then challenge his audience to find the one which contained the nut. All hands would point to the obvious one but Brookie would then triumphantly pick up another thimble to reveal the nut.

In October 1937 Errol Holmes, our captain, invited us down to Tandridge Hall, his family home at Oxted, Surrey, for a day's rough shooting. Both Brookie and I told Errol that we were novices with a gun so he paired us up and sent us out in charge of the butler, George, who was an expert shot. As we entered the wooded area allocated as our beat, Brookie fired his gun frightening off dozens of pigeons. 'Why did you do that?' asked George, 'Just testing,' was the reply.

George then told us that we would have a long wait now before the birds would come back. They never did come back, though we waited for two hours without firing a shot of any kind. I think Brookie must have scared even the rabbits into their burrows.

Errol's mother was a charming and gracious lady who acted as hostess when we sat around in the lounge to take tea. Apart from the butler, now in tail-coat and black trousers, they had a teenager they addressed as 'Buttons' so named, we presumed, because of his double-breasted coat which was adorned with many shiny silver buttons.

During tea, Brookie, then weighing around fourteen stone, noticed a game board with the latest gimmick of a pyramid puzzle on it. He asked for, and was given, permission by Mrs Holmes to have a crack at solving the puzzle. He placed it on a small table and then looked around for something to sit on. One of us pushed forward what he thought was a coffee table, and Brookie plonked his full weight on it. The table collapsed and those of us who had recognized it as one of the several antiques in the room were horrified. But dear old Brookie, in all innocence, looked at Errol and said, 'Cheap furniture you have around here, Skipper.' The rest of the 'heavies' in the team thought, 'There, but for the grace of God, go I'.

HOWARD LEVETT

Kent have always had a tradition of great wicketkeepers: Jack Hubble, Les Ames, Godfrey Evans and Alan Knott. When Les Ames was England's regular 'keeper Kent were lucky to have a substitute in amateur Howard Levett, arguably the best amateur 'keeper ever, nicknamed 'Hopper' as his business was connected with the Kent hop fields.

Hopper was also quite a character, always full of fun, who never stopped talking, even when keeping wicket. He was a useful late-order batsman too, always ambitious to knock up a respectable score. During one Surrey versus Kent game I was fielding at my usual short leg post and Stan Squires our number 3 bespectacled batsman, was bowling to Hopper. Stan bowled what his team-mates described as a 'sort of leg break' and a 'sort of off spin' both with a deceptive flight. Hopper pushed and jabbed without scoring a run and eventually turned to me saying, 'Alfred, Stan's bowling piss, but I still can't hit it.'

STAN SQUIRES

Stan Squires was another who would keep the dressing room amused. He wrote humorous songs and rhymes. When we resumed cricket at the Oval in 1946 the ground and pavilion had only just recovered from being a prisoner-of-war staging camp (in the event it was never used as such). Whenever we had practice nets the whole place would apparently be deserted, apart from a solitary ground assistant working on the middle so Stan produced a song for the whole team to sing. The words were written to the tune of 'The Mountains of Mourne go down to the Sea'. It went:

They tell me the Oval is a terrible place
And the organization is a ruddy disgrace,
They stand with their hands in their pockets with nothing to do –
The President, the Secretary and the Assistant Secretary too.
And for all the good they are
They might as well be
Where the mountains of Mourne go down to the sea.

They tell me the Oval is a terrible place
And the organization is a ruddy disgrace,
They stand with their hands in their pockets with nothing to do –
The office staff, Bosser Martin (head groundsman) and the gate keeper too.
And for all the good they are
They might as well be
Where the mountains of Mourne go down to the sea.

Let me hasten to say that the whole chorus was sung in fun. The ground and administrative staff were all working hard behind the scenes to put the club back on an even footing after the war.

Another of Stan's rhymes was about our numbers 9, 10 and 11 batsmen who had all registered two ducks in each innings of their two previous matches. It went:

Who does the bowler like to see
coming out of the P.A.V.?
Why, Geary, Gover and Fennerly.

SANDY TAIT

Sandy Tait, our masseur and trainer, was another cheerful character in our dressing room. In his early days he had been a stagehand at the Old Lewisham Empire in the great days of variety and became familiar with the popular songs of that era, so on rainy days he would conduct the 'Surrey Choristers' – six of the players. The 'microphone' was an abdominal guard on the handle of a bat tied upright on to the table. Sandy stood in front and conducted. As time went on we could sing in harmony although lacking any treble voices. Then we came down to earth with a big bump. In those days the home team's very large dressing room was split into two, divided by a wooden partition. We were playing cricket against the boys from Glamorgan and rain had stopped play so the 'Surrey Choristers' were in full flow when suddenly from next door the Welsh voices burst into song with tenors and baritones, singing with perfect timing and harmony. We stopped and listened and at the end of their recital gave them an ovation. Turning to Sandy we said, 'And we thought we could sing, after that we will go back to playing cards when rain stops play.'

Sandy was an old-fashioned chap who always wore his blue suit on Sundays when Surrey were playing away from home. This habit nearly got him arrested during a Yorkshire versus Surrey game at Leeds. The players had arranged to play golf at Sandmoor Golf Club on Sunday afternoon. The Moortown Golf Club starts off alongside the Sandmoor Golf Club and the two club-houses are very close together. Sandy decided to walk round with us having left his old mackintosh in the Sandmoor locker room. After nine holes he announced that he was tired and was going back to the team's hotel but unfortunately he walked into the wrong clubhouse. He went into the locker room to collect his mac. At that time there had been a spate of pilfering in both club locker rooms, so when Sandy was discovered in the Sandmoor locker room dressed in his blue suit and not looking like a weekend golfer, the club secretary would not believe his story of looking for his mac or that he was trainer to the Surrey cricket team. The secretary was about to call the police when Sandy mentioned that the Surrey players had invited him to walk round Sandmoor Golf Club, that he had walked nine holes and feeling tired had left them to go home. The Moortown secretary tumbled Sandy's error at last but, even so, accompanied him into the Moortown dressing room to identify the old mac, much to the relief of poor Sandy!

DON BRADMAN

'Who was the best batsman you ever bowled against?' This is the question I am always asked whenever I sit as a member of a sports panel and I always reply, 'Don Bradman'.

I bowled at many great batsmen: George Headley of the West Indies and V. J. Merchant of India, but the outstanding run-getter was Don Bradman. The Australian had all the shots, he was quick on his feet and saw the flight of the ball early from the bowler's hand. When under attack from the bowlers he would counter-attack with remarkable stroke-making. He was deadly on any ball pitched just short of a length, putting his left foot to the on side and opening his stance to give himself room to pull the ball hard to the on side between mid-on and mid-wicket. He would amaze, and at times annoy, bowlers with his cutting of the good length ball pitched on the off stump. He kept his score going so consistently that when his fifty came up it often took the fielders by surprise.

When the ball was swinging away Don gave it the full face of the bat. Against the off spinner he often turned the bottom hand to close the face of the bat in order to hit the ball with the turn. He could use his full repertoire of shots to keep his score moving quickly and I witnessed, among his other batting feats, his 309 runs in 300 minutes against England at Leeds in 1930.

JACK HOBBS

The best batsman I played with was undoubtedly Jack Hobbs. I was fortunate to play alongside him in the Surrey team for six years. He was an artist with the bat as he stroked the ball to various parts of the field. I once asked Sir Pelham Warner, who played with him in the England side, to describe Jack's style of batting in his earlier days. 'He was similar to Denis Compton, making all the shots and was a powerful hitter of the ball.' Len Hutton was the closest I saw to Jack for perfection in batting skill and the ability to pick up the line and flight of the ball as soon as it left the bowler's hand. I always enjoyed bowling at Denis Compton, even when he was in full flow, as I felt that I had a chance because he was prepared to take risks to keep the score moving. Like Hobbs and Bradman, Compton was quicker on his feet than the ordinary batsman.

FRANK WOOLLEY

Frank Woolley, the Kent and England left-hander, was nearly six-and-a-half feet tall. He was known as 'Stalky', and bowling to him called for a fine degree of accuracy, especially on the front foot, because of his long reach. On the back foot he was severe on any delivery slightly short of a length outside the off stump. It was almost impossible to bowl a bouncer at him because of his height. The ball had to be pitched so short to bounce him that he had plenty of time to judge the ball. He was always looking for runs. I remember a game in 1935 at the Oval on a plumb pitch when Frank was in his 48th year. He had hit 240 runs, including three huge 6's over the West Stand, a long-distance hit rarely made. Freddie Brown now bowled at him and pitched the ball in the bowler's rough outside the off stump. Frank was obviously tired and made no effort to offer the bat to the ball, which came back and hit his off stump. I immediately said to the skipper, Errol Holmes, 'After seven years of bowling at Frank I have at last found out how to get him out.'

'How?' asked Errol.

'Tire him out,' I replied. Errol was not a bit amused.

Frank was one of two batsmen that I always found difficulty in keeping quiet when bowling to them. The other was Patsy Hendren.

PATSY HENDREN

Patsy Hendren, of Middlesex and England, was another of my 'Jonahs'. Stockily built with broad shoulders, strong hands and forearms, he was one of the best players of fast bowling in the world. I never bounced the ball at him as, when I was a young player, I was taught a sharp lesson by Patsy in my first encounter with him at Lord's. Patsy always used the visitors' dressing room, and when Surrey walked in I recognized the great man and gave him 'Good morning, Mr Hendren.' He asked me my name and what I did, and I replied that I was a fast bowler. He then asked me if I was very fast, and I said 'Yes', with all the cockiness of youth. Patsy said, 'Well, I'm getting on a bit so don't bowl any short ones at me.'

Surrey lost the toss and managed to get an early wicket and in came Patsy. The first three balls I delivered were played gently back, I bounced the fourth ball short and straight at him, only to be hooked hard to the leg-side boundary. He looked up the wicket, shaking his head at me. So the next delivery was another bouncer in the off-stump area. Patsy stepped back and thrashed it to the third-man boundary. 'Hello,' I thought, 'now he is running away,' and bounced the last ball of the over straight at him. This he hooked for a six high up in the Mound Stand. As the field were changing over, Jack Hobbs said, 'Why are you bowling short at Patsy?'

'He is frightened of short bouncers,' I replied.

'Who told you that?'

'He did,' I said, pointing down the wicket at Patsy. Jack laughed: 'He's the best player of short-pitched fast bowling around!'

I got to know Patsy very well as time went on, and he would often say, 'When are you going to bowl me a bouncer, Alfred?' I would reply, 'You had your ration a long time ago!'

Even to the best-length deliveries he had an answer. In his last game against Surrey at Lord's, just before retiring from the game, he hit a magnificent 100, collecting his usual contribution off my bowling. I was at mid-off when he eventually got out; I was clapping vigorously as he walked past me. 'That's very generous of you, Alfred,' he said.

'It's not generosity, Patsy,' I replied, 'it's relief that I won't have to bowl at you again!'

PERCY FENDER

The other question always put to me is, 'Which players of your era would be a success in modern one-day cricket?'

Percy Fender, my Surrey captain for four years, was another mighty hitter of the ball. His record of 113 runs in 35 minutes against Northampton stood for many years until beaten by Ian Botham. I batted with Fender against Nottingham one year on a day when runs were at a premium for Surrey. I played the 'prop and cop' role while he took on the pace of Larwood and Voce, eventually getting out just short of his hundred. He was one of the originators of hitting the ball through the covers with the bat face slightly open to send the ball wide of cover's left hand.

Percy was basically a leg spinner but I have seen him turn to off spin to good effect and, when a bowler short, open up with inswingers with the new ball. He had a safe pair of hands in the slips and had a good arm from the deep.

CHARLES BARNETT

Charles Barnett, the Gloucestershire and England cricketer, was unusual for an opening batsman. He never played himself in, attacking the bowling directly he had taken guard. He also bowled medium-pace inswingers and was a good fielder with a good arm. An ankle injury forced him to retire from first-class cricket, but, on migrating to the Lancashire League, his name became a by-word for his outstanding success with bat and ball, and he would be equally outstanding in today's one-day game.

WALTER HAMMOND

Walter Hammond, the great Gloucestershire and England cricketer, would match any modern batsman. He hit with tremendous power, especially off the back foot. Standing at short leg in a game at the Oval, I once watched Wally hit a full toss from slow leg spinner Bob Gregory off the back foot into the Vauxhall Stand, a distance of about 90 yards. He had a reputation of being primarily an off-side player but he could adapt and use the leg-side area to promote his score when necessary. He bowled medium-fast off- and leg-cutters and when in the mood could send down a genuine fast delivery. One of the great slip fielders, he was a good mover capable of filling any place in the field.

FREDDIE BROWN

Freddie Brown, the Surrey and Northants cricketer who skippered England in 1950 in Australia, would hold his own as an all-rounder in any modern side. He was a fine attacking batsman against any type of bowling, a powerfully built chap who favoured the front foot. I saw him hit many a six on the big expanse of the Oval playing area. When he went to Australia in 1950 he reverted to medium-pace seamers in place of his normal leg spin. He was quick on his feet and had a powerful return from the deep field.

STAN NICHOLS

Stan Nichols of Essex was a magnificent all-round cricketer who did the double of 1,000 runs and 100 wickets in a season seven times. A right-arm fast bowler, off the comparative short run of 13 paces, he could swing the ball both ways. He batted left-handed at number 5 in the order and there were numerous occasions when he would have to look for quick runs when the lower order of the batting was disintegrating. He had a good pair of hands and could field equally well in the deep or close to the bat. Stan was slightly round shouldered and did not look like an athlete until he started moving around. I remember a Surrey versus Essex game at Clacton when Stan bowled throughout the Surrey innings with only four overs rest, apart from the lunch and tea breaks. In the Essex second innings he batted through from number 5 to the end of the innings. He then bowled through the two hours left for Surrey to bat on the last day of the drawn match.

LEARIE CONSTANTINE

Learie Constantine from the West Indies would be a top star in one-day cricket. He became a legend as a fielder, catching impossible chances, and many tales are told of him, such as fielding in the covers off his own bowling. He was an unorthodox batsman and many an astonished bowler saw his best ball hit for six.

ARTHUR WELLARD

Arthur Wellard, the Somerset and England smiter of 6's, took a comparatively short run of 13 paces for a fast bowler. He moved the ball both ways and as a fielder had a good pair of hands. He did the 'double' twice although rarely batting above number 9. He, too, would be in my one-day team.

VINNO MANKAD

Vinno Mankad, the great Indian all-rounder, would undoubtedly be a success. An opening batsman with many Test hundreds to his credit, his left-arm bowling kept a tight rein on the batsman and he was a first-class all-round fielder.

ALL-ROUNDERS

As for all-rounders, the trio of Keith Miller, Gary Sobers and Ian Botham stand out from all the others. Keith, like Gary, enjoyed the game, and it was obvious for all to see. He retired before the advent of one-day cricket, but, as one of the game's great all-rounders – fast opening bowler, attacking middle-order batsman and exciting fielder – he would have very easily adjusted to it. Ian Botham and Gary Sobers are proven one-day cricketers: Ian, the modern Goliath, and Gary the same a generation back. It is a moot point who was the better of these two greats. Gary probably has the edge with his both fast and slow bowling, but Ian has a wonderful record as a wicket-taker and a devastating batsman. I'll stick my neck out and declare it a draw between the two of them.

ONE-DAY CRICKET

When cricket folk ask my opinion on one-day cricket, I always remind them that I first suggested one-day cricket back in 1958 in my *Sunday Mirror* column. I said that spectators wanted to be involved in the game by seeing the start and the finish. The suggestion was not received well at headquarters, one leading administrator said that cricket could do without gimmicks. Three-day cricket had lost much of its support, and many games had contrived finishes, with declarations on the third day. There is no doubt that the thrills of the one-day competitions have helped to sustain interest in the game. Three-day cricket would not survive if it had to stand on its own feet.

THE MODERN GAME

Some people expect to hear from me, as an ex-player, a dissertation on the game not being the same as it was in my day. Of course it is not the same, changes have always happened, going back to the days in the 1880s when the five-ball over replaced the four-ball over, and was in turn replaced by the six-ball over. During my career the pitches were covered only at the bowler's end, now they are sensibly covered for the whole of the match, helping to ensure play after rainfall. In 1929 the stumps were made larger and the ball smaller, to redress the balance of the game in favour of the bowlers, who for years had toiled on pitches made in favour of the batsmen. Today the bowler's foot holes at the crease are repaired during the game, a sensible change in the law, as in my day the front foot hole on the third day spelt danger for the fast bowler if he landed on the edge of the 'crater' and turned his ankle over.

Fielding in today's cricket has an athletic look about it – the infielders diving about like soccer goalkeepers and the outfielders making a 'sliding tackle' on the boundary, both in an effort to save the odd precious run that could bridge the gap between victory and defeat in a one-day game. This fielding has crept into three- and five-day cricket with some old players denigrating this but I enjoy watching these 'antics', and of course it is good television.

The standard of batting in the counties has undoubtedly suffered, batsmen being asked to perform on sub-standard pitches. However, season 1990 saw the pitches change from the ridiculous to the sublime. Maybe the groundsmen will now strike a happy medium in season 1991 and give both bat and ball an equal chance. It is probably only a pipe dream on my part hoping to see the type of pitch Yorkshire provided on all their home grounds during my career. A firm pitch on the first two days and and then taking spin on the last day. This usually produced a finish to the game, and the skills of batsman and bowler were given an equal chance.

If there is anything that irks me about today's cricket it is the players' habit of rushing from all parts of the field to cuddle the bowler or the catcher at the fall of a wicket. So often have I seen the deep fielders rush across the field and cuddle and slap the 'keeper when he has made a simple catch off a top edge. Such bouts of enthusiasm should be kept in check unless some outstanding performance has been made by bowler, 'keeper or fielder.

One of my young pupils at the School once told me that I could not have been competitive because he had seen a film of me in a county game bowling and taking a wicket. He said, 'Just after you had bowled the ball you leaped in the air with your arm raised high in appeal, the wicketkeeper caught the ball, but to my surprise you did not go down the wicket to congratulate him. Instead you waved a hand at him and turned back to the bowling crease and started kicking the ground.' I explained that this was to level the bowler's foothold instead of making an unnecessary journey down the pitch. I told him that I would say 'Well caught' at the change over. Quite frankly, if I had rushed down and cuddled my regular 'keeper, Ted Brooks, he might have kicked me where it would have hurt!

The histrionics on the field today could be because of the prize money involved, but I prefer to believe it is the winning of the game which is of paramount importance, as it was in my days when our win bonus was 'peanuts'. The one big difference now is the conditions of a player's employment. In my day, to move to another county meant a qualifying period of two years' residence in your adopted county. This was, of course, in restraint of trade, and was scrapped in the immediate post-war years. Now players can move to another county at the beginning of the year.

Unfortunately, players are now offered additional cash to make the move, and some counties are being deprived of players they have fostered for several years. The only way to stop this practice must be the introduction of a transfer system, something I expect to see within the next two years.

18

Cricket's a Funny Old Game

SOME YEARS AGO Andrew Sandham and myself travelled down to Farnham in Surrey to give a demonstration on the opening day of a new indoor cricket school. The school had two nets, and for the purpose of the demonstration, one side net had been lifted to make room for the spectators. Bob Relf, the old Sussex all-rounder and resident coach, joined myself in bowling to Andrew. Unfortunately, Bob wanted to demonstrate his own skill of leg-cutters and a very late inswinger, and on a matting pitch laid on a wooden floor, Bob was lethal. Andrew had to concentrate on keeping his wicket intact. So I came to the rescue. Using pre-conceived signals to let Andrew know the length and the width of the delivery I was about to send down, Andrew was able to demonstrate the drives on both sides of the wicket and his famous late cut. By this time the spectators had pushed past the safety barriers and were close up to the net on the leg side. The last ball was due and I was to bowl it, so I gave the signal to Andrew for the pull shot. He was quickly in position and gave a perfect demonstration, hitting the ball hard in the middle of the bat and whack into the face of a young spectator tight up against the netting.

There was blood all over the place. Andrew rushed across to say how sorry he was, but the lad's father said, 'It was an honour', and could he have a picture of his boy holding his handkerchief to his lips together with Andrew. The astonished Andrew obliged, and to soften the blow spent a long time talking cricket to the lad. 'That took a long time,' I said, 'Well,' said Andrew, 'it was difficult because the poor lad couldn't answer back and I had to do all the talking.'

Before the advent of the one-day knock-out games all counties played twenty-eight championship matches. The Oval has the longest cricket square in England, so the county games were always played on the same strip of turf on the square every year. When we played Gloucester and I went in to bat, the umpire called out, 'What guard, Alfred?' I simply replied: 'It's all right, I was here last year.' The players around the bat thought this was a great joke, but I was quite serious. All previous batsmen had taken middle and leg guard, as indeed they did every year, excavating the same spot in the batting crease. So why should I, batting at number 11, bother to dig 'yet another hole'.

A cold mid-winter morning with heavy snow falling and a man with a suitcase stands by the bus stop at Clapham Junction, a patrolling policeman approaches. 'What have you got in that suitcase', to receive the reply, 'My cricket clothes.'

'Don't give me that nonsense, open up,' said the officer. The case is opened for the officer to see cricket clothes neatly folded plus bat and pads.

'You see,' said the owner, 'I am off to play cricket.'

'You must be mad,' said the officer, 'you can't play cricket in this weather.' Back came the reply, 'I am going to play at Alf Gover's cricket school.'

'I have never heard of it,' said the officer. 'In that case,' said the owner of the cricket bag, 'you must be mad.'

In a Surrey versus Notts game at the Oval I went in as nightwatchman on the first day of the game. I went out next morning to face the fiery pace of Harold Larwood and Bill Voce. I had been batting for six overs when I suddenly realized I had forgotten to wear my abdominal guard. I panicked and ran straight off the field. On my return, Arthur Carr, the Notts skipper, said, 'Alfred I don't mind you going off for a pee but you might have had the courtesy to first ask me.' I explained my horror at finding myself 'boxless'. 'Then' he said 'In that case you must be a BF.'

Surrey play two matches a year away from the Oval at Guildford. On arrival on the ground for the game to be played against Hampshire in June 1946 I went out to inspect the pitch and I could hardly believe my eyes: it had so much grass it looked like a bowling green. I had a slight strain to the muscle just below the ribcage on my left-hand side but this had happened before during my career and I had always strapped it up with three-inch elastoplast. This gave me sufficient support to bowl flat out. Alec Bedser had reported unfit with a similar strain and was prepared to cry off. So I took him out to the middle and said, 'You must have a go on this, the skipper is going to put them in if he wins the toss and I will strap you up and guarantee you will be able to bowl flat out.' I strapped Alec up. The elastoplast stretched from the middle of his back to his front covering the strained area. 'It's too tight, Alfred, I can't breathe.'

'Come on,' I said, 'let's get cracking!'

And get cracking we did. Alec took five wickets for 22 runs and I had the other five for 21 runs. Hampshire were all out for a measly 48 runs. Back in the dressing room I took off the three strips of elastoplast on my back with one large pull. I have a smooth skin with no hair on that part of the body and there was no discomfort in pulling the support away. Alec, on the other hand, has lots of hair on his trunk.

'Stand still,' I said, 'and I will take your strapping off.' Getting three fingers under the end of the sticky strappings, I gave a tremendous heave. Off came the strapping and Alec gave a loud shriek and nearly hit the roof. 'I'm not going through that again,' said Alec. He turned to our trainer, Sandy Tait.

'You had better give me plenty of treatment to get me ready to bowl in the second innings.' It had a happy sequel when Alec was selected for the first Test against India at Lord's – the first of many in his distinguished Test career.

When the throwing controversy was at its height in the late 1950s and early 1960s it was the duty of the square-leg umpire to watch the bowler and if necessary call 'no ball'. Brian Statham, the great Lancashire and England bowler, was playing against Worcestershire at Worcester. As he delivered the ball there was a cry of 'no ball' from the square-leg official. Brian stared in horror, his action had always been beyond reproach. Then the umpire called out to Brian, 'You have three fielders behind the wicket on the leg side, you should know you are only allowed two.' A relieved Brian made a hurried adjustment to his field placing and, the colour having come back to his cheeks, got on with his bowling.

In 1922 the lunch-time became flexible in county cricket and counties could if they wished change from 1.30 p.m. to 2.00 p.m. Notts chose to make their interval 2.00 p.m. In their first game of the season George Gunn, one of the great characters in the game and Notts' opening batsman, opened up as usual and by 1.30

p.m. he had hit 64 runs then he deliberately got himself out. 'Why did you do that, George?', he was asked on his return to the pavilion. 'Because' said George, 'my lunchtime has always been at half past one.'

My old friend Joe Hardstaff the Notts and England batsman told me about an incident when his father was standing umpire at square-leg in a county game. Young Joe had reached 97 and went for a risky third run and was run out by at least four yards. Father Joe went through the motions of raising the forefinger to give him out. Joe told me that after that game Notts had a three-day rest, and coincidentally his father had a three-day rest from umpiring. Young Joe decided to visit his mother, and, on going into the kitchen, greeted her and then asked: 'Where's dad?' In a very off-hand way she said: 'Oh, he's in the garden.'

Joe's parents got on well together, so Joe sought father out in the garden. 'What's the matter with mum?' he said.

'It's that run out the other day.' Joe went back to his mother. 'That run out the other day was entirely my own fault – trying to get my hundred.'

'I know that, son,' she replied, 'but his own flesh and blood!'

In the 1934 Surrey versus Australia game at the Oval, I took the wicket of Alan Kippax, then one of Australia's leading Test batsmen, with a freak delivery. As a fast bowler, my natural delivery was the ball moving away from the batsman. I say a 'natural' ball from a fast bowler because, if he's going through the correct motions of delivery, he will be in position for away-swing at the moment of releasing the ball. The cricket writers described me as a fast away-swinger with an occasional break-back. This break-back was not something I tried to do, it just happened probably when I was trying to get too much body into the action and the seam would be upright in my hand instead of pointing towards first slip at the moment of releasing the ball. The break-back was very small, a matter of an inch or so. On this particular day I had been moving the ball away to Alan for several overs, some, however, of the bad deliveries had started outside the off stump and to these Alan simply padded up and watched the ball go by. Then came my freak delivery, the ball pitched at least twelve inches outside the off-stump and as Alan padded up the ball moved in and knocked his off stump out of the ground. At close of play Alan came over to our dressing room to congratulate me saying, 'That's the best ball that has ever been bowled to me. I assured Alan it was a complete fluke but he would not have it, 'You are too modest, Alfred,' he said.

Some twenty years later, on my first visit to Australia as a journalist and broadcaster, I called in to see Alan at his large sports emporium in Sydney. He was delighted to see an old friend and introduced me to the staff as the chap, 'I often told you about – who bowled me with the best ball in the whole of my career.' I knew it would be useless trying to explain the luck in the whole incident, so in respect to Alan, and with tongue in cheek, I received the plaudits of his staff.

Have you ever seen a batsman flat on his back in the middle of the pitch? Well, it happened to Arthur Carr, ex-captain of England and captain of Notts – a useful hard-hitting number 5 batsman, capable of making 2,000 runs per season.

Surrey were playing Notts at the Oval. Arthur had the fast bowling 'terrible twins' of the short bouncer, Harold Larwood and Bill Voce, in his team. The game was going on quite sedately, the runs coming in singles and twos, when suddenly there was an explosion. Maurice Allom let go a bouncer at Arthur. Maurice's bouncer was always quicker by two yards than his normal delivery. This was accentuated by his bowling the ball from his full height of six feet three inches. Arthur, unprepared for the bouncer, flung himself backwards, the bat flying out of his hand towards slip, and landed flat on his back. Then, sitting up on his haunches, he turned his head and said to Percy Fender, our captain, standing in the slips, 'Percy, this is no way to play cricket.' These words, from the high priest of the short-pitch bouncer brigade, caused convulsions among the close-in fielders, and his professional partner at the other end had to turn away to hide his laughter.

'Come on, get up, Arthur,' said our skipper, 'take the bouncer like a man.'

This infuriated Arthur even more and so, as soon as he got up, he started thrashing around wildly and within an over holed out at mid-off.

Did Percy Fender, our wily skipper, make that remark to get Arthur going? The Notts skipper had a reputation for being a very tough chap, and Percy's remarks could be interpreted as an accusation of Arthur's cowardice in running away from the bouncer. Jack Hobbs thought this was so when he said to Percy, 'Well done, skipper. You certainly talked him out.'

Maurice Allom, who bowled the other end to me, was an amateur whose career lasted only six seasons owing to the calls of business. In these six seasons he was selected for two overseas trips – South Africa and New Zealand – and it was on the New Zealand tour that he took four wickets in five balls, and thus became the only cricketer ever to have a Test match hat-trick, and, at the same time, a jazz record at the Top of the Pops. Just prior to his overseas tour he had made a record with band leader Fred Elizalde at Cambridge University. When Fred left Cambridge, his band became one of the Savoy Hotel's resident bands and released the disc made with Maurice at Cambridge. It was an immediate success and stayed at the top of the pops for several weeks.

Stan Squires, who scored many runs batting at number 3 for Surrey, was among the few players who batted in glasses, Geoffrey Boycott, at the start of his career, and Mike Smith were others. Stan was involved in an amusing incident when batting with Ted Whitfield against Lancashire at the Oval. Ted played the ball behind the wicket and Stan called him for a run but as they went half-way up the wicket Ted turned his head away to look backwards to follow the ball about to be fielded at leg slip. This resulted in a collision with Stan in the middle of the pitch and Stan's glasses flew off. With Ted underneath trying to get out and the now short-sighted Stan groping for his glasses it was all arms and legs by the two of them. Stan was heard to mutter, 'You BF Ted, I can't see a damn thing.' The fielder with the ball in his hand came up to the pitch area and enquired of square-leg umpire, 'Which end do I throw to get the run out?'

'Please yourself,' was the reply, 'by the time these two have sorted themselves out it won't really matter.' In the event Stan had to go and on his return to the dressing room his team-mates were entertained at some length by Stan using flowery language to describe Ted's eccentric running between the wickets.

Ted Whitfield could have lost his wicket under the three-minute rule when we played Derbyshire at Derby on the old racecourse ground. It was on the third day, just after lunch, with Surrey playing their second innings of the match. The players on the batting side had seats on top of the pavilion to watch the play. It came Ted's turn to bat and off he went but we did not see him emerge from the usual place out of the pavilion onto the field. After an interval Richardson the Derby captain walked over to the pavilion and called up to us 'Where is your next batsman?

It's two minutes already.' At that moment Ted appeared from the far end of the pavilion and all was well. 'What happened to you?' we asked, when he came in at the tea interval. His reply was, 'I turned the wrong way at the bottom of the stairs and found myself in the kitchen; the chef comes from Kennington adjacent to the Oval and he kept me talking.'

In my second season at the Oval I had a 'phone call from my maternal grandfather, aged 70, a retired master builder, who said he would like to come to the Oval to see me play. I had not seen him since I was a teenager but made the necessary arrangements and met him at the back entrance to the players' dressing room. He was a splendid sight, dressed in the fashion of the day for an elderly gentleman, the light grey felt hat, the grey summer suit, a cravat to match complete with the diamond tie pin, black patent leather shoes and silver-topped stick. His first words to me were, 'I expect you to do well today, my boy, now that I am here.' Typical of a self-made successful business man, I had to put on a show for his special benefit. I gave him his pass into the pavilion and the members' dining room. Grandfather had enjoyed a reputation as a ladies' man in his younger days, and even at the age of seventy he was still a handsome looking man. While I was talking with him, a young girl walked past on her way to the entrance to the ladies' stand. He gave her a quick 'look over' and, twirling his moustache said, 'Nice looking filly, my boy.' I protested. 'Grandpa, not at your age.' He was most indignant, 'What do you mean, "not at my age"?', and followed the girl into the ladies' stand. Late in the morning, just before the lunch interval, I was fielding in the deep in front of the members' dining room, and through the plate-glass window saw Grandfather drinking with the filly he had admired. They were leaning forward, wine glasses touching, toasting each other. The old rascal. (This habit does not run in the family.)

There are many stories told about Bill Reeves, one of the leading umpires during my career. I like this one best of all. A young amateur batsman, making his first-class debut, was having a rough time struggling to get off the mark, continually playing at and missing the ball just outside the off stump. The first straight delivery he received beat his abortive defensive shot. There was a loud appeal for lbw and up went Bill's forefinger. The youngster, obviously unhappy with the decision, walked past Bill at the bowler's end. 'I did not think much of that decision, umpire,' he said. Quick as a flash, cockney Bill said, 'To tell you the truth, I just wanted to put you out of your misery.'

On one occasion, Tom Pearce, the Essex captain, 'phoned me just after a season had ended to say, 'Come and play for your old county in a one-day game against the pick of several Essex club sides.' I accepted and opened the bowling with Stan Nichols at the other end. After seven overs I had taken two wickets and Stan the odd wicket. Tom then said, 'I am going to have a bit of fun with Stan at the end of your next over. I'll call out for you to put your sweater on, and I'll take Stan off and put a spinner on at his end. After that over I'll tell you to resume bowling.' So, as soon as I peeled off my sweater, Stan rushed across to his skipper protesting, 'You can't do this to me, keeping Alf on after taking me off!' He was so upset that I thought the joke may have misfired, so I volunteered to come off in his favour, and he bowled as though he was in a Test match, and skittled the rest of the unfortunate club's batsmen within the next hour.

In my early days at the Oval there was a pub called the Clayton Arms which stood on the gasholder side of the ground. It had a flat roof on which was mounted a small open-air stand which gave the pub customers a good view of the Oval playing area. On many a hot day when the pub customers had sunk varying numbers of pints they would be our severest critics yelling both advice and abuse. Now we players could cope with barracking from the folks inside the ground but not from the outsiders who had not even paid for that privilege.

19

Manifestations in The Manor House

DO YOU BELIEVE in ghosts? No? Well, I do. We had one in my former residence next door to the School – Wandsworth House, in bygone days, the Manor House. It was a Grade 2 listed building, with sixteen large, high-ceilinged rooms. The Ghost was not a figment of my imagination, or indeed of anyone in the family, but a manifestation that occurred from time to time, usually in the early hours of the evening. The Ghost took the form of a 'feeling' of its presence and the sound of 'tip tapping' running feet up the staircase, plus the rustling of a dress. On rare occasions they all happened at the same time. We assumed our visitor to be female because of the rustling of the dress.

One evening, my wife was sitting with friend Betty Surridge in a downstairs room, with Betty's son 'Tiger' (then aged six, now over forty and head of the bat-making family firm) asleep in a first-floor bedroom. The Surridge dog, Monty a black labrador, was keeping the little lad company, stretched out on the bottom of the bed. The girls suddenly heard the 'tip tap' of feet running up the stairs, and Betty, who had always treated our ghost stories with 'a pinch of salt', immediately jumped up, thinking someone had entered the premises by the back door. She tore up the stairs, only to find Monty outside the bedroom door 'on guard', with hackles up and teeth bared. Inside the bedroom Tiger was still fast asleep. Marjorie, who had belatedly followed Betty up the stairs, said, 'I don't know why you panicked. It was only our Ghost, and now perhaps you will believe me when I tell you we do have something that occasionally makes its presence felt.'

I used one of the rooms at the top of the house as a storeroom for our cricket equipment for the retail shop. One early evening, one of our staff, Joe Skelton, who had been with us for many years and was my senior coach at the time, went upstairs to collect a bat. He came down and said, 'I am not going up there again in the dark. I felt something go past me and it scared me.' We assured Joe it was only our Ghost who was quite harmless, but he was adamant in his refusal to visit the storeroom except during the day.

My eldest son David and his wife, Leah, came to stay one weekend. Leah and my wife were talking together in the lounge at the top of the house when they both felt something go between them. Leah was quite definite. It was her first experience of our ghostly lodger and she was very definite in describing the movement between her and my wife.

Did the Ghost have a physical presence? Maybe it was the cause of a mystery concerning a piece of jewellery which my wife put away amongst clothing in a drawer of her dressing table. A week or so later, when she went to the drawer to take it out, it was missing. She enlisted the aid of her daily help of many years, Mrs Penfold, to turn over all the items of clothing, but there was no trace – it had disappeared into thin air. Our claim for the missing piece to the insurance company was quickly settled, but a few weeks later, my wife was most embarrassed when, going to the same dressing table drawer, which was in constant use – lo and behold, there was the missing brooch underneath the top piece of clothing. A cheque was sent back to the insurance company with an accompanying letter trying to explain the mystery of the burglary that had apparently not taken place.

The only people with access to the dressing table would have been my wife, myself and Mrs Penfold. So what was the explanation? Could it have been the Ghost playing tricks?

It must have been responsible for a happening to our daughter-in-law Leah, a year after she had first felt the Ghost's presence. With husband David she was sleeping in our twin-bedded guest room. Leah's bed was two feet from the side wall, which had a picture suspended by wire on a curved picture hook. During the night the picture came off the wall and landed on the bottom part of Leah's bed. The wire was unbroken and the hook still in position. There was no logical explanation for the 'moving picture'.

The front part of our old house had been built in Tudor times for Queen Elizabeth's armourer, hence Armoury Way, just behind Wandsworth Town Hall. The back part, added much later, in Georgian style, had the magnificent bay windows of the period. The hall, seven feet wide, went through the house from back to front, with a flying arch half-way down. This flying arch was so designed to take the stress and strain of the front portion of the building. The dividing wall between the two parts was two feet thick. A flying arch is a rare feature of a house, found only in old country houses. From the stone cellars underneath the house, a tunnel ten feet high and eight feet wide ran down to the River Wandle some four hundred yards away. The residents of the house in far off days would travel up the Thames and on to the tributary River Wandle on their barges, and then disembark at the entrance to the tunnel, and walk to the house in safety, without fear of being attacked by footpads, the muggers of the day.

In the early 1900s, a workman wielding a pickaxe, to dig a hole for a gas main in York Road, two hundred yards towards the Wandle, suddenly disappeared when the ground collapsed, revealing the existence of the tunnel from Wandsworth House. As a result, with the owner's permission, the tunnel was blocked off at both the house end and the York Road end, and the remaining part down to the River Wandle filled in.

Our house had a six foot wide staircase with attractive carved bannisters. The house was my wife's pride and joy. She had furnished it with antiques and appropriate sized furniture for a big house. Antique shops and sales rooms gave her many a happy hour hunting for bargains. Paintings came from the same source and many proved valuable as the years rolled by. One was an early French canvas, five feet by three feet – a garden scene with a chap dressed in frilly clothes and pantaloons, playing on a mandolin to two girls and a boy dressed in clothes of the Stuart period. My cricketing friends would, at first sight of the tapestry, label the mandolin player a 'poof', whereat, to their amusement, I would tell them that unlike myself they did not appreciate art. This would call for drinks all round to toast their 'artistic' host.

My wife was fortunate in having the daily help of Mrs Maude Penfold. She came for a week's work and stayed forty years, becoming part of the family and helping in the bringing up of my family. It was a sad day for all of us when she had to retire to look after a sick husband.

At the time of writing, the house has been standing empty and desolate for the past eighteen months. I have often wondered if our Ghost now feels lonely, missing the people who occupied the house for fifty years, the children who grew up there, and our many 'Out of Town' visitors. Does the sound of softly running feet still go up the stairs when it makes its occasional visit?

I wonder.

I left another legacy when I moved out of the house on my retirement. The legacy is the many 'spitting images' of my old cat, Bobo, who was part of the establishment of the School. I had taken a very sick Bobo on his last journey to the vet shortly before vacating the premises. Bobo had a big head and broad shoulders, with a white waistcoat and white paws. The first time I saw one of his progeny I almost believed in reincarnation! Bobo was a stray when he first came into my life – thin and hungry. We had a Yorkshire Terrier in the house so Bobo was given accommodation in my lock-up garage. I left the shutter open at the bottom just wide enough for him to get in, he slept in a wooden box lined with straw which was changed every week. He had remarkable faith in me. Whenever he was feeding from his bowl at the side of the lock-up, I could back the car into the garage within a few inches of him and he would never move, but out in the rest of the garage premises (I had 24 lock-ups beneath the cricket net area) he would move smartly out of the way whenever another car was driven in.

He was a magnificent animal and the scourge of all the other Toms who invaded his territory. He got himself into trouble on one of his amorous trips when pursuing one of his 'harem' into an empty house. He got locked into the upstairs front room and apparently the 'lady' ran away through the bedroom door which then closed with the force of the wind. He was missing for six days. I advertised in the local shops and had my staff helping me to search the side streets, but all in vain, until we had a report of a cat being seen at the window of the empty house. When we rescued Bobo he was emaciated and obviously dehydrated and under 'doctor's orders', but with careful nursing he was back to himself within a few weeks and he went, tail up, back to his old habits of consorting with his 'harem' – you can't keep a good man down!

Bobo would follow me in dog-like fashion and was part of the School routine. When I was working late he would sit outside the

School door waiting to accompany me on the short 50 yard walk to 'our' house. He was a character known to all the neighbourhood as 'that Cricket School cat' but he was never a cat to 'socialize' with everyone. He got on well with my family so long as they did not give him too much affection, but I could handle or mishandle him as I pleased, much to the amusement of my family.

I have a habit of taking a 'cat nap' after lunch each day on the sofa in my bedroom and as soon as I laid on my back I would hear a padding of paws on the stairs and in would come Bobo. With one mighty leap he would land flat on my chest, two paws would go around my neck, his head would be tucked under my chin and his purring would gradually subside into a gentle snore in harmony with mine.

I always knew when he had lost a temporary interest in the opposite sex as he would follow me around all day and at meal times insist on sitting on my shoulders. A most uncomfortable procedure for me but he never attempted to scrounge any food.

My daughter, Lis, had a black labrador about ten years old and one day when the cat was eating his meal in the kitchen, Lis came round with the dog, who had not been in contact with Bobo before. The dog went ahead into the kitchen and I was expecting a spitting, with arched back, from the cat, but found the dog sitting, watching Bobo eating his meal. When he had finished, Bobo strolled across to the dog, a gentle old labrador and, after a full inspection raised himself on his back feet and rubbed his head in affection against the dog's jaws. Thereafter they were great buddies. Separate meals were put down but they would never touch the other's food – they were both perfect gentlemen.

I must confess that for a few days after Bobo had gone I found difficulty in concentrating on my work. He was my friend.

20

Thanks for the Memory

DURING THE SUMMER of 1944 I was able to play many games of cricket with my sons, David and John, and made many appearances for 'Australia' against 'England'. They wanted to play cricket as often as possible, and naturally I was pleased that they liked the game and gave them every encouragement. They always insisted that they must be England and both had an innings against my single knock, with the non-batter on their side having to field for me as I was somewhat immobile. We played our games on the Winkfield Cricket Club ground opposite our house. I, as Australia, rarely beat England in the six or seven daily tussles.

The boys were also encouraged to play at their prep school in Windsor by their headmaster, Sydney Beckwith, who was a cricket enthusiast. They both played in the school first eleven and, going on to their public school at Cheltenham, they eventually made the first eleven there too. I say 'eventually' because they had the handicap of my name. They were told, 'Do not think you will get your colours simply because your name is Gover.'

David had ambitions as a fast bowler and I taught him swing and cut; John was a useful off spinner and middle-order batsman. Both went on to play for Richmond. David moved on to business in Devon where he took many wickets for Paignton, one of the county's strongest clubs and John went on tour to Bermuda under Stuart Surridge, who came back convinced that John could be a success in first-class cricket. However, after a few games in the Surrey second eleven he decided he must devote all his time to his business.

John had joined me in my cricket school to run the retail shop side and within five years he had built up the largest shop sales of cricket equipment in the south of England. He became my full partner and we had a happy relationship until we both decided to retire. Apart from his expert knowledge of the retail shop side of the business he also became a first-class cricket coach, assisting me with pupils whenever he had the opportunity.

The youngest of my three children, Elisabeth, always called Lis, might have developed into a good woman cricketer as she would often see me bowling in the nets and could give a lifelike impression of my bowling action. However, she showed little interest in the game and when the time came to select a girls' public school for her, my wife and I decided on Queenswood in Hatfield, Hertfordshire, famous as one of the leading girls' tennis playing schools.

Lis, who now lives in Portugal, still plays tennis and at the moment of writing has just been successful in a tournament at her club in the Algarve.

One of Lis's school friends, Jane, shared her enthusiasm for snow skiing and it was on one of those trips with brother John that Jane also went along. A romance blossomed and Jane married John, and, at the time of writing I am looking forward to the 21st birthday celebration of their son, James, and the 18th birthday celebration of their daughter Julia.

James has followed father's footsteps as a cricketer and after leaving Bradfield College he joined his Dad's old club, Richmond.

I have had lots of good fortune in my life, but none more so than having a wife who has been my right hand all fifty-eight years of our married life. Marjorie was destined for a career on the stage, having been trained at the famous Italia Conti Stage School. After starring in the annual Christmas show 'The Windmill Man' for several years, and in James Barrie's 'A Kiss For Cinderella', she subsequently played many West End theatres with the stars of those days: Sybil Thorndike, Louis Casson, Jack Hawkins, Jimmy Hanley, Lillian Braithwaite, Nelson Keys and Athene Seyler. Marjorie also performed at a Royal Command Performance at Drury Lane.

After the birth of our eldest son, David, she gave up the theatre. The famous actor, Jack Hawkins, once said to me, 'Alfred, you have robbed the stage of a very fine little artist.'

When we re-opened the School after the war years, we wanted someone to run the office and Marjorie volunteered, although she had our big house with sixteen rooms next door to the School to run and a family to bring up. It was a strange new world in tackling a business with account books, ledgers, and the diary for booking in the school, a vastly different proposition from having to learn lines. In my playing career I made it a habit never to take my 'work' home with me, but my 'Missis' could always sense how the day had gone for me. When I went on my frequent overseas trips in the winter, I went with the confidence and warmth of knowing my affairs were left in the capable hands of Marjorie, my 'right hand'.

I have enjoyed writing my autobiography. It has brought back memories of happy days spent in my various activities, and the friendships I made, especially in my sixty years' association with the greatest of games – cricket. If I have one regret it is that I cannot start it all over again.

Index

Index